# ERODING LOCAL CAPACITY

## International Humanitarian Action in Africa

*Edited by*
Monica Kathina Juma and Astri Suhrke

*Indexing terms*
Humanitarian assistance
Emergency relief
Capacity building
Local planning
Regional cooperation
Kenya
Somalia
Tanzania
Uganda

Cover photo: Jørn Stjerneklar/PHOENIX.
Food distribution in Benaco refugee camp, Tanzania.

Language checking: Elaine Almén

© the authors and Nordiska Afrikainstitutet, 2002

ISBN 91-7106-502-4

Printed in Spain by Grafilur Artes Gráficas, 2002

# Contents

# 1. Introduction

*Monica Kathina Juma and Astri Suhrke*

A curious pattern emerges from the voluminous statistics that trace the financial appeals of the international Red Cross movement during the last century. In the 1920s, the graph jumps wildly from one year to another. The Red Cross appeals in 1921 for 180 million Swiss francs for victims of famine and civil war in Russia. In 1922, it appeals for only 72,000 francs, this time for earthquake victims in Chile. The next year the graph shoots up again; the total appeal is for 355 million to assist victims of the earthquake in Japan, and social unrest and famine in Germany. And so it goes, up and down, until World War II, and into the 1950s. The crises appear to occur with great unpredictability—one year demanding very large expenditures, while other years requiring only a minor appeal or none at all (1933). By the 1970s, however, a new pattern emerges that by the end of the century has solidified. The appeals no longer vary sharply from one year to the next. Instead, they have stabilised into an almost straight line: the Red Cross appeals almost every year for about the same amount of assistance to meet humanitarian emergencies (www.ifrc.org).

The changing shape of the curve is more interesting than the absolute level of financial appeals. Does it signify a general change in the incidence of earthquakes, wars and famine from the first to the second half of the 20th century? Or is it rather the response of aid institutions that has changed for other reasons? In other words, is this a supply or demand driven pattern?

The literature gives no conclusive answer to the question of whether war, conflict and emergencies have become more frequent, destructive and regular in the second half of the century as compared with the first. Much depends upon the definition of the event being counted and the periods considered. For instance, one oft-cited study found that the number of armed conflicts (as defined) had decreased throughout the 1992–97 period (Sollenberg and Wallensteen, 1999). Other observers cited US official figures for "people at risk", claiming these were three times higher in the 1990s as compared to the early 1980s (Maynard, 1999:4). What is undisputed, however, is that a set of general developments—notably decolonisation and globalisation in communications—have made the international aid community concern itself with more conflicts and disasters of all kinds than before. To illustrate: Vietnam in 1930 experienced both a massive famine and rebellion, but the country was still colonised by France, which requested no assistance, and the international Red Cross movement therefore launched no appeal. In 1975, by contrast, the Red Cross appealed for 94 million francs to aid refugees and displaced persons in Indochina. The pattern was repeated globally. In the closing decades of the 20th century, virtually no major conflict went unnoticed, and most governments or self-proclaimed authorities welcomed relief assistance. The end of the Cold War further encouraged collective international action to deal with the humanitarian consequences of conflict, and sometimes the conflict itself.

Sensing both the need and the opportunities, international aid organisations developed into large, professional institutions with stable bureaucratic procedures. Many expanded their functions from immediate emergency to longer-term provision of social services, becoming reliable welfare providers in what Mark Duffield (1994) has aptly called an international safety net. While still dependent on annual appeals, the budgets of aid organisations started to fluctuate within fairly narrow margins—rather like the "snake in the tunnel" pattern of managed foreign exchange rates. In institutional terms, the result was to markedly strengthen what is commonly called the international humanitarian regime. This phenomenon is what the changing curve of the Red Cross appeals statistics during the last century signifies: it is essentially a shift from emergency relief to welfare.

This international, humanitarian welfare regime has a dominant Northern imprint. Using OECD, the UN and ad hoc fora, the industrialised states and Northern-based aid organisations have primarily been responsible for articulating common norms, providing financial resources, and developing institutions and strategies to both identify the problems and address them. Relief and protection activities on the ground are dominated by Northern-based organisations. Most of the operations, by contrast, take place in the South as conventionally defined, more recently including Southeast Europe and the Caucasus, and the assistance activities there. This structure raises some critical questions regarding the role that local or "Southern" actors can and should play in the international humanitarian regime. The dominant rhetoric on all sides has long emphasised the need to build more "local capacity", yet this is generally followed by non-action. Even long-term, semi-permanent emergencies have not generated significant local capacity to assist. In some cases, whatever local capacity did exist in this arena has been overwhelmed by the international aid presence and eroded. Why is this so? What is the case for a more even division of labour between North and South, and why is it so difficult to bring about?

This volume addresses these questions with respect to experiences in Africa. The book is very much a collective endeavour, growing out of a three-year research project supported by the Norwegian Development Agency (NORAD) through the Chr. Michelsen Institute, Bergen. The substantive themes and tentative conclusions were discussed at three seminars held in the second half of the 1990s: in Dar es Salaam, hosted by the Centre for Foreign Relations; in Cape Town, organised by the School of Government at the University of the Western Cape in Cape Town; and in Oslo, organised by the Chr. Michelsen Institute. Participants included African and Nordic scholars as well as practitioners from government and private aid organisations. All the participants—too numerous to be named individually—contributed to the project by forming, in effect, a constructive and critical panel of experts that helped develop ideas and reacted to the papers presented. This book is based on a selection of the papers prepared for these seminars, as subsequently edited by Monica Kathina Juma and Astri Suhrke. As editors, we wish to acknowledge the contributions of this larger cast of participants in addition to the individual authors.[1]

The papers reflect the diversity of background of the authors as well as disciplinary traditions—two of the authors are lawyers, one is an NGO official, and the rest are political scientists. A modest effort has been made to streamline the presentational style of the various chapters, but not to impose uniformity.

## Defining the Focus

Two key terms should be clarified at the outset. What do we mean by humanitarian *action*, and why do we use that term instead of the more common humanitarian *as-*

---

1. The editors further wish to acknowledge helpful comments from an anonymous reviewer regarding the structure of the manuscript and important points of substance.

*sistance?* To many readers, particularly those familiar with refugee situations, humanitarian assistance has a precise and rather narrow meaning. It refers to provision of material goods and services (food, water, shelter, and medical aid) for certain categories of needy persons. Many of these persons have additional need for protection against physical violence and the loss of legal rights. Humanitarian action covers both protection and assistance and hence conveys more accurately the subject covered in this book. As for *humanitarian*, the term is well established in the legal literature, where it refers to activities designed to protect and assist victims of war—originally international wars, but in some respects also internal conflicts. International humanitarian law codifies such activities in terms of (i) obligations by the warring parties to respect the rights of civilians and military personnel *hors de combat*, and (ii) rules for third parties seeking to aid the victims. Although there is some overlap between this body of law and human rights law, there is an important distinction in that human rights law primarily addresses the constitutive and enduring relationship between individuals and the state, and is not specifically concerned with victims of war. One area of clear overlap between international humanitarian law and human rights law concerns refugees, who may be victims of both state violence and wars. This category is covered by a separate body of treaty law, i.e. international refugee law.

In line with contemporary law, then, we can say that humanitarian action consists of activities to protect and assist victims of wars and similar kinds of physical violence. Moreover, as a matter of practice, the term is frequently used to include support for refugees and, more recently, internally displaced persons as well. Aid organisations usually refer to assistance to victims of natural disasters as "humanitarian", especially since man-made and nature-made disasters often come together. As this indicates, the meaning of humanitarian action in terms of norms and practice has evolved over time and in various directions. Organisationally anchored in the Red Cross initiative in the second half of the 19th century, humanitarian activities have since then exhibited three distinct orientations. These may be called the neutrality, solidarity and peace activist schools of thought; more recently, a developmentalist perspective is evident as well. Yet, the core—aiding victims of violent political conflict—remains and has defined the analytical focus of this book.

*Local capacity*, likewise, has many faces and meanings. Ian Smillie has recently sorted out the most common usage of the term in contemporary practice and the literature and come up with a 3x3 matrix (Smillie, 2001:11). Most common, perhaps, and most easily identified, is local organisational capacity. In the humanitarian arena, "local capacity" is often used to refer to local aid organisations in the affected areas, and which can identify need and meet them as effective service providers. Typically, these organisations are working in competition with large international NGOs (INGOs), or as subcontractor to them. Much discussion of local capacity concerns this relationship, and how to understand its dynamic. It is typically an unequal relationship, with the INGOs dominating (in terms of funding if not in numbers).

Explanations for the underdevelopment of local organisational capacity range from inadequate support and training to build local capacity, to a political economy perspective where obstacles to local organisational growth is seen as a result of structural imbalances, both locally and, more grandly, globally. In this latter view (de Waal, 1997; Duffield, 2001), the INGOs responding to humanitarian emergencies behave rather like certain multinational corporations that have a short time horizon and associated focus on narrow organisational gain. The local aid organisations resemble infant industries that need protectionist policies to survive—which they rarely get—and even then tend to fall by the wayside. State actors and international aid agencies reinforce this dynamic by being unconvinced of the rationale for developing local humanitarian capacity, and at any rate failing to promote it. The main exception to this pattern is the Red Cross movement, which consistently has supported the development of national branches in the South as well as the North. In this respect it appears as the exception that truly proves the rule. Unlike most NGOs, the Red Cross/Red Crescent is also a social movement, and building local chapters throughout the world is an integral part of its philosophy.

As Smillie makes clear, however, local capacity is much more than the existence of organisations as service providers. It entails institutional capacity to engage in a given arena within a) civil society—both the "new" civil society that was heavily promoted in the 1990s by aid agencies, and the "old" civil society in the sense of traditional social structures such as elders, clans, and—indeed—any authoritative body outside the state; and b) the public sector. Both state institutions and civil society structures represent a range of skills and resources that can be utilised and strengthened to deal with humanitarian emergencies. This is particularly the case when emergencies are protracted, requiring support to displaced or otherwise dependent populations for years.

Moreover, and here we depart from Smillie, local capacity can also be understood as knowledge and norms that are relevant reference points for action in a political arena or a public interest sector. Socially approved cognition, as Ernst Gellner argues in a different context, typically has ritual expressions or subtle forms of institutionalisation that may not be obvious to outsiders, yet constitutes an institutionalisation of capacity (Gellner, 1988). In the humanitarian arena, local norms to regulate war and assist victims, as well as socially accepted forms of coping with the consequences of violence and disaster, may constitute important types of local capacity. Unless expressed in Western-style institutions or other familiar forms, however, these types of capacity are readily overlooked by outsiders.

This book includes all these types of capacity. The context should make clear what kind is being discussed, i.e. organisations as service providers (including protection of rights), civil society structures to influence humanitarian action and underlying causes of war and disasters, public sector capacity to define and promote humanitarian action, local coping mechanisms, and local acceptance for traditional or contemporary humanitarian norms. As we shall see, the conditions for survival and growth of local capacity in the humanitarian arena depend in part upon the kind of capacity being addressed.

## Outlining the Arguments

To contextualize the question of local capacity in the African humanitarian arena, the book starts by examining how the international humanitarian regime has developed and how it functions. The chapter by Astri Suhrke demonstrates how changes in the international political system have influenced the development of the international humanitarian regime. Various models of humanitarian action emerged; in none of them were issues of local capacity a major concern. The international humanitarian regime has been rather self-absorbed with issues of organisational ethics and efficacy, defined in terms that are central to the operations of the large, Northern-based NGOs and the UN aid agencies concerned.

The chapter concludes by identifying the principal issues in the humanitarian discourse at the turn of the century. As aid agencies increasingly operated inside conflict zones—whether in the midst of civil war, in the chaos caused by an imploded state, or under the surveillance of a hostile state—they were confronted with the question of how to reduce the unintended, negative consequences of their action. Fearing their presence might unwittingly prolong the conflict by bringing large relief resources to contested areas or populations, the aid agencies reiterated a commitment to "do no harm", but did little else. The changing conditions of humanitarian action highlighted issues of protection (difficult to ensure) versus material assistance (easier to provide). The international humanitarians became more aware of local capacity questions, but were also alerted to the limitations of the concept. Local organisations might have difficulties operating in a conflict situation or be more vulnerable than foreign aid actors. They might also be corruptible or partisan in their approach. In Somalia in the early 1990s, the mushrooming presence of local NGOs designed to milk the foreign aid presence became a caricature of local capacity in the humanitarian arena. The refugee camps in (the then) Northern Zaire demonstrated in mid-decade how local power structures in the camp used the aid for partisan purposes and to prepare for a new round of the war. Of course, foreign NGOs were also competing for aid money, and some had sectarian or political interests—not unlike the "solidarity" tradition of humanitarian work noted above—but it was a different factor that brought the issue of local capacity to the forefront in a positive manner.

The proliferation of situations which called for humanitarian assistance and subsequent reconstruction during the 1990s encouraged aid agencies to reconsider the costs of humanitarian aid and contemplate structural reforms. Local capacity was promoted as a more cost-effective approach than wholesale reliance on international NGOs. Moreover, developing local capacity was viewed as a means for creating sustainable forms of assistance and bridging what became known in the international aid discourse as "the gap" between relief and development. In this way, developmentalist humanitarianism contributed to the rationale for building local capacity that in the late 1990s had come to dominate the rhetoric of aid.

The international humanitarian regime is founded on a set of norms that affirm the rights of victims to assistance and protection, as well as the obligations of the belligerents towards both victims and those assisting them. Discussing the status of international humanitarian law (IHL) in Africa in chapter 3, Mutoy Mubiala points to a stark dualism: African governments show a strong formal commitment to the law, but a manifest failure to respect it in practice. Of increasing importance, moreover, states are neither the only, nor the most critical, players in the wars on the continent, as there is a growing number of rebel groups, militias and private armies. A state-centered legal framework does not cover these actors and has no mechanisms for holding them accountable. This, Mubiala notes, is a main weakness of the IHL structure as it pertains to Africa today.

The single most important way of strengthening the status of humanitarian law in Africa, Mubiala argues, is to develop the links with customary law of war in the continent. Mubiala identifies critical points of convergence between IHL and customary law of war in Africa that could serve as building blocks for this purpose. Noting that African customary law of war largely disintegrated during the colonial period, he argues that restoring it as a foundation for current norms must be pursued as a matter of deliberate policy. In other words, utilising and strengthening local capacity in the norm sector is a necessary condition for more legitimate, sustainable and effective humanitarian action.

States in various parts of the world have found regional co-operation useful as a means to regulate humanitarian assistance and protection issues. This is particularly the case with respect to mass inflows of refugees, as Bonaventure Rutinwa discusses in chapter 4. Rutinwa explores the potential role of the now revitalised East African Community (EAC) in building and enhancing local relief capacity, particularly in response to mass inflows of refugees. The chapter synthesises the evolving thinking and practice relating to disaster response in the EAC, establishes the extent to which the EAC pursues common responses to emergencies, and identifies the linkages between the Secretariat and various governmental and non-governmental institutions in the region. Rutinwa suggests ways in which the regional framework can assist the development of local relief capacity and points to the various articles of the EAC treaty on which a regional response can be based.

The second half of the book examines the dynamics of building local relief capacity level in Eastern Africa. The evidence shows that local capacity has not been growing, but rather, has eroded over time. This applies particularly to capacity in its organisational and civil society forms. In the case of Somalia, humanitarian action in the 1990s attained a peculiar form by being intense politicised in a process that is commonly known as "spoils politics". The dynamic of the erosion of local capacity —or the failure to build new—varied according to the situations, as the country chapters show.

## Why the Focus on Eastern Africa?

In Eastern Africa, as elsewhere in the continent, the 1990s saw emergencies multiply and relief response assume a permanent rather than transient nature. Indeed, the new issues in the aid discourse relating to the prolonged nature and negative effects of some relief interventions were largely generated by experiences in Africa. An emerging conventional wisdom among donors and NGOs proclaimed—at least at the level of rhetoric—that strengthening local organisational capacity to provide services in the emergency response sector could break the vicious cycle of disaster, relief and dependency (Kathina Juma, 2001). This claim is based on three key assumptions. First, local organisations are more effective in utilising local knowledge, skills, institutions and experiences that have been largely ignored in the past. Second, local capacity in this sense will have externalities that help empower the affected communities to deal with existing and future disasters and ensure the ownership of the relief process. Third, local capacity can provide a basis for transition from relief to sustainable development, especially in the face of the practice by many aid agencies of shifting resources from the development to relief sector.

The case studies drawn from Kenya, Tanzania and Uganda present a good opportunity to examine these claims and ascertain the extent to which the formal commitment of donors and NGOs to build or utilise local capacity for humanitarian response is followed in practice. While each case study is country specific, all are guided by several broad concerns. They examine the nature and dynamics of local humanitarian capacity since independence, analyse how it was built and sustained during and after emergency situations, and assess the impact of international capacity on local capacity. In each chapter, the challenges and prospects for building capacity are identified, followed by recommendations on how the process can be strengthened.

Kenya, Tanzania and Uganda share a long history of responding to emergencies, including those caused by drought and famine. However, the compounded emergencies in the 1990s presented particular challenges. By 1995, the three countries were host to more than a third of Africa's 6 million refugees. In addition, Kenya and Uganda generated a significant number of internally displaced persons throughout the 1990s. These experiences provide a basis for examining what happens to local capacity when emergencies become large-scale and complex. Although the countries pursued different political trajectories soon after independence, the revitalisation of the East African Community in 1999 led to conscious attempts to create policy convergence in the treatment of forced migrants.

Compared to much of Africa, the three countries had stable political environments and functioning states in the 1990s. They share a history of substantial local relief capacity after independence, although this was less the case in Uganda in the 1970s and the 1980s. Nevertheless, the three countries were incapable of responding on their own to the emergencies that arose, necessitating the involvement of international actors. Within a short period, international organisations and aid agencies dominated the humanitarian scene. Concomitantly, assistance was emphasised at the expense of protection, which in several cases was neglected. Although to varying degrees, the response of the states was similar: those with refugee populations abdicated their responsibility to assist and protect, and those with large numbers of internally displaced persons obstructed the activities of aid actors seeking to help. These policies facilitated the entry and subsequent dominance of foreign aid actors in the humanitarian sector.

For Tanzania, Bonaventure Rutinwa traces the steady decline over a thirty-year period of local capacity to assist refugees. Local capacity in this case meant above all local community institutions and the government, on both the national and local level. The refugees arriving in the early 1960s were mainly assisted by the Tanzanian public sector and civil society structures. Importantly, the refugees themselves were involved in what became for the most part successful settlements. It was the response of a benevolent humanitarian system, created under and encouraged by President Julius Nyerere, who conceived of humanitarian action within the Pan-Africanist ideology. However, this capacity was gradually eroded in a process that started well before the massive refugee flows generated by the 1994 genocide in Rwanda. That event only accelerated and cemented a pattern that was already underway, in which international aid actors rapidly came to dominate the scene.

Rutinwa argues that the change was not primarily a function of either the declining administrative capacity of the Tanzanian state, nor the marked increase in the magnitude of refugee inflows. Rather, the Tanzanian government made a decision in the mid-1960s to accept a tripartite model of refugee assistance that effectively turned the main responsibility for aiding refugees over to UNHCR and its implementing partners, most of whom were international NGOs. When massive inflows from Rwanda appeared some three decades later, the pattern was set. At that point, donors and the UN aid agencies—which alone had the resources to assist the huge refugee population—insisted on controlling the funds by channelling them either through their own organisations or their established NGO partners. This proved decisive. The Tanzanian public and local community institutions that previously had been central in assisting refugees were totally marginalised. The result was a costly, conflictual and at times ineffective response to the refugee problem. More fundamentally, it encouraged the Tanzanian state to further abdicate its responsibility under international refugee law by making decisions to provide asylum contingent upon the receipt of foreign humanitarian aid.

The tripartite model and the funding structure had by this time become standard procedure for international assistance to refugees in most parts of the world. The Tanzanian case study provides a provocative illustration of its consequences in a country that at an earlier point had had significant local capacity to address humanitarian challenges.

Discussing reforms that he admits can only modify and not reverse this pattern, Rutinwa again focuses on the role of the state. While the state in the mid-1960s had opened the door for progressive international domination in the humanitarian field, it could equally restrain these actors and revive local capacity by establishing an appropriate legal and administrative framework to this end. In particular, regulations should be made to ensure a clear division of labour between local, national and international actors in the humanitarian arena.

In the Kenya chapter, Peter Mwangi Kagwanja contextualises aid to refugees and internally displaced persons (IDPs) within a security conscious, strong state. Kagwanja addresses the challenges confronting actors when a state relegates its international obligations to aid refugees to external actors, and prevents them from addressing the needs of internally displaced populations. The chapter focuses on the relationship between the state, perceived by humanitarian actors as strong, and humanitarian actors, perceived by the state as its nemesis. Kagwanja finds that assistance—whether local or international—can only be of limited effectiveness when the state views humanitarian crises through a prism of national security and is itself implicated in causing or accentuating the emergency.

Adopting a historical approach, the chapter traces the evolution of local capacity from the early years of independence through the 1990s. Kenya's refugee response was shaped by its self-definition as a place of transit rather than an asylum state: refugees were expected to only pass through the country on their way to third countries or receive temporary refuge before repatriation. Consequently, the government did not concern itself with developing local relief capacity. This left the burden of assisting refugees to the non-state sector, particularly the churches. Slowly but steadily the capacity to deal with refugees grew as Kenya remained a destination of choice for many people fleeing persecution. By the 1990s, when Kenya experienced an influx of large numbers of refugees and generated significant internal displacement, structures and skills for responding to emergencies had already evolved.

However, the pre-1990 relief response structure was fragile and was overwhelmed by the emergencies of the 1990s. International actors arrived to fill the consequent relief gap, but they failed to meet the critical challenge of strengthening indigenous capacity. Once on the scene, international organisations progressively excluded local actors, entrenched themselves and expanded their institutional power and influence, in effect, making their own exit or "devolution" of responsibility to local actors difficult. As in Tanzania, international capacity failed to phase out and promote local capacity building even after the emergency stabilised.

Accused of involvement in causing the ethnic and land clashes that prompted massive internal displacement in the 1990s, the Kenyan government was largely unwilling or unable to respond to the humanitarian consequences of the crises. Local actors were critical as first responders to aid the victims, but the political sensitivities of the conflict exposed them to great risks. This was an opportunity for international aid actors who assisted the IDPs in the early 1990s to boost the local aid sector as well. However, instead of strengthening the role of local organisations, the international humanitarians engaged in an unhealthy competition, duplicated efforts and played down local capacity. The clash among aid actors led to a deterioration in the conditions of the victims, waning of confidence in the solidarity between local and international humanitarian actors, and, finally, the withdrawal of most of the international actors from the IDP arena. Suspicious of international actors, local actors have since attempted to build their own capacities and cultivate some degree of indispensability within this arena.

Kagwanja concludes that the presence of local humanitarian actors with well-developed institutional structures and skilled personnel represents a significant potential to strengthen local relief capacity. This can only be achieved through intervention that focuses on three levels. At the local level technical assistance can help improve the effectiveness and sustainability of indigenous organisations. At the national level there is a need for a policy and administrative framework, which has been lacking since independence, to regulate the protection and assistance of displaced populations. Finally, Kagwanja suggests a re-orientation towards peace building, the rule of law and respect for human rights.

The Ugandan case study explores the role of relief capacity in the context of the rehabilitation and rejuvenation of a collapsed state and equally the civil institutions. Monica Kathina Juma and Bertha Amisi take us through the prospects of building local relief capacity as part of general reconstruction efforts in a country where both state and non-state structures are emerging "from the ashes". Focusing on local community capacity—particularly the potential of the communities most affected to marshal human and material resources to respond to adversity—the authors show that local capacity in this sense requires a minimal level of security and development. With conditions in North Central Uganda providing neither security nor development, local community structures have been fragmented and families dispersed. Violence and displacement have further discouraged the communities from utilising government-supported local institutions for empowerment and relief. In short, the authors conclude, the development of local capacity for relief presupposes the existence of at least a minimally supportive socio-economic and political environment that makes it possible to build an asset base to tide the community over a crisis.

Both national and international humanitarians have tried to alleviate the consequences of the insurgency and displacement in North Central Uganda. Most aid activities are relief-oriented and do not attempt to develop longer-term programmes, including support for local institutions and coping mechanisms. The shortcomings of the aid organisations in this respect also reflect the role of a strong and at times hostile state that wants to assert its control in the insurgency-ridden area. In this situation, humanitarian actors have retreated to a 'do no harm' model, preferring to secure access to victims and engage in minimalist relief interventions rather than confront the state.

In the Somalia case study, Joakim Gundel presents the classic humanitarian dilemmas associated with the complex emergencies that characterised the 1990s. Given the simultaneous collapse of both the state and the economy, the presence of heavily resourced foreign aid organisations became a determining factor in the local political economy. By channelling large resources into the conflict area, Western aid agencies helped create and reinforce structures of violence on the ground. Relief aid and externalities of the humanitarian presence fuelled Somali spoils politics, thereby intensifying the conflict, Gundel argues.

Whether aid was distributed though the local political actors or Somali aid organisations made little difference. Aid was controlled and distributed by and through warlord networks. Under these circumstances—that is, the absence of a functioning state, the presence of intensely competing local warlords, and little or no space for neutral humanitarian assistance on the ground—local organisational capacity became part of the problem rather than the solution. On the other hand, other forms of local capacity functioned positively, and distinctly better than foreign aid actors. Local market mechanisms and clan relations often helped to distribute the food without generating new conflict or permitting large-scale diversion of supplies through looting.

The Somali case exemplifies the dysfunctional aspects of international humanitarian aid and demonstrates the limitations of local capacity under the conditions of ongoing insecurity and spoils politics. There were numerous Somali NGOs, but most were instant creations in response to the inflow of aid and, particularly in the early phases of the emergency, were controlled by the warlords or the political actors. These NGOs, Gundel argues, contributed little to alleviating the humanitarian situation and probably fuelled the conflict. However, it was the context rather than any inherent qualities of local organisational capacity that produced this result.

In a concluding chapter, Monica Kathina Juma explores the dynamic of building local relief capacity in the 1990s. Drawing on the East African cases, she argues that relations among aid actors as well as their role vis-à-vis the host state is a fundamental determinant of capacity building. The chapter is guided by an apparent puzzle. If building local capacity for humanitarian action is more valuable than otherwise, as is frequently said in the international aid community, why have the three East African countries experienced a systematic decline in their capacity to deal with emergencies over time?

The starting point, Kathina Juma argues, is the notion of humanitarianism as a temporary interruption of development processes. A related assumption is that the affected area lacks relevant expertise. Receiving areas are in this respect declared a *terra nullis*. As a result, capacity building is seen as a one-way process of transferring the knowledge of the outsiders by them to the communities concerned. Capacity building projects—to the extent they exist—fail to recognise relevant local structures and knowledge. This approach to assistance typically devalues local actors in both the public administration and civil society. Soon the process becomes cumulative, with a built-in element of self-fulfilling prophecy. The dynamic is reinforced by intense competition among aid organisations for funding, structured in favour of the large, international aid actors. While much aid rhetoric professes a harmony of interest between local and international actors—where the latter find it in their interests to build "equal"and"genuine"partnerships that strengthen local capacity—this is in reality lacking. There is limited development of human resources and institutions for humanitarian action in the South, and little related technology transfer. All factors are critical to enhance local capacity.

The role of the host state in this constellation of forces is complex and at times perplexing. In the East African experience, the state—and especially its line agencies with responsibility for various aspects of humanitarian affairs—has been systematically sidestepped by the international aid agencies. In part, the state concerned has itself opened the door for this process by abdicating its responsibility in some areas, particularly in the refugee sector. On the other hand, the international donor community has been disinclined to recognize the role of the African state in the humanitarian arena, as evidenced by the refusal to channel significant aid funds through the public sector and thereby empower the state to assume responsibility. Instead, the international humanitarian regime has instituted an approach based on direct intervention to provide assistance, with key actors of that regime—the UN agencies and the large Northern-based NGOs—as the preferred channels.

The underlying logic of this regime drives humanitarian actors to show results in terms of immediate performance, which typically entails direct control to produce visible results in the short run. It encourages preoccupation with narrow organizational interests, notably the need to be present in emergency areas to qualify for future funding. In this schema, building local capacity assumes low priority and—in an ultimate sense—would be in fundamental conflict with the dominant interests of the regime.

# I

# Constructing a Framework for International Humanitarian Action

# 2. From Relief to Social Services

## An International Humanitarian Regime Takes Form

*Astri Suhrke*

To appreciate the radical change of humanitarian action in the modern age, it is useful to look at the international response to two fairly similar wars in Europe. During the Spanish Civil War, Madrid was partly or wholly blockaded, shelled and bombed during almost the entire war (1936–39); towards the end, hundreds of residents were dying daily from hunger. Yet there were no food convoys or airlifts to the besieged city. During the siege of Sarajevo during the Bosnian war, five decades later, the city became the end point for "the longest-running humanitarian air-bridge in history, [lasting] from 30 June 1992 to 5 January 1996" (Roberts, 1996:36). During the years of the air-bridge, UNHCR-chartered planes made 12,951 sorties, delivering 160,677 tons of food, shelter material and medical supplies. Observers noted the airlift even included fresh orange-juice (Woodward, 1995:325).

The sharp differences in response reflected systemic changes in the international community, rather than the differences in need or the nature of warfare. As indicated in the introduction to this book, the distinguishing characteristic of the humanitarian response during the 20th century was that it evolved from an ad hoc crisis response into an institutionalised regime with global coverage, numerous actors, state and private sources of finance, rules and principles of action, and structures for identifying needs and charting strategies of response. This development was particularly evident in the 1990s. Yet a longer historical perspective shows that sub-regimes had developed earlier, particularly in the refugee sector and around individual organisations such as the Red Cross movement. The Red Cross already started to diversify its activities in the 20th century, expanding beyond situations in which the movement had originated (to aid combatants and civilians injured in war) to respond to nature-made disasters (e.g. earthquakes) and what today would be called complex emergencies (e.g. concurrent war, famine and displacement). The humanitarian imperative was given diverse institutional expressions and more elaborate legal framework forms after World War II. Both were subsequently developed, and strikingly so in the immediate aftermath of the Cold War. Landmarks in the legal arena included a treaty to ban anti-personnel landmines and moves to prohibit the use of child soldiers. The "right" of humanitarians to intervene where needed to assist civilians was repeatedly asserted at the UN. As a sign of the changing times, the UN Security Council—normally preoccupied with the "high politics" of international peace and security—started to discuss "human security" and in September 1999 it held an open meeting on protection of civilians in armed conflicts. By the end of the 20th century, a wide range of humanitarian activities had come together in a recognisable international regime.

## Characteristics of the International Humanitarian Regime

In its present form, the system satisfies the meaning of 'regime' as it is developed in the social science literature: a system of actors, norms and responses that has emerged to address a common set of tasks (Rittberger, 1993). The formal objectives in this case are to save lives and reduce suffering caused by man-made and nature-made events. The system is international in the sense that the actors—international agencies and nationally-based organisations—operate internationally, and the total coverage is global. It is properly called a regime because it is a loosely organised entity, held together more by common norms and purposes than authoritative arrangements of funding and decision-making, a sort of governance without government in a defined public policy sector.

More tightly structured regimes (e.g. some addressing international environmental problems) have restricted scope and membership, and participants undertake well-defined obligations that are subject to joint monitoring (Haas, Keohane and Levy, 1993). By contrast, the international humanitarian regime as constituted by the end of the 20th century had

— a wide scope—members addressed problems ranging from humanitarian consequences of man-made to nature-made events;
— flexible jurisdiction—since the objective was to assist individuals in need regardless of their location, the principle that access should not be limited by sovereign jurisdiction was invoked; however, access to conflict areas within states remained variable and often had to be negotiated;
— no common membership screening—there was no central mechanism for screening membership based on common criteria for admission. As a result, in the 1990s some major NGOs and analysts stressed the desirability of establishing a credentials process for private aid organisations so as to strengthen professionalism in a rapidly growing "relief industry " (Weiss and Collins, 1996);
— no common monitoring of compliance—while the objectives and methods of humanitarian action were governed by international norms, there was no central, authoritative mechanism to monitor progress (in reducing suffering and saving lives) or compliance (with codes of conduct for humanitarian organisations). Monitoring and evaluation functions were decentralised, ad hoc, and usually undertaken by donors and authorities in the recipient country. Typically, the result was decisions affecting only the individual organisation scrutinised with respect to its future funding or permit to operate;
— uncertain and ad hoc financing—both the UN agencies and the aid organisations were heavily dependent upon annual allocations and ad hoc campaigns to raise funds for operational activities. While this produced a fairly steady level of funding, the budgetary process became increasingly regularised, this was the outcome of a competitive process rather than stable structures of financing. The financial relationship between the major donors and the humanitarian actors was essentially that of a spot contract. Lacking sequential obligations, these are the most limited kind of contracts, as Kratochwil has pointed out (Kratochwil, 1993). The humanitarian actors could not be certain that funds would be forthcoming to maintain current operations, or anticipate what amounts would be available for new emergencies.

The loose structure produced a regime riven by internal rivalry among the executive actors—humanitarians and human rights organisations, national and internationally based NGOs, and UN agencies. In high-visibility crises, the competition widened as states sought to demonstrate a humanitarian presence and military establishments became humanitarian actors as well (e.g. in Kosovo 1999). In addition to competition for funds, the power of presence became a major source of rivalry on the aid scene.

The regime had three principal types of actors: (i) UN organisations providing humanitarian assistance (mainly the United Nations High Commissioner for Refugees, UNHCR, the United Nations Children's Fund, UNICEF, the United Nations Development Programme, UNDP, the World Health Organization, WHO, the World Food Programme, WFP), and the main UN co-ordinating entity, Office for the Coordination of Humanitarian Affairs (OCHA), which replaced the UN Department of Humanitarian Affairs, (ii) non-governmental organisations and the Red Cross movement, and (iii) the donors, both bilateral and multilateral organisations such as the European Commission Humanitarian Office, ECHO. The regime rested on two major bodies of international law—humanitarian law and refugee law—and, to a lesser extent, human rights law. These norms provided a legal framework for action and legitimised the activities. For operational purposes, some organisations had developed common principles of conduct—notably the Code of Conduct in disaster relief promoted by the Red Cross movement and subscribed to by the principal NGOs—and the code of conduct of the International Committee of the Red Cross (ICRC). In the mid-1990s, major NGOs developed detailed common standards for provision of basic necessities during emergencies, down to the amount of water (litres per day) and space (square metres) per person (the SPHERE project).

The regime worked according to a general division of labour and principles of co-ordination. The division of labour was defined by formal mandates (especially for the UN agencies), as well as by political, financial or organisational interests. Many organisations showed considerable flexibility in adjusting to new operational requirements and funding possibilities—thus demonstrating a measure of organisational learning as Ernst Haas would have argued (Haas, 1990). In the 1990s, for instance, organisations that previously had focused on development assistance expanded into more clearly humanitarian activities (e.g. UNDP) while the humanitarian agencies moved into longer-term development-related assistance (e.g. UNHCR). The change was facilitated by the term "relief-to-development", which entered the aid vocabulary of the 1990s and encouraged organisations from both ends of the spectrum to take on new tasks to ensure a smooth transition from one to the other.

The division of labour between the UN agencies and the NGOs reflected operational and funding considerations. All the UN agencies used NGOs as implementing partners. Some relied very heavily on NGOs, especially UNHCR, which in a relatively slow year in the early 1990s—just as its engagement in Bosnia was starting, and before the Rwanda emergency—had around 350 implementing partners (UNHCR, 1993:178). Although looking to the UN agencies as major sources of funding, the private organisations had additional financing from state governments and public campaigns that made them independent of the UN system and, UN agencies complained, very difficult to co-ordinate. This was particularly the case in high-visibility crises when funding was plentiful and incentives to be present were strong. In the refugee emergency following the 1994 Rwanda genocide, for instance, the international NGOs independently mobilised almost as much funding as did UNHCR, controlling 20 per cent of total humanitarian resources committed to the emergency as compared with 24 per cent for the agency (Suhrke et al., 2000:85). At the opening of the 1990s, the funds contributed by or through NGOs to humanitarian programs were equivalent to over half of the amount allocated by OECD member states, or 3 billion dollars compared with 5 billion (Danida, 1999:3; Eliasson, 1992).

In some situations, the nature of the conflict rendered the UN agencies more dependent than normal on NGOs for relief distribution and project implementation. For instance, the continuing war in Afghanistan in the mid-1990s and UN security regulations made it difficult for UN officials to move freely in the country and operate effectively. International NGOs, by contrast, had their own security regulations that permitted freer movement and could draw on accumulated local knowledge from a long presence in the country. National NGOs had mushroomed as well. As a result, the large UN relief operation—amounting to about half a million dollars a day at the end of the 1990s—was mostly channelled through projects planned and operated by NGOs (www.pcpafg.org). The UN decision to headquarter its Afghanistan-operations in neighbouring Islamabad during the Taliban-period made it further dependent on NGOs, which maintained offices inside Afghanistan.

The proliferation of activities and actors on the humanitarian scene generated demands for a more coherent response—effectively for a more institutionalised regime. "Coherence", "co-ordination" and "connectedness" became central criteria for OECD programme evaluations in the humanitarian sector (OECD/DAC, 1999). The calls originated in mounting donor concerns about rapidly growing humanitarian budgets. OECD donor budgets for emergency/humanitarian assistance increased dramatically from less than 2 billion dollar (US) in 1989, to almost 5 billion in 1991. This level was maintained in the first part of the 1990s, peaking in 1994 at some 6 billion before flattening out (Danida, 1999:3).

Efforts to economise fed into a parallel process started in the 1990s to reform the UN. Culminating in 1997, it introduced new co-ordinating mechanisms for the humanitarian sector, principally a new office for co-ordination (OCHA), a more elaborate structure of inter-agency co-ordinating committees at the UN headquarters level, and a more ambitious common appeal for fund raising (the Inter-Agency Consolidated Appeal, CAP). For exceptionally difficult cases, special co-ordination structures were established that included donors and NGOs as well as the UN agencies: the Strategic Framework for Afghanistan was the first and supposedly model case. More co-ordination did not necessarily follow, however (Daedring, 1996, ODI, 2001).

The increased availability of funds in the early 1990s permitted rapid expansion of humanitarian activities, which generated an equally rapid growth of critics who disparaged the "disaster relief industry" (de Waal, 1997). The competitive market dimension of the regime became more pronounced, highlighting the loose nature of the common structures that made actors compete for funding and spheres of operation—niches in the market, so to speak. In this game, new aid organisations were pitted against old, locals against internationals, and UN agencies against each other, although there was a closing of the ranks in matters of resource allocation to humanitarian programs generally. The ability to attract funding depended only partially on quality, efficiency or core mandate of the organisations. Visibility in the media and closeness to donor governments were important as well.

Elements of a competitive market notwithstanding, the overall trend during the second half of the 20th century was towards an institutionalised regime with global reach and wide coverage of services. From the Spanish Civil War to the siege of Sarajevo, humanitarian assistance had essentially been transformed from ad hoc relief assistance to a predictable system of social services.

## The Dynamic of Change

What explains this change? Theories of how international regimes take form identify different types of dynamics, related to respectively a) political realism (national power interests), b) utilitarian, usually collective interests, and c) normative concerns (Rittberger, 1993). These are not mutually exclusive, and all explain to various degrees the growth of the humanitarian regime during the second half of the century. Need in and of itself, it should be noted, is not assumed to be a principal explanation for regime growth. Rather, it is recognised that there is no straightforward relationship between humanitarian needs and humanitarian responses; the former may be a necessary but certainly not a sufficient condition for assistance, as the siege of Madrid in 19936–39 demonstrated. Needs have to be acknowledged, weighed against other demands and interests, and resources have to be mobilised for assistance to materialise. For this reason, it is only an apparent paradox that the level of expenditure for humanitarian purposes stabilised at a high level in the mid-1990s even though the need—as indicated by the number of conflicts and related casualties—started to decrease (Sollenberg and Wallensteen, 1999). Similarly, the argument that wars in the late 20th century were more barbarous than earlier wars in their impact on civilians, and hence generated more humanitarian action, does not hold up well. The Spanish Civil War is again instructive.

By erasing the distinction between combatants and civilians, systematically and on a grand scale, the Spanish Civil War was one of the first truly 20th century conflicts. Referring to the fading distinction between combatants and non-combatants, Hobsbawm notes that the war represented an "unfortunately accelerating return to what our nineteenth-century ancestors would have called the standards of barbarism" (Hobsbawm, 1996:13). Descriptions of the war are disturbingly familiar. Civilians—including their means of subsistence—were primary targets of attack. The Nationalist (Franco) forces took few prisoners, and staged mass executions to "clean up" (limpieza) territory they had conquered and to rid the country of "the evils which had overtaken it" (Thomas, 1986:279, Ellwood, 1991). Republic supporters murdered thousands of clergy, devout members of the laity and other presumed "reactionaries". Cities were besieged. In Barcelona, swollen with a million refugees from areas that had fallen to the advancing Franco forces, disease and malnutrition were rampant; deaths from malnutrition alone doubled between 1937 and 1938. Cities were indiscriminately bombed, most dramatically Guernica in the Basque region. Yet the massive humanitarian needs of the war went largely unattended.

The Quakers established a fund to assist refugee children, but had money to feed only 40,000 of the 600,000 identified as needy. The international Red Cross movement donated a modest 4 million francs (compared with 277 million for victims of the earthquake in Japan some ten years earlier). The International Committee of the Red Cross worked mainly in the traditional area of prisoner exchange. Sympathetic political groups in Western democracies provided some assistance to the Republic, as did the Soviet Union. "Friends of Spain, Spanish medical aid committees, committees for Spanish relief were established everywhere" to proclaim solidarity with the Republic (Thomas, 1986:461). The German and Italian governments supplied the Franco forces with both military and medical aid. But the large international, presumptively neutral and impartial humanitarian apparatus, financed by states and intended to aid the victims of war, simply did not exist.

Humanitarian assistance during the Spanish Civil War constitutes what can be called "the traditional mode" of response, and is a useful starting point for assessing later change. It was predominantly "aid as solidarity", undertaken mainly by civil society. The League of Nations, which could have provided the backbone for an international state-financed system of humanitarian assistance, was inherently weak and practically defunct in the late 1930s. The League did have an office to aid refugees, but its mandate was limited to certain nationalities and did not include internally displaced persons.

## The Post-World War II Period

Most of the factors critical for regime development that were absent during the League-period gradually came into place after World War II. The horrors of war and persecution itself contributed significantly by creating aspirations for a more humane post-war order, and were articulated in international norms that promoted humanitarian action and human rights (the 1949 Geneva conventions, the 1948 Declaration of human rights and the 1951 Convention on the status of refugees).

International arrangements established to assist refugees and persons displaced by World War II constituted a forerunner of the present humanitarian regime in a chronological as well as ontological sense. The office of the UN High Commissioner for Refugees (UNHCR) subsequently expanded its role because states recognised that it provided a public benefit in line with their interests—that is, providing immediate assistance and brokering proposals for longer-term solutions to displacement that, if left to itself, would likely create further disorder. At the same time, these activities were in line with the universal language of human rights articulated after the war. In retrospect, it is evident that the expansionary dynamic harmonised with theories of how regimes develop, and how international public goods come to be recognised as such (Kaul et al., 1996). From assisting refugees and displaced persons in Europe after World War II, UNHCR moved on to aid refugees from Africa's wars of independence in the 1960s and 1970s. During the next two decades the agency underwent a massive expansion. This was occasioned, first, by the large number of refugees from Cold War-related conflicts in the Third World, and, in the 1990s, by numerous victims of new wars, including populations besieged or displaced within the conflict area (Loescher, 1993, 2001). In the course of this period, UNHCR gradually widened its definition of beneficiary from the specific category of "refugees", who by legal definition had left their country to seek assistance and protection in other states, to the more general term "people of concern". At the same time, the coverage in terms of services expanded rapidly. Measured in constant (1970) dollars, the agency's per capita budget per beneficiary had risen from 3 dollars in 1970 to around 17 in 1990 (Suhrke, 1995:119).

## Biafra

The civil war in Nigeria (1967–70) is sometimes viewed as the first modern humanitarian crisis. The war sparked a large international media campaign to provide relief to civilian victims; this in turn focused attention on the right of humanitarian organisations to operate in an internal conflict without the consent of the belligerents. At the time, UNHCR was not assisting persons within the country of conflict (as it later did in Yugoslavia). Still in the grips of the Cold War, other UN agencies stayed out as well. Humanitarian intervention was still a concept of the future. But the private aid organisations and the Red Cross moved into the void with great alacrity. Indeed, the crisis opened a new growth period for humanitarian NGOs; Médecins Sans

Frontières, today one of the largest multi-national NGOs, was established to aid the Biafra victims.

The Biafra case brought out the conflicting principles of humanitarianism that later created agonising divisions in the international aid community. The solidarity tradition dispensed with concerns of impartiality and neutrality, while the Red Cross tradition required that aid actors be impartial (by assisting victims on both sides of the conflict), and neutral in relation to the political issues in the conflict. In the Biafra conflict, the victims were concentrated on one side; famine developed only in the secessionist enclave of Biafra, which was blockaded by the central Nigerian government. Impartiality was consequently not an issue. But neutrality was. Struggling to be neutral in relation to the conflict, the International Committee of the Red Cross (ICRC) stood firm on the principle that both belligerents must consent to aid operations and guarantee that assistance would not be used for military purposes. When the central government obstructed aid deliveries to Biafra, and the rebel government flew in arms in the shadow of relief supplies, the ICRC suspended operations (Forsythe, 1977). Other NGOs defied the Nigerian government and set aside the neutrality principle in order to aid the Biafra population, thus operating in the solidarity mode of assistance as classically defined by the Spanish Civil War.

Biafra became a historic marker for the policy debate on neutrality-versus-solidarity of humanitarian action. It set a precedent for the right claimed by humanitarian agents to freely assist civilians in an internal conflict, without limitations imposed by jurisdictions of sovereignty or political authority. Biafra was the first modern emergency in another sense as well. By brilliantly manipulating the famine for propaganda purposes, the Biafra leaders demonstrated the political significance of suffering in a world of mass media and humanitarian consciousness (Stremlau, 1977). The result was that Western relief aid was rushed to the Biafra side and in a small measure compensated for the material weakness of the secessionist side.

## The Cold War in the 1970s and 1980s

During the next 20 years, humanitarian assistance expanded massively, on the heels of the Cold War and partly as its instrument. Indeed, a distinct feature of this period is the frequent overlapping between the humanitarian and the political spheres. Much of the assistance was in the mode of solidarity aid; the difference from the Spanish Civil War period was that this time the aid was largely financed by states, mainly in the West.

Local or regional wars in Africa, Asia and Latin America in this period produced large movements of refugees in need of long-term assistance. Many found it in neighbouring countries where political conditions made it safe and easy for humanitarians to operate. The first large refugee movements from Indochina (late1970s), and Afghanistan (early 1980s), were followed by large and sustained displacements in the Horn of Africa, Southern Africa, and Central America. During the decade of the 1980s, the refugee population in Africa, Asia and Latin America as counted by UNHCR doubled, reaching 14.7 million in 1990 (UNHCR, 1993:8–9).

The rapidly accumulating refugee population, of which many were confined to camps requiring long-term care and maintenance, generated a comparable growth in the international humanitarian regime. UNHCR's budget increased ten-fold over six years in the 1970s and doubled in the next two to stabilise around 500 million dollars annually in the 1980s (UNHCR, 1993). Other UN agencies provided relief as well, particularly WFP (food deliveries) and UNICEF (water). In some cases such as Afghan refugee camps in Pakistan, UNDP and the World Bank assisted in rehabilitating campsites and the affected localities. The ICRC's budget went through a comparable expansion; from a modest annual budget of about 19 million francs in the early 1970s, to a budget for relief supplies alone totalling 219 million in 1985 (ICRC, 1985). Although precise data are not available, the NGO sector grew rapidly as UN agencies and bilateral aid agencies needed partners to implement projects on the ground. Some estimates suggest an increase from 1,600 in 1980 to 2,500 in 1990, including both development and humanitarian NGOs (Weiss and Gordenker, 1996:44) The NGO growth was even more dramatic in the early 1990s: NGOs of all kinds registered with the Union of International Associations as operating in three or more countries and receiving finances from sources in more than one country, doubled from 1991 to 1993/4 to reach 16,142. Nevertheless, the 1980s appear in retrospect as a critical take-off phase for the international humanitarian regime in terms of organisational growth and budgetary expansion

While the need for assistance was obvious, its recognition was clearly aided by the fact that the refugee movements resulted from conflicts that were closely related to the superpower rivalry of the Cold War. The Cold War, it will be recalled, was pervasive in its reach. As the division of Europe stabilised during the 1960s, the superpowers extended their rivalry to other regions, offering patronage to even small and hitherto overlooked parties. Directly, or at some steps remove, the United States and the Soviet Union became involved in all the major conflicts in Asia, Africa and Latin America in this period; the East-West ideological divide was in some measure reproduced in the local conflict dynamic. As a result, humanitarian assistance to the victims was often used by states to promote interests other than reducing suffering and saving lives. Aid could serve a propaganda function by highlighting the culpability of subjecting countries to conflict or oppression while demonstrating one's own moral worth. It could appease regional allies that provided large-scale asylum, and, in some cases, aid enabled a population in exile to continue fighting. While such interests did not reduce the life-saving impact of assistance, they explain the extraordinary surge in funding for Western-based NGOs and UN humanitarian agencies.

The ideological overlay of the Cold War affected the neutrality-solidarity issues of humanitarian action in other ways as well. The statutes of the relevant UN agencies and the Red Cross movement prescribed adherence to the traditional humanitarian principles of neutrality and impartiality, but NGOs were at the outset more open with respect to choice of locality and activity. In practice, NGOs that were funded directly by state governments typically worked on one side of the conflict. In certain situations, however, even agencies and organisations committed to the principles of neutrality and impartiality found it difficult to observe them, and—like the ICRC in Biafra—some contemplated withdrawing rather than compromise.

The dilemma appeared starkly in situations where refugee camps were closely linked to the ongoing conflict, either directly by serving as a sanctuary and conduit of material supplies for military groups, or indirectly by providing manpower for military recruitment and basic services for a civilian community that gave political legitimacy to the military struggle (Zolberg et al., 1989; Terry, 2000). "Refugee-warrior" communities, as they came to be called in the literature, appeared most obviously on the border between Pakistan and Afghanistan, between Thailand and Cambodia, in countries neighbouring El Salvador, in various countries in the Horn of Africa and in southern Africa (Mason and Brown, 1983; Shawcross, 1984, Baitenmann, 1990). Such situations painfully exposed a humanitarian dilemma that re-emerged in the 1990s, above all in the Rwanda–Zaire case. By almost directly benefiting one party to the conflict, humanitarian assistance was not neutral and arguably served to perpetuate the violence. Withdrawing aid, however, might have endangered the lives of innocent civilians.

The growth of the humanitarian regime in this period meant greater attention was given as well to some of those who could not flee. In the Sudan, the combined effects of war and drought produced a massive famine in the mid-1980s, prompting over one hundred organisations, mainly Western-based NGOs and UN agencies to offer assistance. Heavily dependent upon U.S. support for survival, the government of Numayri reluctantly permitted humanitarian assistance to reach the rebel-controlled South as well as other regions. His successors were not as co-operative, however. An agreement for humanitarian assistance to victims in both the North and the South was concluded in 1989—the first Operation Lifeline Sudan—but languished (Burr and Collins, 1995; Keen, 1994). A new agreement was concluded in 1994 under UN auspices, but implementation was uneven.

## After the Cold War

The end of the Cold War entailed structural and doctrinal change in the international state system that facilitated collective intervention under the aegis of the United Nations. At the same time, the end of the Cold War reduced the strategic significance of many ongoing conflicts (e.g. Afghanistan), while some new ones that erupted (e.g. in Central Africa) were marginal to the interests of the major states. Closer to the Atlantic-European power centres, disagreement over objectives and strategies prevented decisive political-military intervention (the Balkans), or old spheres of influence prevailed to preclude it (Caucasus). Yet in all cases demands were made that "something be done". The demands reflected globalised communications that instantly transmitted images of human suffering, and resonated with a progressively transnational civic culture of human rights and humanitarian action. The force of such demands was heightened by unusually large displacements—e.g. when 2–3 million Iraqi Kurds and Shi'ites streamed towards the borders of Iran and Turkey in 1991—or particularly horrific events, such as ethnic cleansing in the former Yugoslavia and genocide by machete-wielding paramilitaries in Rwanda.

The conjuncture of humanitarian imperatives and strategic marginalisation that appeared as the decade opened translated into demands for humanitarian intervention of various kinds. Although the UN and the major powers were reluctant to intervene to address the causes of conflict, humanitarian assistance could be provided. In the humanitarian community, there was both elation over the new significance attached to their work, and anxiety that the humanitarians could serve as a fig-leaf for more fundamental indecision. The tendency for humanitarian action to substitute for efforts to regulate the conflict itself was particularly evident in Yugoslavia and Rwanda (Higgins, 1993; Danida, 1996).

A related development was the diminishing opportunity for protection and assistance in other countries. The large refugee camps that had emerged as a biproduct of the internationalised internal wars of the 1980s were being reduced as these conflicts wound down. While new conflicts emerged, and some of the old ones simmered on, Western states were less willing to pay for long-term refugee camps, and neighbouring countries accepted the asylum role with increasing reluctance. The restrictions on conventional asylum were particularly harsh in Europe, as had been evident for some time. When a major war erupted on the doorstep of the European

Union in 1992, the UN High Commissioner for Refugees concluded that a new, "comprehensive approach" to the Balkan victims of war and ethnic cleansing was necessary. Greater protection to displaced persons within the conflict area was part of this strategy, designed to increase protection while simultaneously pre-empt a massive refugee flow into the rest of Europe and the United States.

The notion of internal protection fitted nicely with a broader doctrinal development that emphasised the right of humanitarian actors to freely provide assistance within the country of conflict. While previously articulated in non-state circles, the "right"—or even duty—to intervene in pursuit of humanitarian objectives was now raised at the state level. The idea had already been introduced by the French government in the form of a draft General Assembly resolution in 1989–90 at the initiative of Bernard Kouchner, founder of Médecins Sans Frontières and at the time Minister of Humanitarian Affairs in the French government. The notion was cautiously embedded in the authorisation of the new UN Department of Humanitarian Affairs in 1992. The idea legitimated the appointment in 1992 of a special representative for IDPs who reported to the UN Secretary-General and the UN Commission on Human Rights. The representative, Francis Deng, untiringly promoted the rights of IDPs through studies, lobbying and eventually a set of guidelines of response (Cohen and Deng, 1998; ASIL, 2000). By the end of the decade, the reformulation of principles had clearly eroded the right of sovereign states to refuse foreign humanitarian assistance. In the UN system, the new thinking received much support at the level of the Secretary-General. In 1998, for instance, Kofi Annan unequivocally asserted that refugees, displaced persons and other victims of armed conflict had "a right" to receive international protection and assistance (UN, 1998:par. 15).

A parallel development was the doctrinally separate but similar idea of the right of states to intervene militarily in support of humanitarian objectives (Ramsbotham and Woodhouse, 1996; Roberts, 1996). While the claim of humanitarian agents to assist victims of conflict was based on international humanitarian law and human rights law, the right of UN member states to intervene militarily was founded on considerations of international peace and security as specified in Chapter VII in the UN Charter. In an unprecedented resolution (Res. 688/1991), the Security Council first invoked Chapter VII to establish a "security zone" for Kurds and Shi'ites forcibly displaced inside Iraq in April 1991. Chapter VII was subsequently used to authorise other military interventions in formal pursuit of humanitarian objectives, starting with Somalia. Drawing together the two strands of interventionist justifications, the UN Secretary-General put forward a concept of "two sovereignties". Placing the sovereignty of individuals on an equal footing with traditional state sovereignty, Annan called for humanitarian interventions whenever this was necessary to halt "massive and systematic violations of human rights" (UN, 1999:2).

The result of these developments was a stronger and more diversified humanitarian regime. There was greater readiness to assist civilian populations caught in internal conflicts, whether the wars were new (the former Yugoslavia), seemingly nonending old ones (the Sudan and Angola), complex emergencies with war and famine (Somalia) or previous conflicts emerging in a new form (Afghanistan, Rwanda). In some semi-permanent emergencies, the international aid community de facto took over social service and welfare functions normally provide by states. Peace settlements entailed substantial assistance as well, particularly for rehabilitation and reintegration (e.g. in Cambodia, Central America and the former Yugoslavia). By the mid-1990s, some 45 million beneficiaries were supported, compared to 15 million ten years earlier.

## Divisions and Issues in the Contemporary Regime

The massive growth of the international humanitarian regime towards the end of the 20th century magnified its good as well as its problematic aspects, and brought its inherent contradictions into public view. A new, critical literature appeared, generated by both outside analysts and practitioners (Brauman, 1996; Barber, 1997; de Waal, 1997; Maren, 1997; Rieff, 1996). Aid could serve as a fig leaf not only for non-intervention in dealing with a particular conflict. As humanitarian assistance became an international welfare safety net in semi-permanent crises in the South, the rich and stable North came to regard conflict as a normal state of affairs in the South, as Mark Duffield argued (2001). Addressing the symptoms of conflict, humanitarian aid had an anaesthetising effect that distracted attention from underlying causes and cures.

Operating within conflicts posed particular dilemmas for humanitarian actors. As noticed in the Biafra case, aid could serve to prolong war. On the operational level the dilemma was addressed with the 'do no harm' principle; on the ideological level it touched the old solidarity-versus-neutrality divide in the humanitarian com-munity. A related issue concerned the imbalance between protection and assistance. Whether facing a strong state or fragmented authority, aid agencies found it much easier to materially assist their clients than to physically protect them. Finally, the massive and often prolonged presence of international aid agencies in conflict areas or adjacent refugee camps brought up issues of local capacity. Did international aid presence undermine the capacity of both local state and civil society to respond? What were the dynamics of the relationship between local and international aid capacity, and under what conditions could the former be strengthened? Could more use of local capacity reduce the costs of humanitarian operations and reduce the gap between relief and subsequent development?

### Impact of Aid on the Conflict

For almost three decades, the logic of superpower competition had complied with the needs of local protagonists by liberally financing their wars. Since most states already had an apparatus for extracting resources, financing a war was most problematic for the rebels (or for all warring parties when the state imploded). When the Cold War ended, humanitarian assistance with its large inventory of food, medicine and infrastructure for delivery (including vehicles and radios) became a substitute for superpower financing. As the warring parties increasingly sought to control the relief resources that were channelled into the conflict area, humanitarian actors became hostages to "unwilling solidarity" with one or the other side, or found themselves indirectly feeding the war.

Some belligerents had other resources. As Jean-Christophe Rufin notes, rebel economies have shown considerable ingenuity and adaptation (Rufin, 1996). Insurgencies on the political left had traditionally tried to live off the people on whose behalf the struggle was waged. Rebels of all shades taxed the local economy, particularly smuggling routes, or supervised illicit, lucrative production. The role of poppy in Afghanistan, coca in Colombia and timber and gemstones in the Khmer Rouge-controlled sector of Cambodia are oft-cited cases; more recently Angola and Sierra Leone, where access to local raw materials financed a protracted war (Berdal and Malone, 2000). Communities with established out-migration traditions had important diasporas that helped finance the struggle, notably the Palestinians, Armenians,

Tamils and Eritreans. But where there were neither diamonds nor migrants, and where people lived close to subsistence level, external resources became critically important. It was above all in these areas that humanitarian assistance in the 1990s picked up the slack from Cold War financing.

As a principal source for keeping the local communities alive, humanitarian aid became inextricably tied up with the struggles fought by, or on behalf of, those communities. Assistance was taxed, sold or seized or—more indirectly—reproduced the social basis for continued violence. The resultant dilemmas for humanitarian actors had been observed in the 1980s with reference to "refugee warrior" communities in exile; now they were internal to the country and appeared as a generalised feature across most conflicts. As the problems of "doing good without doing harm" mounted, some organisations withdrew or suspended their work (e.g. in Eastern Zaire and Liberia). The dangers of working in a war zone, particularly in conflicts where civilians and relief supplies were central targets in the conflict, similarly compelled agencies to withdraw (for instance, UNHCR and ICRC temporarily suspended their operations in Sarajevo; ICRC did likewise in Burundi after four of its delegates were killed in 1997, and all aid agencies withdrew when six foreign Red Cross workers were killed in Chechnya in 1997).

## The Protection Gap

Large-scale infusion of assistance highlighted the disproportionate lack of protection. Traditionally, the protection and assistance functions of the humanitarian presence had been distinct and separate. Assistance meant providing material goods and medical services to save and sustain life. Protection meant protecting human and humanitarian rights by promoting the relevant bodies of international law, monitoring the treatment of prisoners of war and other victims of armed conflict, providing refugees with legal protection to secure their formal rights and, ultimately, deterring violence against civilians and military hors de combat with whatever means were at hand. Many humanitarian organisations provided material assistance only, partly because this typically was easier than to effect protection. Protection was central to the Red Cross/Red Crescent movement, particularly the ICRC, but the protection function was backed only by the power of the symbol, by testimony and presence, and by long-term promotion of international humanitarian law. It was hoped that this would deter violence against persons in clearly designated humanitarian zones (notably Red Cross/Red Crescent hospitals), and to have a civilising influence on warfare and treatment of victims more generally. UNHCR's central and original mandate was to protect refugees, but until the 1990s it customarily worked in asylum areas outside the theatre of conflict.

The difficulties of providing both protection and assistance within a conflict area were exemplified during the war in Bosnia; the two functions became fused in a way that highlighted the imbalance between them. The lead humanitarian agency (UNHCR) was for the first time specifically mandated to protect civilians within a war zone. To prevent expulsion of people ("preventive protection"), and to protect those who had been displaced, the agency had at the height of the conflict in late 1993 a total of 25 protection officers—unarmed, civilian UNHCR-staff, mainly lawyers. The much larger assistance operation indirectly served protection purposes as well (Cutts, 1999), but its main purpose was to provide material supplies. A massive relief effort co-ordinated by UNHCR supplied food and medicines to almost four million "persons of concern". The humanitarian mission operated in a context where the UN Security Council had designated certain areas as "safe havens" and deployed military units (UNPROFOR) to protect them. In the end, UNPROFOR did not implement its protection mandate, and the civilian humanitarian actors were totally unequipped to withstand the targeted onslaught on civilians, which was a principal feature of the war. While starting from what in retrospect seem like unrealistic expectations, critics responded by expressing doubt and disillusionment with humanitarian assistance generally. What was the purpose of humanitarian aid when the UN protected itself and the relief convoys rather than the victims of war, and kept people alive who might soon be killed? The term "the well-fed dead" appeared (Rieff, 1996). A similar "protection gap" was evident elsewhere, including Somalia (Prendergast, 1997).

## Local Capacity

The massive foreign aid presence in many of the conflicts of the 1990s not only dwarfed local relief structures, but in some areas became a local shadow government and profoundly influenced national policy priorities as well. The development generated a small body of literature on the political economy of humanitarian assistance (de Waal, 1997; Tvedt, 1998), and a more policy oriented discussion on the implications and strategies of developing local capacity (Danida, 1999; Smillie, 2001). In this discourse, the main reasons cited for utilising and strengthening local capacity were effectiveness, costs, ownership and sustainability. The main obstacles related to conditions in the conflict area, the nature of emergency situations, and a political economy of aid that favoured the large, international actors.

Budgetary conventions were a limitation in the early 1990s, when most donors had separate budgets for humanitarian and development purposes, and most aid actors specialised in one or the other. Building local capacity for humanitarian action did not seem to fit into either category. Yet it was clear that the two areas constituted a continuum. Structures built through relief assistance (e.g. roads, schools, clinics) could be a contribution to development if properly integrated with national strategies. Many emergencies were semi-permanent, which called for longer-term solutions. In all cases, studies showed that involvement of the beneficiaries and local authorities was essential for the sustainability of the project. As the decade wore on, many aid organisations adjusted their activities to address overlapping areas between relief and development. Humanitarians started to focus on the longer-term implications of aid projects, while development organisations recognised the need for a relief perspective when operating in areas emerging from crisis. Both positioned themselves to participate in "post-conflict" reconstruction and peacebuilding, which by the early 2000s had become firmly established as a new aid niche (Forman and Steward, 2000). Multilateral and bilateral funding institutions alike developed specialised units and flexible mechanisms to serve projects operating in the twilight zone between relief and development. The World Bank, for example, established a special "post-conflict unit" (World Bank, 1998). In theory, institutional developments of this kind should make it bureaucratically easier to obtain funds for building local capacity for humanitarian action, particularly to ensure that relief projects can be integrated with broader reconstruction strategies and translate into development assets.

The declaratory policy and practice of UN aid organisations regarding humanitarian capacity is discussed in a recent study commissioned by the Danish Ministry of Foreign Affairs to evaluate Danish humanitarian assistance (Danida, 1999). The findings show that the UN agencies are firmly committed in principle to using and building local capacity in the humanitarian sector, but that practice lags far behind.

Articulating the pros and cons of building local humanitarian capacity, the study noted the main advantages:

— Involving local people and utilising local knowledge and resources lead to better and more efficient solutions for the affected populations, thus increasing the overall effectiveness of the aid.
— Making use of local manpower, businesses and local NGOs is more cost effective than relying on highly-paid expatriates and imported goods.
— Local involvement enables people and organisations to become stakeholders in the process, which encourages project integration with national strategies and a sense of ownership of aid structures.
— Local capacity building means greater self-reliance and less dependence, thereby creating conditions for sustainability when external actors withdraw.

Most of the counter-arguments relate to conditions in the affected areas. Massive emergencies require large, professional and immediate relief assistance that typically are not available locally. Once large foreign aid organisations have established themselves on "Day One" of the crisis, it is difficult to bring in local partners and work through local authorities in the "Day Two" phase, as local capacity advocates call for. Turning over a large operation to smaller local partners will likely disrupt service. Creating new institutions is a slow and difficult process. Working through local authorities and organisations is problematic if the latter are incompetent or corrupt. Contracting out technical parts of a relief project to local NGOs (e.g. food distribution, building of schools and bridges) blurs the difference between a non-governmental organisation and a private contractor, and might hamper the development of a more viable business community. Finally, local authorities and NGOs may be closely associated with the parties to the conflict. Using or building local capacity under these conditions makes it difficult to insulate the humanitarian sphere from the politics of the conflict.

Given the strong tradition of solidarity-humanitarianism in the West—since renamed the North—this particular argument is disingenuous. The other arguments point to the difficulties of using or building local capacity, but do not question its desirability as a goal. It is mainly an ends-means dichotomy: using local humanitarian capacity is better than international aid, the problem is getting there.

The Danida study showed that the agencies were a long way from their stated goals. As a development agency, UNDP has traditionally focused on national and local capacity building. During the 1990s, the organisation gradually reoriented itself to a broader engagement in crisis-affected countries. Greater priority was given to support for local coping strategies and recovery programmes. Yet the general obligation to work with existing state authorities limited the agency's manoeuvrability when operating in conflict areas where the state remained strong. Only when the UN restricted co-operation with the regime for political reasons did UNDP work more actively with local organisations (Myanmar, Afghanistan, Somalia).

UNHCR is above all a relief agency with no tradition of local capacity building. Agency practice by the end of the 1990s showed a distinct dualism, weakening claims that UNHCR emphasised working with local actors. In 1997, 72 per cent of the agency's implementing partners were local organisations, but they received only 30 per cent of the total funds. The figures improved only slightly in 1998: 79 per cent were local organisations, receiving 36 per cent of the funds (Danida, 1999:82). In

Afghanistan, the dualism was so marked as to border on formalism, another study showed. UNHCR had 37 implementing partners for its country programme in 1998, of these 21 were local NGOs. However, the funds channelled through the local NGOs represented only 16 per cent of UNHCR's total disbursement to its implementing partners, the remaining 84 per cent went to international NGOs (Danida, 1999:81).

UNICEF routinely works with both government institutions and NGOs. A critical multi-donor evaluation in 1994 recommended that UNICEF should strike a better balance between activities for capacity building, empowerment and advocacy, on the one hand, and service delivery on the other. Agency officials responded that the principle of supporting local capacity was not in doubt, the problem was how to implement it. The difficulty of working with local partners in situations of violent conflict and chronic instability was one concern, and was echoed by a 1998 report prepared by outside consultants. "[I]n this environment, choices about partners become extremely difficult. Not only does UNICEF often face considerable political pressure in-country regarding its choice of partners, but the range of partners usually declines as violence increases, and civil groups retreat or their personnel are killed or flee" (Macrae and Bradbury, 1998:61). However, even when UNICEF in one case chose to work with an undisputed party to the conflict—the humanitarian wing of the rebel movement in southern Sudan—studies found that little systematic effort was invested in local capacity building (Danida, 1999a).

In the World Food Programme, local capacity issues mainly meant local procurement of goods and services (including transportation) for food distribution. Criticism that the agency did not sufficiently use local organisations and resources made the Executive Board recommend in October 1997 that the organisation invest more in this area, particularly local NGOs and community groups, and work closely with NGOs to strengthen programming. The result was a clearer division of labour between the local and international partner. An agency assessment in early 1999 found that "the type of partner chosen by WFP depends on the timing and nature of the food aid operation. Projects requiring a rapid and logistically heavy emergency intervention or a significant technical capacity are often managed by international NGOs, while national NGOs are well prepared to implement activities which require contact with communities, such as income-generating activities and rural development" (WFP, 1999).

The gap between declaratory policy and actual practice is partly explained by conditions in the affected areas, as accounted for under the counter-argument side in the discourse on local capacity building. There are also powerful obstacles rooted in organisational mandates, institutional cultures and the broader political economy of funding. By virtue of their organisational mandate and experience, the development-oriented agencies are more capable of investing in institution and capacity building than are the humanitarian ones. UNDP, as noted, is the most likely candidate to undertake capacity building, yet is constrained by its orientation of working closely with national governments. That leaves capacity building in the public sector only. The principal UN agency for humanitarian emergencies—UNHCR—is steeped in an organisational culture of top-down, externally directed assistance, where the standard response is to send in "service packages" from the outside. No UN agency has a mandate to develop local capacity for humanitarian action.

As long as donors did not urgently call for local capacity building in the humanitarian sector, no agency strode in to take up the challenge. While generally affirming the principle of local capacity building, donors tended to promote their nationally-based NGO organisations, either directly or indirectly. More generally, increased donor insistence on efficiency and effectiveness in the humanitarian sector—which in itself reflected mounting UN appeals for funds to meet emergencies in the 1990s—encouraged aid agencies to focus on tangible and immediate results. Innovation and risk-taking and long term projects were discouraged or placed in the "development" portfolio.

The limited achievement of the UN agencies in using and developing local capacity in the humanitarian sector illustrates the fundamental difficulties of the process. One might not expect international NGOs to be in the forefront of this process. They are competing for the same funds as local NGOs, and often for the same local staff. As long as "presence" in the conflict area is a critical condition for organisational survival, international NGOs have an interest in developing local expertise, but not in institutional forms that would compete with their own presence. The Red Cross/Red Crescent case is the exception that truly proves the rule. The Red Cross is more than an organisation; it is a movement, and building local chapters throughout the world is an integral part of its philosophy. As for the donors, they would gain in the long run gain if local capacity meant a more efficient and effective humanitarian response. But donors are also guided by short-term considerations to show immediate results, particularly in high-visibility crises, and most have a close relationship with their own NGOs.

The UN agencies have comparatively less vested interest in maintaining the current division of labour that heavily favours northern NGOs. While needing to show presence in conflict areas to preserve their organisational position in the humanitarian sector, they are heavily dependent upon implementing partners. Yet even the UN agencies have made little progress in using or building local humanitarian capacity. In some parts of the world they have rather contributed to the erosion of local capacity, as the case studies from East Africa in this book suggest.

# 3. International Humanitarian Law in the African Context

*Mutoy Mubiala*

There is an apparent paradox in the African situation. On the one hand, most of the research and evidence recognises the ingrained humaneness of the values of tradi-tional (pre-colonial) African societies and the extensive formal acceptance by mod-ern African states of the principal instruments of contemporary international hu-manitarian law (IHL). On the other hand, the serious and mass violations of IHL in several recent conflicts (Burundi, Rwanda, Congo-Kinshasa, Congo-Brazzaville, Liberia, Somalia, Sierra Leone, etc.) reveal the ineffectiveness of such law in Africa.

This chapter explores the reasons for this contradiction and possible ways of re-solving it. The study is divided into three parts: 1) humanitarian principles in African customary law and their relevance to the promotion of contemporary IHL; 2) Afri-can perspectives and interests in contemporary IHL, and their relevance to current African conflicts; and 3) issues of enforcement and promotion of IHL in contempo-rary Africa. The chapter concludes with some recommendations. These take account of the special features of the African situation, not in order to reduce the impact of the universality of IHL but rather to deduce from that situation some means of strengthening the understanding and enforcement of IHL in the continent.

## Humanitarian Principles in African Customary Law and their Relevance to the Promotion of Contemporary IHL

As several studies have shown, the traditional African societies of the pre-colonial era had three important social values: humanity, solidarity and interdependence. These values had a decisive influence on the conception of law and justice in general and on human rights and humanitarian law, as well as on concepts of social and po-litical leadership.

Although African legal systems bear the imprint of the different customs of the entities in which they evolved, they have common characteristics in terms of their foundations and their operation. Traditional African laws are oral laws, transmitted by word of mouth from generation to generation. Hence the importance, in most of the traditional lands of the pre-colonial era, of the *griots* (minstrels), whose function was to perpetuate the collective memory, in particular by means of juridical dance songs. These juridical traditions inherited from ancestors also had a strong magical-religious connotation, and to violate them was regarded as transgressing both the so-cial and the divine order of things (Sohier, 1955). In terms of their content, these le-gal traditions governed relations both between individuals and between individuals and society. In view of the collectivist and mutually supportive nature of traditional African societies, rules that may be described as rules of public policy were by far the more important (M'Baye and Ndiaye, 1982). They influenced the application of private laws themselves, in particular with respect to criminal and civil responsibility.

In contrast to European systems, the systems of responsibility in traditional Africa is a collective one. An individual who commits a misdemeanour or crime which causes harm to someone else or who defaults on his debt triggers the responsibility of the group (lineage, clan, etc.) to which he belongs. It thus becomes the responsibility of the group to ensure appropriate compensation (Kalongo, 1972). Such a system of tort law has two consequences. The first is that, being legally responsible for the acts of all its members, the group keeps a close watch on their behaviour both within and outside the group. The second, a corollary of the first, is the preventive effect on every individual, who will try to avoid being the "Jonah" or the black sheep of the group. Thus the traditional system of responsibility is in itself an institution of social control which supports the conflict settlement system.

In traditional Africa, the function of the judge is less to settle disputes and designate winners and losers than to conciliate and reconcile the parties in dispute. We may cite, for example, the peacemaking role played by such institutions as the *gacaca* in Rwanda (Ntampaka, 1995), the *bambaku* in Congo (Mubiala, 1990), the *ubushingantahe* in Burundi,[1] or the *tougouna* in the Sahel. A more general conflict resolution element in traditional African justice is evident as well. Many traditional communities had developed judicial services, sometimes operating in conjunction with the political administration and sometimes separate or even independent, which seem to have had the common feature of being much less concerned with laying down the law and imposing it by force than with finding a solution acceptable to the litigants. In fact, African law consists of a set of procedures according a central place to conciliation.

Traditional justice reflects very strongly the ways of life and the conceptions of social relations, in short the whole civilisation of the ancestral world. As the Wolof proverb "*Nit nit garabam*" ("man is a cure for man") indicates, this ancestral world placed a high value on the dignity of the human person whose rights were recognized and guaranteed, especially by the judicial system. There is no doubt that the magical-religious dimension of traditional African law, the prevailing system of collective responsibility and conciliatory function of justice played a decisive role in the emergence and development of human and community rights.

Contemporary research confirms the existence in pre-colonial Africa of a well-established system for the protection of human rights (M'Baye, 1992; Ouguergouz, 1993). While it was true that the legal personality of the individual was inseparable from that of the group to which he belonged, the group did not bring tyrannical pressure to bear on him. Quite the contrary, the group allowed the individual to assert himself, guaranteeing the enjoyment and exercise of his rights and freedoms by

---

1. Concerning the ubushingantahe in Burundi, the Special Rapporteur of the Commission on Human Rights on the situation of human rights in Burundi, Professor Paulo S. Pinheiro noted in his first report: "As several Burundian intellectuals explain in a study published in the magazine Au coeur de l'Afrique, January-March 1995, pages 55–58, the institution of the Ubushingantahe used to hinge on values such as devotion to truth, experience and wisdom, a sense of the common good, of justice and of equity, a sense of responsibility, of measure and of balance in both word and deed, as well as devotion to work and self-sufficiency. In other words, the institution was a factor of social cohesion, of order and of conflict-control, and embodied a code of conduct which guaranteed social harmony and stability. For their part, the Bashingantahe were the authentic guardians of social peace. Their function was to remain vigilant so as to preserve social harmony and to contribute to reconciliation and co-operation and to the protection of individuals and property. In the juridical sphere, the Bashingantahe were responsible for settling conflicts, for investigating and deciding cases, for settling litigation, in particular over land or livestock, for reconciling individuals or families in conflict, for authenticating all types of contract (marriage, inheritance sale, bequests) and for securing safety and justice around them". (United Nations, E/CN.4/1996/16/Add.1, pp.19–20).

means of appropriate machinery, including the judicial system described above and the "councils of wise men", which limited and controlled the powers of the traditional chiefs. It was generally understood that the protection of the human person and of communities continued in time of war.

## Humanitarian Principles in Pre-Colonial Societies

Rules governing the conduct of hostilities and the protection of the victims of war existed in pre-colonial Africa. Scholars have not merely identified the rules, but also draw attention to the similarities and differences with the principal rules of contemporary IHL, commonly known as "The Hague law" and "Geneva law".

Among the most important pieces of research based on juridical sociology surveys published to date, the ones produced by Yolande Diallo and Emmanuel Bello deserve particular mention. In a preliminary study on the Peul society in Senegal, Yolande Diallo has shown the existence of a "law of war" (Diallo, 1976). She begins by noting that, contrary to some then current views, war is not a normal state in Africa but used only as a last resort, following intensive discussions dealing with the consequences of commencing hostilities. Once war had been declared, it was regulated by several categories of rules, expressed orally in the form of maxims and proverbs. The first category consisted of rules on personal conduct during armed conflicts. For example, combatants had to respect certain places regarded as holy (houses of prayer, cemeteries, sacred woods, etc.) and must never enter such places in pursuit of persons taking refuge there. The second category of rules governed the treatment of the defeated party. When taken prisoner or made house slaves, the losers were treated humanely and very often became part of the family of the persons into whose power they had fallen. The third category of rules addressed conflict resolution. This was achieved by means of negotiation between the representatives of the groups involved or of arbitration by third parties, conducted in the conciliatory African spirit discussed earlier.

In a more detailed study made at the request of ICRC in West Africa, Diallo confirms the existence of such traditions among most of the peoples of the region. With regard to the rules on the conduct war, the author notes that in Senegal "there was a genuine ethics of war which was taught to any young nobleman for his future calling as a warrior. He was taught never to kill an enemy on the ground [...]" (Diallo, 1976a:394). The study also highlights other rules on the prohibition of certain weapons, in particular poisoned ones, the protection of non-belligerents—removal from the combat zones of women, children, old people and serfs, identifiable by the facial markings applied for their protection (as in Ghana)—observance of truces for agricultural reasons (as among the Mossis), and respect for asylum zones (Upper Volta, Ghana, Mali, Niger, Senegal and Togo). The fate of the vanquished was usually improved by the practice of ransoming prisoners of war, the designation of a number of slaves, or the cession of animals or land. In most of the kingdoms mercy prevailed over hatred and integration of the vanquished over vengeance.

On the firm foundation of this field research, Diallo concludes:

> As can be seen, many principles expressed in the Geneva Conventions are to be found in the law of war in pre-colonial Africa. It was only after the introduction of slavery and the inroads of colonialism into Africa south of the Sahara that traditional societies began to disintegrate, causing the code of honour to fall into disuse in war. However, the memory of this code of honour is kept alive in the narratives of the storytellers, and the code perhaps could be revived as a means of humanising present-day conflicts.

Perhaps Africa will remember, now that it is reviving its own cultural values, that this sense of humanity is one of its permanent values and that it must accept the obligation not to let those values be forgotten (Diallo, 1976a:400).

A later study undertaken by Emmanuel Bello under the auspices of ICRC, and covering the whole of the African continent, confirmed the general validity of these findings. While mentioning a number of minor differences in contemporary IHL and in traditional African humanitarian law (which accepted the legality of espionage, for example), Bello found several similarities between the relevant principles of traditional legal systems and IHL (Bello, 1984; Okoth-Obo, 1988). Adamou Ndam Njoya arrived at the same conclusion in a 1988 article: "International humanitarian law as it stands today is not a law which is alien to Africans. It is in line with their most ancient humanitarian traditions" (Ndam Njoya, 1988:11).

Several studies of the Maghreb (North Africa) have established the existence and application of humanitarian principles since ancient times. For example, a recent document produced by the ICRC regional office in Tunis notes that one early source mentions the rules of conduct laid down by Hannibal, the Carthaginian general and statesman (246–183 BC) during the Punic Wars. One rule required respect for places of worship during hostilities. According to Pliny, *"infra ipsum oppidum id habent, cui percepit religione indectus Hannibal"* ("one of the temples of Saguntum stands at the foot of the town, and Hannibal spared it out of respect for religion"). The rule is similar to contemporary humanitarian principles contained in The Hague Convention of 1954 for the Protection of Cultural Property in the Event of Armed Conflict and in article 53 of Protocol I of 1977. Another rule attributed to Hannibal concerned respect for the dead and wounded. According to Polybius, "after the battle of Trasimeno he sought out the body of the consul Flaminius in order to have it buried; after Cannae, he came to pay his respects to the remains of Aemilius Paulus; and he sent to Rome the ashes of Marcellus". These acts were precursors of the protection afforded to the victims of war by articles 15 and 17 of the First Geneva Convention of 1949 (ICRC, 1997a).

Sources on more recent epochs mention the cases of King Idriss I of Morocco in the 8th century and of Emir Abdelkader (Algeria) in the 19th century. The former advised the Berber tribes to follow the teaching of God, the Merciful, and condemned the actions of "those who have taken the power of the *'umma'*, shed Moslem blood, violated our private life, caused suffering to our children and rendered them orphans, killed our old ones, and made sad widows of our women". The concerns expressed by Idriss I are codified in the contemporary instruments : respect for physical integrity (art. 3, para. 1, of the Fourth Convention of 1949) and special protection of members of vulnerable groups: children (Fourth Convention, art. 24); old people (Fourth Convention, art. 17); and women (Third Convention, art. 27, and Protocol I of 1977, art. 76, paras. 2 and 3). Similarly, Emir Abdelkader issued a decree protecting French prisoners of war, a text which prefigures in particular the contemporary rules contained in article 12 of the Third Geneva Convention on the responsibility of the Detaining Power (ICRC, 1997a).

The fact that massacres took place, and that practices such as the taking of human trophies as well as blind acts of vengeance were recorded in various places, does not deny the existence of traditional humanitarian law. Rather, such occurrences must be understood as flagrant violations of that law.

Several social and political structures were in place to support the enforcement of traditional humanitarian principles in pre-colonial societies. As a Luba (Democratic Republic of the Congo) proverb has it, *mukalenga wa bantu, bantu wa mukalenga* (the chief is to the people what the people are to the chief). The saying suggests a measure of security and protection for the people; although the chief possesses important powers, he can in principle exercise them only for the good of his subjects and guests. This is the reason as well why the output from compulsory labour and the taxes levied on individual production are used to build a "strategic food stock", administered by the chief and redistributed in time of famine. The stock is also drawn upon to feed passing strangers.

The chief plays an important role as mediator. As head of the "traditional council of the magistrate", the chief often presides over important cases. He also serves as the institution of last resort in cases of abuse not punished by the courts. In the ancient Empire of Mali, for example, the King used to tour the various lands to hear complaints about such abuse—a custom that has been revived in contemporary Mali in the *espace d'interpellation démocratique,* an annual event at which citizens harmed by the authorities can state their complaints (Poulton and Ibrahim, 1998). In its ancient form, the function predisposed the traditional chief and his entourage of dignitaries (*abia* among the Yansi of the Congo) to play a moderating and responsible role, which made an immense contribution to the resolution of conflicts, including armed conflicts, both within and between communities.

The effective enforcement of traditional humanitarian law thus rested on the community, through its system of collective responsibility, the justice system, through its conciliation procedures, and the mediation role of leaders. Collective responsibility—and hence the fear of collective reprisal—consequently acted as a deterrent for individuals not to violate the rules governing the conduct the war and the treatment of prisoners. Simultaneously, the spirit of conciliation that pervaded the justice system in the settlement of disputes, and the tradition of responsible governing leadership, tended to restrain possible extremist behaviour.

Colonisation dislocated traditional society and relegated African law to the sidelines. Once independent, however, African states formally reaffirmed the principles of contemporary IHL, and in some areas helped bring their codification forward.

## African Perspectives on Contemporary IHL

African states have contributed to the reaffirmation and development of contemporary IHL in both global and regional fora. Efforts at the global level focused on the International Conference on the reaffirmation and development of IHL applicable in armed conflicts (CDDH), held from 1974 to 1977, resulting in the 1977 Additional Protocols to the 1949 Geneva Conventions.

In the 1960s and 1970s, African states showed their determination to complete the decolonisation of the continent and to safeguard their newly acquired independence. These objectives were to influence their attitudes at CDDH. In the *travaux préparatoires,* African delegations gave priority to humanitarian issues affecting Africa as a result of external factors (colonization, neocolonialism, apartheid, mercenarism). They devoted much attention and energy to the status of wars of national liberation and mercenaries, while showing little interest in, or even resisting, work on Protocol II concerning non-international armed conflicts. In other words, African states were opposed to the internationalisation of internal conflicts, but in favour of the internationalisation of wars of national liberation.

Governments in the third world were generally reluctant to deal with Protocol II, which addressed the humanitarian order in internal conflicts. Their attitude was summed up well by Georges Abi-Saab:

> Draft Protocol II was not examined so to speak during the first session of the Diplomatic Conference in 1974, a session which was practically wholly devoted to the controversy over wars of national liberation, and which ended up by the adoption in committee of an amendment to article 1 of draft Protocol I, recognising the international character of such wars.

> However, even in the opening general debate, both in plenary and in the first committee during the first session, but particularly after the adoption of the above-mentioned amendment, strong doubts were expressed towards the very idea of a Protocol wholly devoted to non-international armed conflicts. The two most populous states of the world, China and India, in addition to Indonesia, the Philippines, Iran, several Latin American and African countries criticised the idea either in its principle, or, more frequently, in a roundabout manner, by suggesting very limitative conditions for its application or drastic reductions in its content

> Though basically reflecting a concern by many (but not all) Third World countries lest the projected Protocol would in fact serve as an instrument of internationalising their internal problems and as a basis for foreign intervention in such situations, a more limitative approach to certain aspects of the Protocol was also adopted both by the socialist states and by some Western countries, particularly Canada. To start with, this approach took the form of restrictive amendments to draft article 1, defining the material field of application of the Protocol (Abi-Saab, 1988:227).

As for Protocol I, the support given to African states from other parts of the third world reflected the distinctive situation in the continent in the 1970s. Its main features were unfinished decolonisation, apartheid in South Africa, and frequent incursions by mercenaries. Thus, Africa's battle gave a new dimension to the exercise of the right of peoples to self-determination and contributed to the global recognition of the legitimacy of the armed struggle of colonised peoples for independence (Fall, 1972). That had an influence on the IHL applicable in wars of national liberation.

Before the CDHH and its culmination in the Additional Protocols, the humanitarian status of wars of national liberation was regarded as falling within the category of conflicts covered by Article 3 common to the Geneva Conventions of 1949. In this matter, and particularly concerning the status of freedom fighters, the CDHH was decisively influenced by resolutions promoted by African states at the UN General Assembly with regard to the humanitarian status to be accorded to persons and/ or peoples fighting for their freedom. For example, a resolution on South Africa (Res. 2396 (XXIII)) requested "that the population of South Africa as a whole should be able to exercise its right of self-determination and that, as their struggle is legitimate, the freedom fighters there should be treated as prisoners of war under the terms of international law, particularly the Third Geneva Convention of 1949" (Sandoz et al., 1986:45). In fact, according to article 1, paragraph 4, of Protocol I of 1977, this instrument on international armed conflicts applies "to armed conflicts in which peoples are fighting against colonial domination and alien occupation and against racist regimes in the exercise of their right of self-determination, as enshrined in the Charter of the United Nations and the Declaration on Principles of International Law concerning Friendly Relations and Cooperation among States in accordance with the Charter of the United Nations" (Abi-Saab, 1979).

African delegations at CDDH also played a leading role on the subject of the status of mercenaries, i.e. whether they should be treated as combatants or prisoners of war in the event of capture (Boumedra, 1981). Their contribution was a continuation of the legislative work already begun in OAU. African states had prepared a draft convention on the elimination of mercenarism in Africa for the Conference of Heads of State and Government of OAU in Rabat in 1972. The text was widely known and had helped the UN to firmly condemn the activities of mercenaries. The Rabat draft had defined mercenaries and criminalised their activities at the international level, denying them the status of combatant or of prisoner of war in the event of capture. It is therefore no surprise that it was an African state, Nigeria, which introduced at CDDH draft article 47 of Protocol I concerning mercenaries. After bitter debate the Nigerian proposal was adopted. Article 47, paragraph 1 of the Protocol bears the imprint of Africa in that it transfers to the global level the African solution formulated in the Rabat draft: "a mercenary shall not have the right to be a combatant or a prisoner of war". As in the case of wars of national liberation, African regionalism had a specific impact on the global solution.

## Affirming IHL in OAU and Other Regional Fora

When discussing African contributions to IHL made at the regional level, a distinction must be made between the legislative work of OAU—often called "Addis Ababa law"—and that of other regional institutions, conferences and seminars.

The legislative work of OAU in the humanitarian sphere can be divided into two categories. The first concerns the response to humanitarian problems stemming from the external factors mentioned earlier (wars of liberation, mercenaries, etc.) and covers the 1960s and 1970s (first generation). The second was developed more recently in the 1980s and 1990s (second generation) and deals with the current humanitarian problems in Africa and the world.

The first-generation legislative activities consisted essentially of the adoption of two regional conventions, the OAU Convention governing the Specific Aspects of Refugee Problems in Africa and the 1977 Convention for the Elimination of Mercenarism in Africa. The 1969 OAU Convention on Refugees is an excellent combination of African thinking and the continent's social and political realities (Bedjaoui, 1979; Mubiala, 2001). In the 1960s many countries were faced with a mass exodus of people fleeing from fighting unleashed by wars of national liberation. It became apparent that the host countries by themselves could not solve the problems resulting from such influxes. Moreover, the individual treatment of asylum, as envisaged in the 1951 Geneva Convention relating to thestatus of refugees, seemed unsuited to mass influxes. These considerations constituted the basis for the "socialisation" of refugee law in Africa. The development took place at three main levels: the definition of refugee was expanded, the granting of asylum was seen as a manifestation of African solidarity, and the burden of providing material care for refugees was to be widely shared. These key elements in the 1969 Convention—and the subsequent practice of granting collective asylum in Africa—adapted refugee law to both contemporary African realities and the continent's humanitarian community traditions (Martin, 1995).

The term "refugee" in the 1969 OAU Convention does not apply solely to any person who, fearing persecution by reason of his race, religion, political beliefs, etc., finds refuge outside his own country, as stated in the 1951 Convention. The OAU definition applies equally to any person who finds himself in a similar situation, "owing to external aggression, occupation, foreign domination or events seriously disturbing public order in either part or the whole of his country of origin or nationality" (art. 1, par. 2). Moreover, for practical reasons connected with the size of the refugee flows, the member states of OAU had recourse to the collective determination of the status of refugee. Lastly, the 1969 OAU Convention states the burden-sharing rule in article 2, paragraph 4, which reads

> Where a Member State finds difficulty in continuing to grant asylum to refugees, such Member State may appeal directly to other Member States and through the OAU, and such other Member States shall in the spirit of African solidarity and international cooperation take appropriate measures to lighten the burden of the Member State granting asylum.

It should be noted that the principle of burden-sharing has influenced doctrinal developments in UNHCR. The Executive Committee of UNHCR increasingly affirmed that the international community had a responsibility to aid countries receiving mass refugee inflows. Responding to the refugee emergency caused by the Rwandan crisis, the Executive Committee in October 1996 explicitly acknowledged that this principle was anchored in African regional law:

> Il s'agit là d'un système *novateur* aux conséquences bénéfiques pour l'institution de l'asile. En effet, le concept d'"indemnisation' compensatrice des dommages causés par les réfugiés dans les pays d'accueil émerge ainsi progressivement comme un principe universel répondant à celui du partage du fardeau, déjà ancré en droit régional africain [...] (Mubiala, 1996:506).

The subject of mercenaries had become a pressing problem of international law in the early 1960s, sparked by the Katanga secession (Congo-Kinshasa) in 1960–1962 when "neocolonial" mercenaries made their appearance. While mercenary activities had repeatedly been condemned in several United Nations resolutions, "mercenaries" had not been defined: it simply emerged from the case in question that they were foreigners recruited individually to the Katangan secessionist forces to fight against the central Government of Congo (David, 1977). The Katangan experience was to have a contagious effect on the African continent. Between 1967 and 1970, mercenaries fought in Nigeria (in the Biafra war) and in Sudan. Over the next several years mercenary incursions designed to destabilise the regimes in place were reported from Guinea (1970), Mauritania (1976), Angola (1976), Zaire (1977), Benin (1977), Togo (1977), etc. In the Angola case, thirteen mercenaries were tried and convicted by a special court in 1976.

The use of mercenaries, which violates the right of peoples to self-determination and the principle of the prohibition of the use of force in international relations, was condemned at the United Nations and third world regional organisations, notably OAU, which was particularly worried about mercenary activities in Africa. In 1971 the OAU Council of Ministers put on its agenda the question of adopting a regional convention on the elimination of mercenarism in Africa. The draft convention was introduced in 1972 at the Conference of Heads of State and Government of OAU in Rabat. The text was formally adopted at Libreville in July 1977. It has three important elements: the definition of mercenary, the humanitarian legal status of mercenaries, and the arrangements for cooperation for the prevention, suppression and elimination of mercenarism in Africa.

According to Article 1 of the Convention:

> "A mercenary is any person who:
>
> a) is specially recruited locally or abroad in order to fight in an armed conflict;
> b) does in fact take a direct part in the hostilities;
> c) is motivated to take part in the hostilities;
> d) is neither a national of a party to the conflict nor a resident of territory controlled by a party to the conflict;
> e) is not a member of the armed forces of a party to the conflict; and
> f) is not sent by a state other than a party to the conflict on official mission as a member of the armed forces of the said state."

The Convention considers mercenary activity a "crime against the peace and security of Africa" (art. 1, para. 2). The criminal nature of the activity precludes a mercenary from enjoying the diplomatic protection of the state of which he is a national. The Convention specifies aggravating circumstances applicable to leaders of groups of mercenaries and recruiters of mercenaries (art. 2). Article 3 of the Convention denies mercenaries the status of combatants and prisoners of war. Lastly, the Convention imposes obligations on African states to punish and prevent mercenary activity, and to cooperate to eliminate the phenomenon in Africa (Owona, 1982).

Apart from influencing the work of CDDH, the Rabat draft convention also acted as a catalyst in the subsequent legislative work of the United Nations in the General Assembly and the Commission on Human Rights. By resolution 44/34 of 4 December 1989 the Assembly adopted the International Convention against the Recruitment, Use, Financing and Training of Mercenaries, which was based broadly on the African regional Convention (A/44/766, 4 December 1989). In resolution 1987/16 of 9 March 1987 the Commission appointed a Special Rapporteur on the topic. It is significant that in his first report the Special Rapporteur, Enrique Bernales Ballesteros, stressed that:

> Africa is without doubt the continent most seriously affected by mercenaries. In the past, an attempt was made to paralyse the historical process by which it achieved independence through the use of mercenary forces linked in some cases to colonialist and racist powers and in other times to private interests. Similarly, after independence, many countries were victims of mercenary aggression aimed at infringing their sovereignty, right to self-determination and territorial integrity.

> These events justify the great effort made by the African States to gain international support for their cause and for the condemnation of mercenarism, a problem that still exists today in a number of African countries which report that they are victims of mercenary aggression. The Security Council and General Assembly resolutions condemning mercenarism were brought about by the result of strong pressure from African States (E/CN.4/71988/14, 20 January 1988).

Since 1988 the Special Rapporteur has submitted annual reports to the Commission on Human Rights and the General Assembly. In his report to the fifty-second session of the Assembly he stressed the fact that, far from declining, mercenarism was spreading and now involved many private enterprises, whose activities constituted an obstacle to the exercise of the right of peoples to self-determination. He also stated that Africa remained the continent most affected by mercenaries, noting their recent interference in the conflicts in Zaire and Sierra Leone. More recently, the scourge of mercenaries has been linked to the increasingly numerous internal African conflicts, i.e. genocide, crimes against humanity, mass recruitment of child soldiers, widespread use of anti-personnel mines, etc. These developments prompted OAU to redirect its legislative work in the 1980s and 1990s.

## Second-Generation Legislative Activities (1980–1990s)

This legislative work has mainly taken the form of resolutions by the OAU Council of Ministers and subsequently approved by the Conference of Heads of State and Government. These resolutions address general issues as well as specific situations.

At its 44th regular session the Council of Ministers adopted resolution CM/Res.1059 [XLIV] relating to the International Committee of the Red Cross, by which it called upon "[...] Member States, in co-operation with their National Societies, to support efforts to make public opinion more familiar with all the activities of the International Red Cross and Red Crescent Movement" (IRRC 1986). Following the conclusion in April 1992 of a formal cooperation agreement between ICRC and OAU, the latter's legislative work on IHL has developed. Four regional seminars on IHL have been organised jointly by OAU and ICRC in Addis Ababa in the 1994–98 period, dealing with (i) IHL and ICRC activities, (ii) IHL, water and armed conflicts and (iii) IHL enforcement and the international criminal court. The OAU has frequently referred to the recommendations of the seminars. More generally, at its Tunisia meeting in June 1994, the Council of Ministers adopted a resolution stating that it:

— Deplores the fact that the civilian population in general, and women and children in particular, are the main victims of hostilities and of acts of violence perpetrated during armed conflict;

— Affirms its conviction that respect for the basic rules of international humanitarian law helps not only to relieve the suffering of all the victims and provide them with effective protection, but also to create an atmosphere conducive to dialogue and the restoration of peace;

— Invites all States that have not yet become party to the instruments listed below to consider, or reconsider, without delay the possibility of doing so in the near future:

— (a) the two Protocols additional to the Geneva Conventions of 1949; (b) the Convention of Prohibitions or Restrictions on the Use of Certain Conventional Weapons which may be deemed to be Excessively Injurious or to have Indiscriminate Effects, of 10 October 1980; (c) the Convention for the Protection of Cultural Property in the Event of Armed Conflict, of 14 May 1954;

— Requests Member States to educate their population on the fundamental rules and principles of international humanitarian law (IRRC, 1994:495–96).

Attention must also be drawn to the recommendation adopted at the conclusion of the joint OAU/UNHCR symposium on refugees and forced population displacements in Africa, held in Addis Ababa from 8 to 10 September 1994. Citing the Additional Protocol II of the Geneva Conventions, the conference urged "all parties involved in armed conflicts to respect the principles and norms of humanitarian law, particularly those aimed at protecting civilians from the effects of war, preventing their being subjected to attacks, reprisals or starvation, or being displaced..." (IJRL, 1995:307).

OAU has adopted resolutions on particular conflicts which include appeals for respect for IHL. The 1996 resolution on Liberia, for instance, (CM/Res.1657 (LXIV)).

Warns the Liberian warring faction leaders that should the ECOWAS assessment of the Liberian peace process during its next Summit meeting turn out to be negative, the OAU will help sponsor a draft resolution in the UN Security Council for the imposition of severe sanctions on them including the possibility of the setting up of a war crimes tribunal to try the leadership of the Liberian warring factions on the gross violation of the human rights of Liberians (par. 12).

In addition to country-oriented resolutions, OAU has adopted several thematic resolutions on IHL. They include CM/Res.1628(LXIII), in 1996 on the revision of the 1980 United Nations Convention on certain Conventional Weapons and Problems Posed by the Proliferation of Anti-Personnel Mines in Africa; CM/Res.1659(LXIV) at the same Council of Ministers meeting on the plight on African Children in Situation of Armed Conflicts; CAMH/Res.14(V) on health and war, adopted in April 1995 by the Conference of Ministers of Health of OAU; and CM/Res.1662(LIXV) on IHL, water and armed conflicts adopted in 1996 (ICRC,1997a).

Other bodies have been active in this area as well. Instituted by the African Charter on Human and Peoples' Rights, the African Commission on Human and Peoples' Rights (hereinafter the "Commission") has protection and promotion functions (Ankumah, 1996). In this capacity the Commission has *inter alia* produced studies on human rights and adopted resolutions on specific aspects (by country or topic) of the human rights situation, including during armed conflicts. Like the OAU Council of Ministers, the African Commission has in several of its resolutions on recent African conflicts called for respect for IHL. For example, at its regular session in Banjul (18–27 April 1994) the Commission adopted a resolution on Rwanda, and at its 19th regular session in Ouagadougou (26 March–4 April 1996) resolutions on Burundi and Liberia. Although drafted from the standpoint of respect for human rights, these resolutions take into account the humanitarian aspects of the conflict.

In addition, the Commission has adopted several thematic resolutions on IHL. A resolution on the promotion and the respect of International Humanitarian Law and Human and Peoples' Rights was adopted at its 14th Ordinary Session (Addis Ababa, 1–10 December 1993) and a resolution on anti-personnel mines at its 17th Ordinary Session held from 13th to 22nd March 1995 in Lomé (Togo). The first "invites all African States parties to the African Charter on Human and Peoples' Rights to adopt appropriate measures at the national level to ensure the promotion of the provisions of international humanitarian law and human and peoples' rights" (par. 1); the second resolution recommends that "concrete and effective steps be urgently taken to prohibit the manufacture of anti-personnel mines and to ensure that existing stocks are destroyed and an international control mechanism is set up" (par. 3).

The African National Red Cross and Red Crescent Societies hold a regional conference every four years. Among matters considered is the promotion of and respect for human rights and IHL. For instance, the second Pan-African Conference of National Societies, held in Dakar from 21 to 23 November 1988, established a committee to address international humanitarian law and African traditions. The result was a Conference decision to support a study on IHL and African traditions, undertaken under the auspices of several African universities and backed by ICRC (ICRC, 1989:76).

The third Conference, held in Mbabane, Swaziland, from 18 September to 2 October 1992, noted that

> assistance to the victims of conflicts in Africa was often seriously impeded and called on National Societies to use their influence with governments to promote respect for international humanitarian law, whether by urging them to accede to the Additional Protocols or by high-lighting the need to apply and ensure application of that law (ICRC, 1992:590).

The Kampala Conference of the Red Cross/Red Crescent societies (23–27 September 1996) recommended *inter alia* that the African governments should take action to follow up commitments made at the 26th International Conference of the Red Cross and Red Crescent (Geneva, 1995), in particular with regard to:

— protecting civilians during war;
— promoting the principle of non-recruitment and non-participation in armed conflict of children under the age of 18;
— moving towards a total ban on landmines;
— encouraging the use of the Code of Conduct for the International Red Cross and Red Crescent Movement and non-governmental organisations;
— permitting relief operations of a strictly humanitarian character in states under sanctions;
— recognising the specific role of national Red Cross/Red Crescent societies in disaster response;
— helping create a beneficial environment for the overall development of national societies (ICRC, 1997b:330).

Another mechanism for promotion of IHL has been created through the Henry Dunant Institute and ICRC, which since 1977 have held regional seminars on IHL for diplomats, teachers, officers, students and persons from other walks of life from all of Africa. These seminars have usually offered the participants an opportunity to confirm that the principles of IHL are universal and find an echo in African traditions. They have also adopted resolutions, including some addressed to the governments of Africa. For example, at the seminar held in 1977 they called upon African governments to ratify the 1977 Additional Protocols to the 1949 Geneva Conventions as well as other humanitarian conventions, and to monitor their dissemination and implementation (Henry Dunant Institute, 1979).

The fifth seminar in 1986 acknowledged that "except for its most recent phase, codification of international humanitarian law has been taking place without any significant input from Africa."The seminar went on to confirm the existence and continuation" in African societies [of] humanitarian traditions deeply embedded in each society's cultural heritage". It was concluded that an overall study of African cultural heritage as regards humanitarian principles and rules should be undertaken as a means to promote a better understanding and acceptance of humanitarian law by African societies, states and peoples.

## Addressing the Eurocentric Origins of IHL

The problem of the acceptance in Africa of law of European origin is a general one, but it constitutes a particular concern for contemporary IHL. The problem has been extensively studied and there is no need to dwell on it here. It must be recalled, however, that the colonial period was characterised by a phenomenon of legal dualism or even pluralism. In most countries the colonisers allowed customary law to survive alongside the written European law, especially in the case of private law. They did so only on condition that such systems were not, in the hallowed expression, "contrary to [colonial] public policy and public morals". This meant that many customary rules disappeared as soon as they clashed with or disturbed the system of law or the authority put in place by the colonisers. But other customs survived, owing to the failure of the colonisers to "assimilate" the peoples completely (Alliot, 1965). This happened, for example, in the case of customary justice in rural and sometimes in urban areas. In order to correct the situation, some colonisers, as in the case of Congo-Leopoldville (former Zaire and current Democratic Republic of the Congo), devised an evolved customary law by establishing indigenous jurisdictions. But this restored customary law had no attraction for the people, for it was anchored in the institution of the state and distorted "authentic" customs.

Independence delivered a fatal blow to this system. But despite the official proclamations of the post-colonial powers about recourse to African traditions in the legislative reforms, most of the legislators reaffirmed the supremacy of the legal system inherited from the colonial past. A situation has thus arisen in which most of the population cling to the vestiges of customary law against a state apparatus that has formally embraced modern law, making more than one writer ask: "What is my law?" (Kouassigan, 1974). More serious, following the failure of modern state structures, including the judicial system, people have turned to African legal traditions which have been distorted and stripped of their quintessential character. In Madagascar, for instance, the revival of the dina (customary courts) is producing a legal system based on popular condemnation rather than on the ancestral spirit of conciliation.

A similar strategy of "tactical" restoration of traditional institutions seems to have been behind the recent promulgation of a constitution by Major Pierre Buyoya, of a Bashingantahe Council in Burundi, and the recognition, albeit entirely symbolic, by President Yoweri Museveni of the traditional authority of some of the ancient kingdoms of Uganda, including the Kingdom of Buganda.

Regarding the specific problems of the acceptance of contemporary IHL, this author has noted elsewhere that this is largely due to its European origin. Africans strongly distrust any European-inspired legal system, let alone a humanitarian law that proved ineffective during the colonial wars. At the same time, it will be recalled that the radical modification of human relations brought about by the colonialist 'divide and rule' policy generated social ills such as acute antagonism among both ethnic groups and states. Partly as a consequence, Africa's current political climate is rife with tribal and international conflicts, which take a heavy human toll.

It is therefore clear that contemporary IHL must be adapted to African attitudes and realities in order to gain popular acceptance. Such acceptance is essential to the enforcement and promotion of IHL on the continent, where they are confronted with major problems.

## Enforcing and promoting IHL in contemporary Africa

Despite the existence of numerous conventional and non-conventional, legal and institutional, means of implementing IHL, its application in Africa is facing major obstacles. These obstacles have deep-rooted causes that only a long-term strategy can eradicate.

### Conventional System (The Hague and Geneva Laws)

There is no formal system for monitoring the enforcement of IHL by submission of reports along the lines of the mechanisms established by the human rights conventions. The states parties to the Geneva Conventions of 1949 and their Additional Protocols of 1977 have always opposed a system of formal monitoring of the enforcement of IHL. Nevertheless, a system emerged under the auspices of the standard-setting activities of the International Conference of the Red Cross and Red Crescent and in the practice of states, national Red Cross/Crescent societies, and ICRC. This system consists of reporting on the measures taken in peace time to develop IHL within states.

Resolution V of the 25th International Conference of the Red Cross and Red Crescent (Geneva, 1986) states that

> reaffirming that the very applicability of international humanitarian law depends largely upon the adoption of appropriate national legislation, [the ICRC]
>
> 1. urges the governments of States Parties to the Geneva Conventions and, as the case may be, to the Additional Protocols to fulfil entirely their obligation to adopt or supplement the relevant national legislation, as well as to inform one another, as stated above, of the measures taken or under consideration for this purpose;
>
> 2. invites National Societies to assist and co-operate with their own governments in fulfilling their obligation in this respect;
>
> 3. appeals to governments and National Societies to give the ICRC their full support and the information to enable it to follow up the progress achieved in legislative and other measures taken for the implementation of international humanitarian law;

4. requests the ICRC to gather and assess the said information and to report regularly to the International Conference of the Red Cross and Red Crescent on the follow-up to the present resolution (ICRC, 1988:127).

Pursuant to the last paragraph of this resolution, ICRC has repeatedly written letters to the states parties to the Geneva Conventions and the National Societies of the Red Cross and Red Crescent in order to put into effect paragraphs 2 and 3 of the resolution. This system has not produced the expected results, and ICRC has received few replies. Moreover, only a few of forty or so replies received between 1988 and 1991 dealt with the substance, the rest merely acknowledged receipt (ICRC, 1991). African states have also contributed to the failure of this mechanism, for only three of them (Egypt, Morocco and South Africa) replied, on the substance, to the ICRC approaches, and another two (Rwanda and Tunisia) merely acknowledged receipt of the letter from the ICRC President. Despite the limitations inherent in the self-assessment system, this is an unambiguous indication of the situation in Africa with regard to the incorporation of IHL in national legislation.

According to the information available to ICRC on 15 June 2000, the following African States had laws and/or regulations on IHL (ICRC, 2000):

a) Applicability of IHL: Botswana (1970), Ghana (1959), Kenya (1968 and 1970), Malawi (1967), Nigeria (1960), Uganda (1964) and Zimbabwe (1981);

b) Repression of breaches and/or universal jurisdiction/genocide and other war crimes:Benin (1982), Botswana (1996), Burundi (1981), Cameroon (1997), Congo-Brazzaville (1998), Congo-Kinshasa (1997 and 1998), Chad (1962 and 1967), Côte d'Ivoire (1981), Ethiopia (1957, 1961 and 1996), Guinea (1995), Kenya (1968 and 1970), Liberia (1956), Mali (1995, 1996 and 1997), Namibia (1991), Niger (1993), Rwanda (1996), Senegal (1996), South Africa (1977 and 1985), Togo (1980, 1981 and 1990), Uganda, Zambia and Zimbabwe (1983);

c) Police and/or Armed Forces: Benin (1969), Chad (1996), Ethiopia (1996), Kenya, Namibia (1990), Nigeria (1986), South Africa (1957), Uganda (1986), Zambia and Zimbabwe (1978, 1979, 1980, 1983 and 1993);

d) Emblem (protection and repression of breaches): Botswana (1997), Burundi (1912), Cameroon (1997), Central African Republic (1996), Côte d'Ivoire (draft law), Ghana (1973), Guinea (1995), Kenya (1991), Malawi (1994), Nigeria (1960), Senegal (1996), Tanzania (1962), Togo (1996), Uganda (1993), Zambia and Zimbabwe (1981);

e) Dissemination: Benin (1991), Burkina Faso (1995), Chad (1996) and Rwanda (1995);

f) National Society: The Gambia (1966), Kenya (1965), Malawi (1994), Tanzania (1962), Uganda (1964), Zambia and Zimbabwe (1981).

The above information was obtained from the documentation unit of the ICRC Advisory Service. This service was created, among other reasons, to offset the deficiencies of the existing reporting system. In fact, the meeting of the Intergovernmental Group of Experts for the Protection of War Victims (Geneva, 30 August to 1 September 1993) recommended that ICRC should strengthen its capacity for promotion, technical assistance, and collection and exchange of information on national measures. The 26th International Conference (3–7 December 1995) endorsed this recommendation, which ICRC had already acted on in early 1995 by creating its Advisory Service to assist states, at their request, with the adoption of legislative and regulatory measures to give effect to IHL (ICRC 2000). The new promotional approach consists of inducing states—by means of bilateral contacts, evaluation studies by national experts, and national and regional seminars—to take preventive steps by adopting in peace time the measures contained in the 1949 Geneva Conventions, their Additional Protocols of 1977, and the 1954 Convention for the Protection of Cultural Property. The promotional activities include subsequent instruments on conventional disarmament, including the Convention on the Prohibition of Anti-Personnel Mines and Their Destruction. Furthermore. As was pointed out by the representative of the Holy See at the signing conference for this Convention in Ottawa in December 1997, "this is much more than a disarmament instrument, it is a humanitarian Convention" (Vatican Radio, 6 December 1997).

Concrete steps on how to implement IHL in a preventive as well as implementing sense have been spelled out by the ICRC Advisory Service for IHL:

1) prepare national translations of the Conventions and Protocols;

2) disseminate the texts of the Conventions and Protocols as widely as possible—both within the armed forces and generally;

3) suppress all violations of the Conventions and Protocols and in particular [...] adopt criminal legislation punishing war crimes;

4) ensure that persons and places protected by the Conventions and Protocols are properly identified, located and protected;

5) adopt measures to prevent the misuse of the Red Cross, the Red Crescent and other signs and emblems provided for in the Conventions and Protocols;

6) ensure the protection of fundamental and procedural guarantees during time of armed conflict;

7) provide for the appointment and training of persons qualified in international humanitarian law, including legal advisers within the armed forces;

8) provide for the establishment and/or regulation of National Red Cross and Red Crescent Societies and other voluntary aid societies; civil defence organisations; national information bureaux;

9) take account of international humanitarian law in the location of military sites, and in the development and adoption of weapons and military tactics;

10) provide, as necessary, for the establishment of hospital zones, neutralised zones, security zones and demilitarised zones.

[...] Some of these measures will require the adoption of legislation or regulations. Others will require the development of educational programmes, the recruitment and/or training of personnel, the preparation of identity cards and other materials, the establishment of special structures or units, and the introduction of planning and administrative procedures. All the measures are essential to ensure the effective implementation of humanitarian law.

[...] Careful planning and regular consultation is the key to ensuring effective implementation. Many States have established national international humanitarian law committees, or similar bodies, which bring together government ministries, national organisations, professional bodies and others with responsibilities or expertise in the field of implementation. Such bodies have generally been found to be an efficient and valuable means of promoting national implementation (ICRC, 1997b:1).

Such committees have been created or are being created in several African states. According to the ICRC's Advisory Service, as at 29 February 2000, the following countries have established a national body on IHL: Benin (1998), Côte d'Ivoire (1996), Egypt (2000), Ethiopia (1997), Mali (1998), Namibia (1995), Senegal (1997), South Africa (1995), Togo (1997) and Zimbabwe (1994). Apparently, the prospects for the promotion of establishing bodies on IHL, thanks to the ICRC's Regional Coordinator of the Advisory Service in Africa based in Abidjan, are encouraging (ICRC, 2000). As an ICRC lawyer told this author, "in no other continent has it been so easy to negotiate agreements or to create institutions as in Africa". (Geneva 20 November 1997). For example, African states are parties to the most important treaties in the field of humanitarian law: all 52 African member states of the United Nations have ratified the 1949 Geneva Conventions, 50 are parties to Protocol I, and 42 to Protocol II.

The widespread formal acceptance of international instruments, however, is apparently not reflected in the reality in the field, to judge by the non-application of IHL in recent armed conflicts. Another paradox is the fact that the flagrant violations of IHL in the African continent have not prompted a strong reaction by international actors.

## Monitoring and Enforcement in the Conventional System

A distinction must here be made between the action taken by foreign states, international non-governmental organisations, and the ICRC.

Foreign states have a general obligation under article 1 of the Geneva Conventions of 1949 and Protocol I of 1977, in which the High Contracting Parties undertake to respect and to ensure respect for these Conventions in all circumstances. This particular obligation of IHL can be fulfilled by adopting a number of measures, ranging from putting diplomatic pressure on the belligerents to coercive measures (retaliation or counter-measures), possibly taken in cooperation with international organisations (Condorelli and Boisson de Chazournes, 1984; Palwankar, 1994).

While recent African conflicts do not offer any examples of unilateral intervention by foreign states, probably for reasons of foreign policy, there are many examples of intervention initiated or authorised by international organisations. Apart from the United Nations, whose role will be discussed later, the interventions of the Economic Community of West African States (ECOWAS) in Liberia and Sierra Leone may be cited. The European Union has so far taken a wait-and-see attitude towards the armed conflicts in Africa: for example, its failure (along with the UN) to act during the Rwanda crisis. The relatively non-committal stance adopted by foreign states and the organisations of which they are members stands in contrast to the activism of international humanitarian non-governmental organisations.

NGOs involved in the monitoring of human rights and/or humanitarian assistance have often witnessed at first hand the atrocities committed during armed conflicts, particularly in Africa. It is an indication of their standing that the UN Security Council accorded a hearing to representatives of humanitarian NGOs in February 1997, when the allegations of massacres of Hutu refugees in the Zaire war (1996–1997) were becoming increasingly persistent. Likewise, the ad hoc bodies set up under the auspices of the United Nations to investigate violations of human rights often use information from humanitarian and human rights NGOs to establish the facts.

The humanitarian NGOs have become the main agents of "humanitarian mobilisation", guiding or eliciting reactions by states, international organisations and the international community to African conflicts. A recent striking example is the mobilising role played by various human rights NGOs in the conflict in the former Zaire in 1996–1997. A combined report Human Rights Watch/Africa and the Fédération Internationale des Droits de l'Homme (FIDH) affirmed the relevant principles in strong and unambiguous terms:

> All parties to the war in Congo, whether rebel or governmental, are bound by international humanitarian law to respect basic norms concerning victims of armed conflict. In particular, regardless of whether a government or an insurgent group, all sides are obliged to apply Common Article 3 of the Geneva Conventions of 1949:

In the case of an armed conflict not of an international character occurring in the territory of one of the High Contracting Parties, each Party to the conflict shall be bound to apply, as a minimum, the following provisions:

Persons taking no active part in the hostilities, including members of the armed forces who have laid down their arms and those placed hors de combat by sickness, wounds, detention, or any other cause, shall be in all circumstances treated humanely, without any adverse distinction founded on race, colour, religion or faith, sex, birth or wealth, or any other similar criteria.

To this end the following acts are and shall remain prohibited at any time and in any place whatsoever with respect to the above-mentioned persons:

a) violence to life and person, in particular murder of all kinds, mutilation, cruel treatment and torture;

b) taking of hostages;

c) outrages upon personal dignity, in particular humiliating and degrading treatment;

d) the passing of sentences and the carrying out of executions without previous judgement pronounced by a regularly constituted court, affording all the judicial guarantees which are recognised as indispensable by civilised peoples.

Furthermore, all parties to the conflict in Congo should respect the principles of UN General Assembly Resolution 2444, which recognises the customary law principle obliging all factions of an armed conflict at all times to treat civilians distinctly from combatants. It states that, "the following are principles for observance by all government and other authorities responsible for action in armed conflicts":

a) That the right of the parties to a conflict to adopt means of injuring the enemy is not unlimited:
b) That it is prohibited to launch attacks against the civilian populations as such;
c) That distinction must be made at all times between persons taking part in the hostilities and members of the civilian population to the effect that the latter be spared as much as possible.

While the above principles apply to all parties to the war in Congo, additional bodies of international humanitarian and human rights law place further obligations on certain parties to the conflict, notably the government of the former Zaire, the ADFL authorities who succeeded to the international obligations of the former government, the government of Rwanda and other governmental allies of the ADFL (Human Rights Watch and FIDH, 1997:11).

The publication of this report had a catalytic effect on the investigations by the UN Secretary-General. Having witnessed the failure of the Joint Mission sent in by the Commission on Human Rights, and alarmed by this report and information from other sources such as UNHCR, the Secretary-General organised a fact-finding mission to inquire into the allegations of massacres in the former Zaire. In this he had the full support of the Security Council, itself under pressure from human rights NGOs. In March 1997, at the height of the war in Eastern Zaire, Amnesty International urged the Security Council to create a commission of inquiry to investigate the alleged massacres in that region. In December 1977 Amnesty International published another report detailing the IHL violations perpetrated there. The report further affirmed that different forms of international law were applicable to the different parties at different stages of the armed conflict, but that the Common Article 3 of the Geneva Conventions of 1949 applied to all parties throughout (Alliot, 1997).

The humanitarian mobilisation work of the human rights NGOs and humanitarian agencies provide a useful complement to the work of ICRC based on the Geneva Conventions and conducted in confidentiality. ICRC is a neutral intermediary in armed conflicts, having been assigned by the states parties to the Geneva Conventions, in article 5, paragraph 2 (c), of the Statute of the International Red Cross and Red Crescent Movement, a mandate "to work for the faithful application of international humanitarian law". Within this framework ICRC has done much work in Africa. Its activities concerning application of IHL, exchange of prisoners, and assistance to refugees, displaced persons and victims of the African conflicts have been described at length in the studies and reports of the organisation, and there is no need to dwell on them here (Lavoyer, 1996). It must, however, be pointed out that the African peoples have welcomed these activities insofar as they constitute assistance and protection, but not intervention. As Zidane Meriboute pointed out, for historical reasons, there is some suspicion among African peoples that humanitarian conditions will be used to justify political or military intervention. However, most African countries do not consider humanitarian assistance a form of intervention as long as it is rendered in an impartial and non-discriminatory manner, and, above all, if it is provided by a neutral mechanism (Meriboute, 1995).

## Non-Conventional System ("New York Law")

In the context of the recent increase in its intervention in the IHL sphere, the United Nations has become closely involved in the African conflicts, mainly in its humanitarian peacekeeping and/or peace-enforcement operations and in the creation of the International Criminal Tribunal for Rwanda (Boisson de Chazournes, 1996).

In the early and mid-1990s, the Security Council authorised the deployment of international troops on humanitarian missions in Africa, and their use of force, if necessary, on the basis of Chapter VII of the UN Charter. Confronted with the deterioration of the humanitarian situation in Somalia, the Security Council adopted resolution 794 (1992) of 3 December 1992, which for the first time in history authorised the use of force to guarantee the distribution of humanitarian assistance (Djiena-Wembou, 1993). Two years later, in the Rwandan crisis, in resolution 929 of 22 June 1994 the Council authorised the Government of Rwanda to deploy a special force of 2,500 men (Opération Turquoise) "aimed at contributing, in an impartial way, to the security and protection of displaced persons, refugees and civilians at risk in Rwanda". On 15 July 1994 the "humanitarian safe zone" created and protected by this force was sheltering between 1.2 and 1.5 million people (Kleine-Ahlbrant, 1996). After the withdrawal of the force the Council expanded the mandate of the United Nations Assistance Mission in Rwanda in order to enhance the security and protection of the people there (Torelli, 1995).

There was an abortive attempt to deploy an international humanitarian force, intended to ensure the security of Rwandan refugees in and around camps in Eastern Zaire (1995) and subsequently assist their repatriation following the outbreak of the crisis in Eastern Zaire (1996). The earlier operations in Somalia and Rwanda, which produced negative results, were largely responsible for the failure of the attempt.

Altogether, these events seem to sound the death knell for the humanitarian peacekeeping organisation (Mubiala, 1996, Sommaruga, 1997). The conclusion is supported by the procrastination of the United Nations in launching an operation of this kind in the 1997 crisis in Congo-Brazzaville and its decision to withdraw in favour of the establishment of an African peacekeeping force or, at least, of the strengthening of the capacity of the African states in this field. The painful experience of the United Nations with regard to humanitarian peacekeeping in recent African conflicts has revealed the essence of the problem: the impossibility of reconciling the use of force with humanitarian action or the enforcement of IHL. Nevertheless, UN efforts did contribute to establishment of the facts concerning the grave violations of IHL in these conflicts.

Another tool used by the Security Council is fact-finding missions on serious breaches of IHL in Africa. Confronted with the re-emergence of serious and massive violations of IHL in Africa, the Security Council created and dispatched ad hoc missions to establish the facts and advise on action to be taken. For example, the Commission on Human Rights and more recently the Secretary-General both took such action in the conflicts in Central Africa.

The Council established two fact-finding missions to inquire into the crimes, including violations of IHL, committed in Rwanda in 1994 and in Burundi since October 1993. The Commission of Experts on Rwanda concluded in its final report (Doc S/1994/1405, 9 December 1994) that the genocide of Tutsis and crimes against humanity did take place during the hostilities in Rwanda in 1994 and recommended inter alia the creation of an ad hoc international criminal tribunal to try the alleged perpetrators of these crimes. In addition, the Commission of Inquiry into the massacres committed in Burundi since October 1993 verified the perpetration of acts of genocide and serious violations of IHL by persons belonging to both the Hutu and Tutsi communities (S/1996/682, 22 August 1996).

By its resolution 1997/58 of 15 April 1997 the Commission on Human Rights decided to create a Joint Fact-Finding Mission consisting of a member of its Working Group on kidnapping or forced or involuntary disappearances, the Special Rapporteur on extrajudicial, summary and arbitrary executions, and the Special Rapporteur on the situation of human rights in Zaire. This Mission was mandated to inquire into the allegations of massacres during the war which had ravaged this country since September 1996. Since the authorities of Congo (former Zaire), initially de facto and then legally from May 1997, were opposed to the dispatch of this Mission, the Secretary-General of the United Nations decided to replace it with another fact-finding mission with a different membership and with a mandate extended ratione temporis to the events which had occurred since 1993 in Eastern Zaire.

Despite the obstacles put in its way, the Joint Fact-Finding Mission of the Commission on Human Rights concluded on the basis of credible allegations that:

> [T] here is no denying that ethnic massacres were committed and that the victims were mostly Hutus from Burundi, Rwanda and Zaire. The joint mission's preliminary opinion is that some of these alleged massacres could constitute acts of genocide. However, the joint mission cannot issue a precise, definitive opinion on the basis of the information currently available to it. An in-depth investigation in the territory of the Democratic Republic of the Congo would clarify this situation.

> Do the incidents described constitute violations of international humanitarian law?

> There is absolutely no doubt that the incidents in question occurred in the context of an armed conflict. None of the parties has denied this and the situation is therefore covered by the Geneva Conventions of 1949, to which Zaire is a party. It is also clear that the conflict involves third countries and has repercussions for other States (return of refugees, new refugee flows, etc.). Nevertheless, the conflict is taking place within the territory of one State. Although the Zairian Government denounced foreign intervention, the entire international community has treated the conflict as a non-international conflict.

> [...] Based on the foregoing, the joint mission is of the view that the provisions of article 3 common to the four Geneva Conventions must be applied to the conflict in eastern Zaire.

> The allegations referred to in this report suggest that while there have been serious breaches of this provision, such breaches can be attributed not only to the Alliance but also to the other parties to the conflict (A/51/942, 2 July 1997).

A number of other United Nations humanitarian operations deployed in the field are inquiring into violations of IHL as well. For example, the human rights operation in

Rwanda was given a mandate, when it began work in 1994, to investigate the genocide and violations of IHL committed in that country during the hostilities in 1994 (Mubiala, 1995). The findings of its special investigation unit were transmitted to the Office of the Prosecutor of the International Criminal Tribunal for Rwanda.

The establishment of the Tribunal is in itself a means of strengthening IHL. Encouraged by the Yugoslav experience, the Security Council, at the request of the new Rwanda Government, created by its resolution 955 (1994) of 8 November 1994 an International Criminal Tribunal for the prosecution of persons responsible for genocide and other serious violations of IHL committed in Rwanda in 1994. The Council decision contributed to the development of international humanitarian law by upgrading serious violations of article 3 common to the Geneva Conventions of 1949 and Protocol II to the status of "war crimes" (S/1995/134, 13 February 1995).

## Addressing the Reasons for the Weakness of IHL in Contemporary Africa

The African continent has in recent years been an experimental laboratory for the legislative and operational activities of the United Nations in the humanitarian sphere. However, the politicisation and militarisation of the enforcement of "authentic" IHL ("Red Cross Law") through the enforcement of "United Nations Law", and the series of failures of such action, has dealt a heavy blow to the image of IHL in the minds of Africans and in international public opinion. Yet the underlying causes of the failure of IHL are to be found in Africa itself.

The root causes of the weakness of IHL lie in the break-up of traditional African society and in the collapse of the post-colonial state, as well as in the crisis of the military. This situation calls for the adoption of a long-term strategy for the promotion of IHL in Africa.

A distinction must be made between the break-up of traditional society and the collapse of the post-colonial state, although the two phenomena are closely connected. As noted above, the arrival of the European colonisers called into question the traditional power of customary chiefs, shattered the social and political structures on which their power rested and marginalised it. However, identification with the (usually ethnic) group to which one belongs and attachment to (traditional/modern) leaders have proved resilient in Africa, even in urban areas. On the other hand, the factors of stability which once existed in pre-colonial Africa—moderating influence of the system of collective responsibility and responsible leadership—have yielded ground to factors of destabilisation. The telescoping of partisan quarrels for the conquest of modern state power and the ethnic struggles from which community leaders draw their support have led to the emergence of a climate which may be described as "ethnocidal". Ethnic conflicts caused by irresponsible leadership have proliferated: Angola, Burundi, Congo-Brazzaville, Liberia, Sierra Leone, Somalia, etc.

In the case of Rwanda, for example, the Special Rapporteur on the situation of human rights in this country has written with regard to the underlying causes of the Rwandan crisis:

> "[...] Although it is not possible to establish any genuine order of precedence among the various causes, the politico-historical dimension seems to be the most important because of its conditioning and determining effect on the others. It is both political and historical in that the basis of the conflict between the two groups, Hutu and Tutsi, is political—i.e. power—and is rooted in the history of this people. Responsibility lies less with the ancestors of past centuries than with the authorities of more recent periods, firstly colonisation and then the African regimes.

[...] It was the colonisers, first the Germans then the Belgians, who as part of their policy of divide and rule, depended on the Tutsi group to govern the conquered territory under a system of indirect rule, thus upsetting the existing social equilibrium. The resulting imbalance gradually became more marked, marginalising the Hutu. Moreover, in order to give an ideological flavour to their concoction and thus consolidate it, they created the myth of the superiority of the Tutsis over the two other ethnic groups, thus institutionalising the ethnic division. This ideology of discrimination was not only reflected in the indication of ethnic group on identity cards, but also reinforced in the schools. The Belgian colonialists supported the Hutu social revolution only because they felt betrayed by their Tutsi allies' demands for independence (E/CN.4/1997, 20 January 1997).

The political and social responsibility of the various Hutu and Tutsi community leaders for the cyclical crises in the Great Lakes region has been broadly established by many pieces of research (Prunier, 1995). It is appropriate that in the case of Rwanda, the International Criminal Tribunal in Arusha is concentrating on prosecuting the leaders. Although this choice has been made necessary by technical considerations (large number of alleged perpetrators of genocide and other crimes against humanity), it nevertheless reflects the reality with respect to the moral responsibility for what happened in that country in 1994 As the Secretary-General mentioned in his interim report to Security Council on 4 June 1995, the tribunal will focus its investigations and prosecutions on 400 identified leaders (s/1995/457, 4 June 1995, 8).

Similarly, in Burundi the Commission of Inquiry established the responsibility of the community leaders, concluding that:

> These considerations lead the Commission to conclude that the wholesale massacre of Tutsi men, women and children in the collines throughout the country could not be imputed to a simultaneous spontaneous reaction of the mass of Hutu farmers against their neighbours. The fact, established by evidence, that many simple Hutu farmers did take part in the massacres can only be attributed to the incitation and example of their leaders, whose presence and activity wherever such massacres took place is overwhelmingly established by the evidence (S/1996/682, 22 August 1996, par. 473).

The baleful influence of African community leaders has very serious implications for the existence of the state understood as the representative of the common interest and, in some cases, even as a geographical entity. As the conflict between the "ethnic" citizenry and the "republican" citizenry became a major factor of destabilisation of the post-colonial African state, the ethnic citizenry gained the upper hand (Yusuf, 1994). Its evident victory at present seems confirmed by the abdication of the state from certain areas essential to national unity, such as education and security. In Madagascar, for example, in order to tackle the resurgence of acts of banditry (in particular the rustling of cattle), the fokonolona (grassroots communities) of Tsaratanāna have concluded a "social pact" (Dynasty mandefitra) consisting of "protection of the people and their property by the people themselves" (L'Express de Madagascar, 2 December 1997). From that point to militias is only one step, and many African communities have not hesitated to take it: Kamanjor (Sierra Leone), Cabras, Zoulous and Ninjas (Congo-Brazzaville), Inkhata (South Africa), the "Sans échecs" Tutsis (Burundi), Interahamwe and Impunzamugambi (Rwanda), etc. The formation of these militias has contributed much to the current crisis of the military in Africa.

The military situation in Africa can be described essentially in terms of the proliferation of small weapons, the large-scale recruitment of child soldiers, and the formation of militias with strong ethnic bases and of armed gangs often totally lacking any responsible command. All these factors have led to the "extension" of the military arts and have made armed conflicts a routine affair. As General Amani

Toumani Touré of Mali pointed out in a recent study, contemporary conflicts in Africa have several important characteristics. One is the prevalence of child soldiers, for whom violence has become a way of life. A second is la banditisation; the recourse to banditry by both the armed forces and rebel groups to replenish their income (Touré, 1997).

The enfeeblement or even disappearance of the state and its corollary (the legal use of armed force), produces a situation of non-law; these factors are at the root of many of the violations of contemporary IHL witnessed in Africa. When the structures have collapsed, any realistic policy for promotion of IHL must start with the rehabilitation of the political, economic and social foundations of the state and its various entities, including the army. In the case of states that are functioning relatively well, it is important to adopt an integrated and long-term strategy for the development of IHL.

Long-term efforts to disseminate and incorporate existing IHL in national law must focus on both the codification of IHL at the national level and the development of the humanitarian culture in society (Mubiala, 1989). Major domestic legislative reforms should be envisaged with a view to incorporating the humanitarian principles and rules in the various relevant codes: criminal code, military criminal code, code of criminal procedure. The adoption of specific codes for target groups such as the armed forces should be encouraged. One positive example is the draft code of conduct for the armed forces being prepared in Mali. Such texts should emphasise the suppression, by specialised national jurisdictions, of war crimes and other crimes against humanity.

Regarding humanitarian culture, the assimilation of contemporary humanitarian rules by African societies should be a major goal of dissemination. To do this, African peoples must be convinced that despite their formal imported character, these rules (Law of Geneva and Law of The Hague) are remarkably similar to African traditions, the virtues and merits of which are currently being extolled across the continent. As for methods of dissemination, they must be carefully chosen and take into account the duality of contemporary African society.

In promoting a humanitarian culture, a distinction must be made between educated and uneducated people. Among the educated, greater use must be made of the customary channels of dissemination, the three main target groups being universities, the medical professions and the armed forces. The efforts should be extended through civic instruction to the primary and secondary schools. In the population at large, oral dissemination must make use of the talent of griots (minstrels), where they still exist, and other resources of traditional folklore. Popular gatherings may be organised with the support of local chiefs; radio programmes may be broadcast and films projected in local languages; recourse may also be had to popular tales and stories and works of naive art, and not least, to the audio-visual means of communication as an essential component of an effective state policy for the dissemination of IHL.

In this regard, the ICRC has taken an important step in sponsoring the production of a CD "So why?", recorded by six leading African musicians: Papa Wemba (Democratic Republic of the Congo), Youssou N'Dour (Senegal), Lagbadja (Nigeria), Jabu Khanyile/Bayete (South Africa), Lourdes Van-Dunem (Angola) and Lucky Dube. This CD, a documentary film, as well as a book "Woza Africa": "Music goes to War", with a foreword by ex-President Nelson Mandela, are supporting a campaign for greater respect for civilians during war launched in 1997 (Kole Omotose, 1997). As the promotional literature of the CD points out (ICRC, 1997c):

The musicians' motivation is to mobilise their enormous influence to combat ethnic discrimination in Africa. The campaign's central message will be the value of promoting respect for victims of war and political violence. This is urgent at a time when a number of countries are in the throes of war, suffering from 'ethnic cleansing', and mass deportation and when countless families are being torn apart. In that 'other' Africa, armed adolescents roam the streets by day, committing cold-blooded murder and terrorising the population, and spend their nights listening to their favourite singers. Liberia and Congo are only the most recent examples.

Africa urgently needs an appeal by its popular idols to 'Wake up' to what is going on. The musicians have teamed up with the International Committee of the Red Cross (ICRC) which is willing to activate its world-wide network to support the campaign.

This project is neither intended to stage another Band Aid-type mega-concert of the 1980s variety nor to promote Red Cross humanitarian activities. What unites the musicians and the ICRC is a commitment to initiate a powerful campaign that will move people and mobilise them for change.

As noted at the outset, African states have contributed significantly to the development of contemporary IHL, both globally and regionally. However, this contrasts sharply with the current realities of warfare in the African continent, which has shown repeated, serious and mass violations of IHL. Some of the reasons are structural and relate to the historical development of the African state. Other causes are operational, connected with the weakness of IHL in Africa. This includes the incompatibility of modern law, including IHL, with African attitudes and realities as well as ineffective promotion of IHL.

Solutions must therefore be sought on two levels. Most fundamentally, the situation calls for the reconstruction of the African state, including the rehabilitation of the army, and the adaptation of the state to African culture. In this connection, a welcome must be given to two recent examples of the genuine incorporation of traditional leadership in the modern institutional system in the constitutions of Ethiopia and South Africa.

The difficulties resulting from operational causes will have to be overcome by implementing measures in three areas: legislative development of IHL in Africa, international cooperation to strengthen the national capacities of African states in this area, and the extensive publicising of this law. In summary form, the central reforms are to be:
— Development of norms on the national and international level to reflect contemporary needs.
— International cooperation to strengthen national capacities in the promotion of IHL.
— Dissemination of IHL in Africa.

## Development of Norms on the National and International Level to Reflect Contemporary Needs

*Country approach.* As repeatedly recommended in official and informal circles, African states should incorporate rules in their national legal systems to ensure, especially in criminal matters, the effective enforcement of IHL. This means ratifying without reservation, if they have not already done so, the international IHL instruments, making the declaration contained in article 90, paragraph 2, of Protocol I, and signing and ratifying without reservation the 1977 Ottawa Convention on the Prohibition of Anti-Personnel Mines and on their Destruction.

*Regional approach.* As recommended in the Yaoundé Declaration, adopted on 3 December 1997 by the participants in the first African seminar on IHL, organised by the Henry Dunant Institute and the Institute of International Relations of Came-

roon, the African states should continue their legislative efforts to improve humanitarian law and the machinery for its implementation. This would be a logical extension of the work already done on the protection of refugees and criminalisation of
mercenarism. Future development of law should encourage the extension of humanitarian protection to all forms of conflict on the basis of the principle of humanity,
and to ensure the protection of victims in accordance with this principle.

In this context, the author recommends the drafting and adoption, under the auspices of OAU, of an African convention on the rights and duties in armed conflicts
of persons and of the ethnic, cultural or religious communities to which they belong,
to supplement article 3 common to the Geneva Conventions of 1949 and Protocol
II of 1977. This humanitarian regional convention might include the following components:

i) In addition to the protection already provided to individuals and peoples under
the universal instruments, they should be accorded further protection by the simple
fact of belonging to communities whose leaders and/or armed elements are engaged
in a conflict.

ii) Where duties are concerned, individuals and communities whose leaders and/or
armed elements are engaged in a conflict should refrain from providing them with
any support and remain unengaged in the hostilities. They should make their neutrality known by colouring their faces with white flour during the hostilities. This
sign should be protected, and the belligerents should respect it, under penalty of
criminal prosecution.

iii) African states should ratify the Statute establishing the International Criminal
Court and establish a regional body within the OAU dealing with a "black list" of
community leaders to be arrested and prosecuted for serious violations of IHL. This
list should be communicated to all member states of the OAU, with a view to arrest-
ing mentioned leaders found on their territory.

## International Cooperation to Strengthen National Capacities in the Promotion of IHL

Measures to strengthen cooperation in this field should be adopted in North-South
operations and relations. This entails developing or strengthening the humanitarian
component of UN human rights field operations, and of regional and sub-regional
mechanisms for conflict prevention, management and resolution and peace-keeping
forces. All the above-mentioned operations and bodies should be staffed by IHL spe-
cialists, invested with functions of prevention in peace time (dissemination of IHL,
technical assistance for states in legal matters, etc.) and of monitoring in war time,
and both types of function in post-conflict situations. In war time, the "IHL observers" should enjoy the same protection as is accorded to ICRC personnel, health personnel, and the personnel of the United Nations and associated bodies. These actions
should be taken particularly for the OAU, Economic Community of West African
States (ECOWAS), Economic Community of Central African States (ECCAS),
Southern Africa Development Community (SADC) and Intergovernmental Authority for Development (IGAD) Mechanisms.

As for North-South relations generally, arrangements should be made to include
"humanitarian clauses" in cooperation agreements where appropriate. However,
"humanitarian conditionality" should not be used as a measure of sanctions in economic relations. Linking aid and trade to observance of IHL would likely yield scant
results or would be counter-productive, as happened in the case of human rights (example: the Lomé Agreements between the European Union and the countries of Af-

rica, the Caribbean and the Pacific). Rather, conditionality should be one of positive incentives, a "conditionality-promotion" offering rewards for the development and observance of IHL to African states that make genuine efforts to enforce IHL.

Regarding military aid, it is necessary to "incorporate the teaching of IHL in military aid and in training programmes for foreign armed forces", as one state suggested during the preparatory work for the meeting of intergovernmental experts on the protection of victims of war, held in Geneva, 23–27 January 1995 (ICRC, 1995).

Lastly, financial and technical support should also be given to the African countries to develop their regional or sub-regional cooperation in the field of "micro-disarmament", including through the adoption and implementation of moratoria on small arms. This has already been done for the West African countries (Ayissi, 2001).

## Dissemination of IHL in Africa

Reinforcement of existing activities in universities and among the population at large is recommended. Education in IHL should be strengthened for target groups and the mass of the population, using in the latter case dissemination methods suited to popular African culture. To this end, as already recommended in the Yaoundé Declaration, mentioned above:

— The African Governments should continue and intensify their efforts to disseminate the principles of IHL, in particular in the armed forces;
— University institutions, primarily the faculties of law, politics, economics and sociology, and medicine, and civil service colleges should include IHL in their curricula;
— This work should be extended to primary and secondary schools, especially in their civics courses; and
— States and private individuals should publicise the basic principles of IHL both through the press and through audio-visual materials and on a weekly basis, especially in the national languages.

Finally, more focused efforts are also advisable. As Professor Emmanuel Bello has already proposed, OAU, supported by the United Nations, the rich countries, including the Nordic countries, and ICRC should create a pan-African IHL research institute with a mandate to carry out research, provide training, and advise African governments (Bello, 1984). This institute should offer further training in IHL for African personnel, somewhat along the lines of the training offered by the ILO Turin Training Institute in other fields for the United Nations and its agencies.

# 4. Regional Co-operation for Humanitarian Action

## The Potential of the EAC

*Bonaventure Rutinwa*

One of the pillars of the present system of refugee protection is the principle of international co-operation and burden-sharing. Historically, this principle has been conceived in global terms, and implemented largely through global mobilisation by UN-HCR for resources to support refugees in countries with limited resources and for provision of resettlement opportunities by third states as a way of relieving the burden of protection on countries of first asylum. Recently, there has been an increased recourse to regional arrangements and organisations as frameworks within which to implement the principle of international co-operation in dealing with the refugee phenomenon. The purpose of this chapter is to examine the role that the East African Co-operation can play in creating and sustaining local relief capacity within the sub-region.

## The Principle of International Co-operation and Burden-sharing

Traditionally, the principle of international co-operation and burden-sharing entails the responsibility to provide assistance to refugees in host countries, and where necessary to remove excessively burdensome refugee populations from the countries of first refuge (Fonteyne, 1987:185; Kibreab, 1991:21). However, in recent practice, international co-operation and burden-sharing is conceived as applying to the entire spectrum of the refugee cycle, that is, from averting refugee flows, to addressing the root causes, providing protection and material assistance to refugees, through to the resolution of refugee problems through repatriation, local integration and resettlement, as well as rehabilitation and reconstruction in host countries and countries of origin.

The principle of international co-operation is reflected in a number of international legal instruments of general nature, including the United Nations Charter,[1] the International Covenant on Economic Social and Cultural Rights (ICESCR)[2] and the African Charter of Human and Peoples Rights.[3]

---

1. One of the purposes of the United Nations is "to achieve international co-operation in solving international problems of economic, social, cultural *or humanitarian character,* and promotion and encouraging respect for human rights and for fundamental freedoms without distinction as to race, sex, language, or religion". (Emphasis added.) See Article 1(3) of the Charter of the United Nations.
2. Article 2 of the ICESCR provides that:
   1.Each state Party to the present Covenant undertakes to take steps, individually and through international assistance and co-operation, especially economic and technical, to the maximum of its available resources, with a view to achieving progressively the full realization of the rights recognized in the present Covenant by all appropriate means, including particularly the adoption of legislative measures.
   Article 11 provides further that:
   1.The States Parties to the present Covenant recognize the right of everyone to an adequate standard of living for himself and his family, including adequate food, clothing and housing, and to the continuous improvement of living conditions. The State Party will take appropriate steps to ensure the realization of this right, recognizing to this effect the essential importance of international co-operation based on free consent.
3. Article 23(2) provides that "States shall have the duty, individually or collectively to ensure the right to development".

The principle of international co-operation is also enshrined in refugee specific instruments such as the 1951 Convention on the Status of Refugees whose preamble provides that "... the grant of asylum may place unduly heavy burdens on certain countries and that a satisfactory solution of a problem of which the United Nations has recognised the international scope and nature cannot therefore be achieved without international cooperation". An express call for burden-sharing is to be found in the UN General Assembly Declaration on Territorial Asylum of 1967, whose Article 2(2) provides that "Where a State finds difficulty in granting or continuing to grant asylum, States individually or jointly or through the United Nations, shall consider, in a spirit of international solidarity, taking appropriate measures to lighten the burden on that State". There are several other General Assembly resolutions in which the principle of burden-sharing has been affirmed.

The principle of international co-operation in addressing refugee matters is enshrined even more strongly in regional instruments adopted for that purpose. In South America, the concept of burden-sharing is referred to in paragraph (k) of Part II of the 1984 Cartegena Declaration on Refugee Protection. According to this, the concerned states reaffirmed the commitments in the Contadora Act on Peace and Co-operation in Central America, including the commitment to "request immediate assistance from the international community for Central American refugees, to be provided either directly, through bilateral or multilateral agreements, or through UNHCR and other organisations and agencies".

A regional instrument in which the principle of international cooperation and burden-sharing is provided for in the most direct and formal fashion is the OAU Convention Governing Specific Aspects of Refugees of 1969 for Africa. Article 11(4) of this Convention provides that: "where a Member State finds difficulty in continuing to grant asylum to refugees, such member State may appeal directly to other Member States and through the OAU, and such other Member State shall, in the spirit of African solidarity and international cooperation take appropriate measures to lighten the burden of their member granting asylum". In 1990, African states reaffirmed their belief in the principle of international cooperation under the Khartoum Declaration on Africa's Refugees which notes, inter alia, that:

> While the African Governments commit themselves to the eradication of the refugee problem in the Continent, a partnership must be forged between the international community on the one hand, and the African peoples and governments on the other. This partnership must be predicated on international solidarity and commitment.

In December 1998, also in Khartoum, the OAU Ministerial Meeting on Refugees, Returnees and Internally Displaced Persons adopted another Declaration which after "Noting with deep concern the growing fatigue of the countries of asylum and the diminishing donor commitment to provide humanitarian assistance to refugees, returnees and internally displaced persons; ... reaffirm[ed] the fundamental responsibility to provide protection and assistance to refugees and asylum seekers and the concept of burden-sharing".

In Europe, the most important development within the European Union with regard to burden-sharing was the adoption of the Council Resolution on Burden-Sharing with Regard to the Admission and Residence of Persons on a Temporary Basis of September 1995 and the Council Decision on Alert and Emergency Procedures for Burden-Sharing with Regard to the Admission and Residence of Displaced Persons on a Temporary Basis of 4 March 1996. The resolution noted the desirability for admission and residence of refugees on a temporary basis to be arranged in a concrete fashion and in a spirit of solidarity between the Member States. Further, the resolution emphasised the "necessity to agree on a sufficiently precise framework which would regulate operational initiatives but be flexible enough to authorise the admission—if necessary outside the normal procedures for applying for refugee status—of persons forced to leave their countries".

Traditionally, international co-operation has been implemented by countries that are willing and capable of providing assistance to those whose capacity is overwhelmed in their effort to host refugees. Usually, this has taken the form of contributions by states to the operations budget of UNHCR, which in turn allocates the resources to various refugee situations. It is for this reasons UNHCR has been described as "the fulcrum of the system of burden-sharing, co-ordinating, monitoring, and supervising the equitable distribution of the burden of responsibility towards refugees" (Beyani, 1997:3). The other way in which the principle of burden-sharing is operationalised is through inter and intra-regional and regional arrangements for dealing with specific refugee situations within particular regions.

An example of a standing inter-regional arrangement for burden-sharing in humanitarian situations is to be found under the 1989 Lomé IV Convention, concluded between the European Community and African, Caribbean and Pacific (ACP) countries whose Article 254 provides:

> 1. Emergency assistance shall be accorded to ACP States faced with serious economic and social difficulties of an exceptional nature resulting from natural disasters or extraordinary circumstances having comparable effects...

> 2. The Community shall take adequate steps to facilitate speedy action which is required to meet immediate needs for which emergency assistance is intended... (emphasis added)

Article 225 of the Convention is specifically addressed to providing assistance to ACP States taking in refugees or returnees. According to one authority, the emergency provisions of Lomé IV Convention, particularly Article 224 represent perhaps the most striking instance of a formal obligation to assist stipulated in a strikingly direct fashion (Goodwin-Gill, 1996:293).

An early inter-regional arrangement on burden-sharing designed specifically to deal with a specific refugee situation was the International Conference on Indochinese Refugees which began with the Meeting on Refugees and Displaced Persons in South East Asia convened by the UNHCR in 1979. The Conference agreed on a burden-sharing system based on intra-regional first asylum and comprehensive extra-regional resettlement. The granting of first reception in the region was made explicitly contingent on the availability of extra-regional resettlement, which was to be provided by Western countries on the basis of a quota system encompassing both immigration and humanitarian criteria. Nearly 700,000 refugees were resettled in third states under this arrangement (IGC, 1995:19) A Second International Conference on Indochinese Refugees was convened in 1989 and resulted in the adoption of the Comprehensive Plan of Action (CPA). The objectives of the CPA were: prevention of organised clandestine departures through, among other means, mass media activities and regular consultations between the countries of origin concerned; encouragement and promotion of regular departure procedures and migration programmes; maintaining guarantees of first asylum; establishment of consistent region-wide refugee status determination procedures; resettlement of Vietnamese refugees, long stayers and new arrivals found to be refugees; and repatriation of non-refugees (Bronnee, 1993:541; Goodwin-Gill, 1996:292; IGC, 1995:19–20). The CPA is generally regarded as a success. By 1995, the outflow from Vietnam and Laos had virtually stopped, almost all those identified as refugees had been resettled, and more than 70,000 persons had been returned to Vietnam (IGC, 1995).

Another instance of burden-sharing arrangements was the International Conference on Central American Refugees (CIREFCA) held in Guatemala in May 1989. The Plan of Action adopted by the Conference outlined a series of commitments by all participating states and established follow-up mechanisms for the process. Unlike the resettlement-oriented CPA, the CIREFCA process sought to achieve voluntary repatriation as the preferred solution, followed by local integration where conditions for voluntary reparation were not feasible. The "return" countries (Nicaragua, Guatemala and El Salvador) guaranteed safety for returnees while host countries (Costa Rica, Mexico and Belize) committed themselves to integrate locally residual caseloads of non-repatriable refugees. Extra-regional participants committed themselves to providing funding to facilitate repatriation and integration. The bulk of funding—over 90 per cent—originated from Europe (IGC, 1995:22). Overall, the CIREFCA process met its objective and it is often put forward as a particularly successful example of regional cooperation to facilitate extra-regional financial burden-sharing in order to achieve durable solutions through voluntary repatriation or local integration (IGC, 1995:21).

A similar initiative was undertaken in the early 1980s in Africa under two International Conferences on Assistance to Refugees in Africa (ICARA). Held in 1981, the first ICARA conference aimed at focusing international attention on the plight of refugees in Africa and had as its purpose to mobilise extra-regional funding for emergency needs in African refugee hosting countries. ICARA I was explicitly conceived as a pledging forum where donors were invited to select the projects they were willing to support. A total of US$574 million was pledged, a sum that included programmes which had already been agreed for funding. Efforts to mobilise additional resources failed partly because of the poor quality of the proposals submitted but mainly because of the non-committal nature of the participating donors. In the end, many failed to meet their pledges.

The second International Conference on Assistance to Refugees in Africa (ICARA II) was convened in 1984 by UNHCR. The Conference adopted Final Declaration and Programme of Action, which emphasised the commitment to burden-sharing:

The Conference recognises that the condition of refugees is a global responsibility of the international community and emphasizes the need for equitable burden-sharing by all its members, taking into consideration particularly the case of the least developed countries.

The principal purpose of ICARA II was to facilitate integration of refugees in the first countries of asylum by providing such development assistance as would enable host countries to absorb them. To improve the low quality of proposals, a problem cited as having undermined ICARA I, a Steering Committee, composed of UNHCR, OAU, UNDP, and the UN Secretary General's Office, was set up. Leading this team was UNDP, whose mandate included the development of guidelines to be used by host countries in drafting project proposals. In addition, a technical team of UN experts was to visit each country to assess needs and determine priorities. UNHCR and UNDP were to co-ordinate donor interest in the various projects, which were mostly funded bilaterally.

Unlike CPA in South East Asia and the CIREFCA process in Central America, ICARA II turned out to be a failure. It was neither able to raise the projected resources nor encourage integration of any significant numbers of refugees into host countries. Many reasons have been advanced to explain this failure. The main ones include the lack of a centralised structure to coordinate and monitor funding pledges, tension between overriding donor preference for funding durable solutions including integration, and the reluctance of African states to permanently integrate refugees (IGC, 1995:25). Above all, there was a lack of serious commitment to the process on the part of donors (Gorman, 1987:Chs 2 and 3; Stein, 1987:47–59).

A recent example of a regional arrangement for burden-sharing is the mechanism established in the European Union under the Council Resolution on Burden Sharing with Regard to Admission and Residence of Persons on a Temporary Basis and Council Decision on Alert and Emergency Procedures for Burden-Sharing with Regard to Admission and Residence of Displaced Persons on a Temporary Basis, discussed above. The criteria for burden-sharing are outlined in paragraph 4 which stipulates that the burden in connection with the admission and residence of displaced persons on a temporary basis in a crisis could be shared on a balanced basis, in a spirit of solidarity, taking into account the following criteria:

— the contribution which each Member State is making to prevention or resolution of the crisis (military resources, local protection and humanitarian assistance)

— all economic, social and political factors which may affect the capacity of a Member  State to admit an increased number of displaced persons under satisfactory conditions.

In a footnote to this paragraph, it is stated that "these criteria are norms of reference that may be supplemented by further criteria in the light of specific situations".

Under the Decision on emergency procedures, the Council, having regard to the above resolution on burden-sharing, and the need for this resolution to be supplemented if the principles set out therein were to be applied effectively when a crisis situation required swift action, decided on a detailed alert and emergency procedure including extensive provisions relating to summoning of emergency meetings in the event of mass influxes, matters that may be covered on the agenda, alternative ways to reach decision on burden-sharing and the monitoring of the situation during the crisis. The provisions of the Council Resolution and Decision read together have consolidated the notion of burden-sharing in the EU context (IGC, 1995:32).

The need for burden-sharing was incorporated in Article 5 of the EU Commission Proposal for a Joint Action Concerning Temporary Protection of Displaced Persons. This article called upon the Council to examine how best to support Member States that were particularly affected by the mass influx of persons in need of international protection. An annotation explaining the background to Article 5 reads as follows:

With regard to the question raised in Article 5, it should be kept in mind that one of the very purposes of the joint action is precisely to create conditions for an effective sharing of the responsibility with regard to situations of mass influx of persons in need of international protection. Article 5 reflects the content of the Council resolutions on burden-sharing which foresee the possibility of taking measures based on solidarity if one or more member states are particularly affected by mass-influx situations. Such measures may for example take the form of financial compensation and/or, if that is not sufficient, a fair allocation of the persons who are fleeing from the crisis regions (European Commission, para 21).

The principle of burden-sharing in refugee situations has been included in the Treaty of Amsterdam whose Article C 2 provides that the Council shall adopt "measures on refugees and other displaced persons within the following areas", and promote "a balance of effort between Member States in receiving and bearing the consequences of receiving refugees and other displaced persons".

From the above review, the practice of states with regard to intra-regional cooperation to address refugee situations may be summarised as follows:

1. Regional arrangements to address refugee situations are likely to succeed if such arrangements are designed to facilitate mobilisation of external resources in order to achieve repatriation of refugees inside or outside the region, or resettlement of refugees outside the region (CIREFCA & CPA).

2. However, regional arrangements to address refugee situations are likely to be rejected or fail if they seek the reallocation of refugees within the region (physical burden-sharing) or if their principal objective is to achieve absorption of refugees into countries of first asylum. (ICARA II).

3. States belonging to regional organisations may be prepared to provide financial and other assistance to one or more member states affected by mass influx situations. These conclusions must be borne in mind in exploring the potential of the East African cooperation as vehicle for cooperation in addressing refugee situations within the region.

## The East African Co-operation

The East African Co-operation (EAC) is an organisation of three member states namely the Republic of Kenya, the Republic of Uganda and the United Republic of Tanzania. These countries once belonged to the East African Community whose origins could be traced back to 1947 and which was dissolved in 1977. Under the Mediation Agreement of 14 May 1984 for the division of the assets and liabilities of the dissolved Community, the three countries had agreed to explore and identify areas for future co-operation and to make arrangements for such co-operation.

On 30 November 1993, an Agreement for the Establishment of a Permanent Tripartite Commission for Co-operation between Kenya, Uganda and Tanzania was signed. This Commission was responsible for the co-ordination of political, economic, social, cultural, security and legal affairs, of the said countries. The Secretariat of the above Tripartite Commission was launched under a protocol to the above agreement, signed on 26 November 1994. On 29 April 1997, the Heads of State of the three East African countries, launched the East African Co-operation Development Strategy (1997–2000), a policy document which gives the direction and programme for the rapid achievement of the aims and objectives of the East African Co-operation. Further, they directed the Tripartite Commission to embark on negotiations for the upgrading of the Agreement to establish the Tripartite Commission as a Treaty. After being drafted and deliberated by various interested actors, the treaty was signed in Arusha, Tanzania on 29 November 1999.

As shown in the chapters on the individual countries in this book, all the member states of the East African Cooperation have been facing acute refugee problems for a long time. This is because they are almost sandwiched between two of Africa's most troubled regions namely the Great Lakes region to the West and the Horn of Africa to the North. The three EAC members have on several occasions expressed their serious concern over the incessant arrivals of refugees on their territory and the impact this was having on the principal objective of the EAC, which is to bring about peace, security and economic development within the region. For example, at their various summit meetings on the situation in the Democratic Republic of the Congo, the Heads of State of the three countries have often observed that the crisis was impacting negatively on the EAC region, through, among other things, precipitating an influx of refugees into the member states. A similar remark was made by Ambassador Fulgence Kazaura, the Deputy Executive Secretary (DES) of the Tripartite Commission, in his statement at the meeting of Immigration and Refugee Chiefs held in Arusha, Tanzania on 29–30 September 1997. Ambassador Kazaura underscored the importance of deliberating on immigration and refugees since these were subjects that related to the EAC's fundamental principle of the maintenance of peace and stability in the region. The DES went on to say that unless handled harmoniously and effectively, the refugee problem had the potential to disturb the peace and security on which the region so much depended in order to move forward with the objectives of economic development and regional integration (EAC, 1997, para 1.4). The rationale of co-operation in peace and security matters within East Africa is stated more elaborately by Allot, the Information and Public Relations Officer of the EAC:

> Defence and security is viewed as an integral part of the regional integration and development. This is based on the premise that a state of conflict and security is the very antithesis of co-operation and development. Only with assured and durable security can the people of the East African region have the necessary enabling environment to maximise their self-expression and utilisation of their resources. Also only with assured and durable security, can gains from the regional integration be preserved, protected and thus sustained (Allot, 1999:6).

Refugee situations do not necessarily constitute a threat to peace and security. However, sometimes they can amount to such a threat, and the refugee dimension in the conflicts in the Horn of Africa and the Great Lakes has been the main reason why the UN Security Council characterised those situations as constituting a threat to peace and security, warranting intervention under Chapter VII of the United Nations (Roberts, 1998:383). Accordingly, it is not inappropriate for the officials of the EAC to link refugee matters with peace and security within the region.

## Enabling Provisions of the EAC Treaty

There are a number of provisions in the Treaty for the Establishment of the East African Community that have relevance to cooperation in the field of humanitarian affairs. The first pertinent provision is Article 4 which sets out the objectives of the Community. In accordance with Article 4(1):

> The Community shall be the principal organ of the Partner States for the development of policies and programmes aimed at widening and deepening co-operation among the Partner States in various fields such as political, economic, social, cultural, defence, security, legal and judicial affairs, for their mutual benefit.

Sub-Article 3 adds:

> For the purposes set out in paragraph 1 of this Article and as hereinafter provided in particular provisions of this Treaty, the Community shall ensure
> [...]
> (f) the promotion of peace, security, and stability within, and good neighbourliness among the partner States.

The scope of cooperation in political matters as provided for under Article 4 is amplified under Article 131, which requires Partner States to define and implement common foreign and security policies. This provision is complemented by Article 132, which relates to regional peace and security and has two provisions that could be pertinent to cooperation in humanitarian emergencies. The first is Article 132(3) which provides that "the Partner States shall evolve and establish regional disaster management mechanisms which shall harmonise training operations, technical co-operation and support in this area". The second provision is sub-article 132(4) under which "the Partner States undertake to establish common mechanisms for the management of refugees".

## Potential Forms of Co-operation

As discussed in the section on the principle of international co-operation in refugee matters, co-operation could take one or several forms. It would involve the sharing of resources and/or the burden of physical protection by distributing refugees arising in one member state throughout the territories of other member states of an affected region. As was also seen, it is difficult to agree on the modalities of physical burden-sharing. Consequently, it would be wise for the members of the East African Co-operation to pursue co-operation in refugee protection in such a way as to enhance the capacity of each member state to cope with influxes of refugees on its own territory. This can be achieved through three main ways: (a) taking joint measures to defuse situations that might result in refugee flows into the territories of member states, (b) taking joint measures to improve the administrative capacity of each member state to respond to refugee influxes, and (c) offering each other mutual assistance in situations of mass influx.

### Taking Joint Anticipatory and Preventive Measures

One way the East African Community partner states could work together to ensure that humanitarian emergencies in the region remain manageable is to take joint action to prevent situations in neighbouring countries that generate refugee flows. This approach would be in line with the current policy of the OAU which puts emphasis on anticipatory and preventive measures, peace keeping and peace building in order to defuse conflicts before they degenerate into intense and generalised conflicts with all the attendant consequences such as refugee flows (OAU, 1993:para 15). EAC's position is reflected in a paper presented by its Information and Public Relations Officer:

> Apart from intra-region conflicts which have immediate and direct effects on our region, situations of conflict and insecurity prevailing in the countries neighbouring East Africa also have spill-over effects. Such cases as exist or have arisen in the past, in Sudan, Somalia, Burundi, Rwanda, Congo and Mozambique have had significant negative effects on our countries. It follows therefore, that for the mutual benefit of all, joint approaches are imperative for the preservation of peace and security (Allot, 1999:4).

So far, the East African countries are co-operating in trying to find a peaceful resolution of the conflict in Burundi. While this initiative involves parties from outside of Africa, it is clear that the three East African countries form a core participating group. As has been clear at almost all the eight regional summits that have been held in pursuit of peace in Burundi, a major reason for this initiative is to prevent refugee flows to neighbouring countries. The signing of a Burundi Peace Accord on 28 August 2000 provides a hopeful sign in this regard.

### Joint Administrative Capacity Building

As argued in the case study chapters, all East African countries need to improve their refugee policies, legal frameworks as well as administrative structures. This is an area where the East African Cooperation can play a vital role in mobilising the necessary resources to enable each country to address humanitarian issues. A joint approach to donors for assistance in this regard, something like a consolidated appeal, is more likely to succeed and to generate greater resources than approaches by individual countries.

The East African Cooperation could also support local capacity building for relief in member states through facilitating joint training activities, information and staff exchange. The need for joint action in these areas was recognised by the meeting of the 6th Commission of the East African Co-operation held on 6 December 1996 (Final Report of the 6th Commission Meeting, 1996, para. 3.7.1.iii(g)) which recommended to the Tripartite Commission that matters concerning capacity building be given serious consideration. At its meeting held on 8 August 1997, the Tripartite Commission decided that a joint meeting of the Member States' Immigration and Refugee Chiefs should be convened by September 1997 for the purposes of deliberating the recommendations made by the Commission at its 6th Meeting.

Pursuant to the above decision, the meeting of Immigration and Refugee Chiefs took place in Arusha Tanzania on 29–30 September 1997. After briefing each other on the positions in their respective countries regarding the matters raised by the 6th Commission, the Immigration and Refugee Chiefs made several recommendations, including the initiation of a regular visit programme for purposes of enhancing capacity for the practical handling of matters relating to refugees and asylum seekers and the utilisation of the Centre for Study of Forced Migration, University of Dar es Salaam, the Centre for Refugee Studies, Moi University, and the Human Rights Centre, Faculty of Law, Makerere University to provide training to personnel both from the public service and the NGO sector in matters relating to refugee management. Towards that end, it was recommended further that the three institutions should coordinate their efforts from a regional point of view and make effective use of the Inter-University Council for East Africa (East African Co-operation Meeting of Immigration and Refugee Chiefs, Arusha, Tanzania, 29–30 September, 1997:5–6).

The official invitation to certain academic institutions to act as training agents of the EAC governments in the field of refugee management is an historic and unique opportunity that should be seized. The said academic institutions are ready and willing to take up the challenge. In fact, even before being called upon to do so, the three relevant institutions had already had extensive consultations and agreed in principle on the modalities of co-operation in matters of staff development, research, standardisation of curricula, staff exchange and capacity building for governments and NGOs. These initiatives were noted and welcomed by the meeting of the Immigration and Refugee Chiefs. What remains is to translate the agreement into action. Between them, and with support from international partners, these three institutions have considerable infrastructure and human capacity to undertake activities related to capacity building within and outside the government. Since then there have been several technical meetings looking at the harmonisation of refugee policy and practices.

## Intra-EAC Mutual Assistance in Humanitarian Emergencies

The other way in which EAC member states could co-operate in addressing refugee issues is to offer each other assistance in situations of mass influx. This could take various forms. It could involve, for example, member states providing financial and material assistance to a member state facing a humanitarian situation, as Kenya did when it provided financial and technical assistance to Tanzania when a vessel, MV

Bukoba, sank in Lake Victoria in 1996 killing over 800 persons. Member states could also offer each other mutual military assistance to deal with refugee emergencies. Already, it is envisaged that under the regional defence and security cooperation provisions of the Treaty, member states will endeavour to achieve collective and rational utilisation of military resources. Ways of dong this include "speedy mobilisation for peace keeping and disaster management operations, preservation of internal stability and enhancement of deterrence and capability in dealing with spill-over effects of external conflicts" (Allot, 1999:8). It is envisaged further that military personnel, equipment and other military resources of member states could be applied to measures such as humanitarian assistance in the advent of adverse situations; beefing up the distribution of food, materials and medicines in emergencies. These states have a tradition to build upon. They have been involved in joint military training exercises and exchange programmes that aim to help build confidence as well as harmonise the command structures.

## Conclusion

Regional organisation provides a useful framework within which member states could co-operate to address refugee and other humanitarian situations. Accordingly, revitalisation of the East African Community provides an opportunity for regional co-operation in addressing humanitarian crises such as emergencies related to forced migration. Such co-operation should involve measures that are acceptable to member states and fit within the broader policies outlined under the treaty of cooperation. These include joint action to prevent refugee flows, improving the capacity of partner states to respond to humanitarian situations and mutual assistance in situations of mass influx of refugees. Such measures can greatly enhance the ability of all states within the East African Cooperation to address refugees and other humanitarian situations occurring in their territories.

# II

# Eroding Local Capacity

# 5. The Marginalisation of Local Relief Capacity in Tanzania

*Bonaventure Rutinwa*

> The development of local capacities is the only alternative to what seems like an unending process of foreigners parachuting into each new crisis spot (USIP, 1996).

Over the 40 years of its independence, Tanzania has had to cope with various humanitarian situations such as influxes of refugees, floods, drought, major sea accidents and more recently a terrorist attack on diplomatic premises in the city of Dar es Salaam. Of these emergencies, the most important and enduring one has been refugee flows. Tanzania has seen six major waves of refugees and asylums seekers. The first were Rwandese refugees in 1959–1962 following the "social revolution" in Rwanda. Then came asylum seekers from the southern African states, Mozambique, Zimbabwe (then Rhodesia), Namibia and Angola in the 1960s and 1970s. The third wave was comprised of Burundian refugees in the 1970s, followed by Burundian and Rwandese refugees in the early 1990s. The fifth was Rwandese refugees after the genocide in Rwanda in 1994. More recently, asylum seekers from the Democratic Republic of the Congo and Burundi have arrived. With every influx of refugees come many issues including the granting of asylum and legal protection, security for refugees and host communities, care and maintenance of refugees and resolution of the consequences of forcible population displacement both on individual refugees and in host communities. This chapter addresses the issues of the administration of refugee assistance projects including those related to rehabilitation of refugee-affected areas.

The evolution of policies and practices relating to administration of assistance to refugees in Tanzania can be divided into three overlapping phases. The first phase falls roughly between 1960 and 1970 during which the principal actors in the refugee relief arena were local authorities and civic groups. While the central government set the policy framework, local governments, in partnership with local institutions such as churches and traditional chiefs dealt with the reception of refugees, relief administration and local settlement. The role of UNHCR, as that of other international organisations, was limited to providing financing.

The second phase, falling between the 1970s and the 1980s, saw a shift in roles. UNHCR and other international actors went beyond funding programmes to actually administering relief supplies and overseeing local integration of refugees. Though characterised mainly by a new approach, known as the "Tripartite Partnership Model", it overlaps with the first model. Its implementation began in the mid-1960s, when the first model still governed certain refugee situations in the country. The third phase began in the early 1990s and continues to date. Its principal characteristic is the total dominance by UNHCR and international NGOs of relief administration, and the concomitant reduction of the role of local actors including government at all levels in refugee relief administration.

This chapter examines the reasons behind the gradual withering of local capacity in the delivery of humanitarian assistance. The focus is on local capacity as it relates to the local community and public sector and only to a very small extent the NGOs. The thesis presented is that while some local policies and developments played a part, the principal reason for the demise of local relief capacity was the involvement of international donors and actors in refugee relief work in Tanzania and the particular policies and approaches they followed in that regard. A number of recommendations are made on how to redress the situation and create space for local actors to reclaim their full participation in the humanitarian assistance arena in Tanzania.

For purposes of presentation, the chapter is divided into six sections. The first is an introduction; sections two to four look respectively at the refugee assistance models in the first, second and third phases mentioned above. In each of these phases, the specific humanitarian situation(s) and the relevant government policy at the time are described and issues related to the organisation of relief operations examined. Particular focus is placed on functions currently dominated by foreign NGOs and expatriate staff because local capacity is presumed absent or inadequate. These are: (a) camp planning and management and (b) delivery of goods and social services such as health care and education. Further, the impact of the practices in each phase on local relief capacity is examined. Section five sums up the main arguments in relation to the evolution of the refugee relief regime in Tanzania, and section six surveys areas where action could be taken to rebuild local relief capacity in Tanzania.

## Phase I: Local Administration of Assistance to Rwandese Refugees

Tanzania began grappling with refugee crises almost at the same time that the country gained its independence. The first large wave of refugees to arrive in the country consisted of Rwandese who fled their country during the political upheavals in Rwanda between 1959–1962. Following closely were refugees from Southern African countries, fleeing from brutal colonial rule, racial domination and the consequences of liberation wars. The administration of relief to both sets of refugees was done within the broader national policy on rural development and undertaken largely by local actors.

### The Emergency Phase: 1959–1962

Refugees from Rwanda began arriving in trickles in the Ngara district of Tanzania in late 1959. Arrival rates picked up between 1961 and 1962 with an estimated 50 to 100 refugees entering Tanzania each day. By the end of 1961 there were some 5,000 refugees in reception centres in Ngara and Karagwe, with several others having spontaneously settled among the local communities. The number of Rwandese refugees entering Tanzania peaked at 10,000 in 1962, with most of them being sheltered at Muyenzi settlement in Ngara District (Gasarasi, 1976:58, Daley, 1989:174, Yeld, 1996:26).

In describing the way policy relating to refugee matters was decided during this period, Rachel Yeld observes:

> Policy decisions on refugee affairs were taken at the central government ministry level (until September 1962 Ministry of Home Affairs and thereafter Vice President's Office), but on the basis of information received from Ngara relayed through Bukoba (the Provincial headquarters). Effectively, with the difficulties of communication, all but major decisions on change of policy were taken at Bukoba (Yeld, 1996:28).

During the emergency phase, the general administration of the refugee centre at Muyenzi was under a district foreman from Ngara. This foreman was responsible for moving refugees to the centre and constructing a hangar for stores as well as grass huts for refugee families. In discharging his functions, the foreman appears to have been answerable to the District Commissioner (Yeld ,1996:29). As numbers of refugees increased with the influx from Burundi, a settlement officer, assigned refugee duties, was posted to Ngara in January 1962.

Settlement officers were assisted in their work by volunteer expatriates, seconded from various international agencies. At Muyenzi there were two expatriate volunteers, one sponsored by the United Nations Association of Britain and another Danish UN volunteer, both of whom lived in tents within the refugee camps. The Danish volunteer was a nurse while the British volunteer was, by her own account, accepted by the local authorities to work as a settlement worker attached to the government (Yeld, 1996:2). The refugees were also involved in the administration of Muyenzi camp. According to Gasarasi, there was a hierarchy of refugee leaders, at the top of which were camp presidents.

> The hierarchy then went from president to vice-president, down to village or commune burgomasters. The role of the camp president was to see that refugees implemented government directives. But he was also supposed to bring refugees' problems to the attention of the government. He also supervised such things as the issue of food rations and other forms of relief aid. The vice-president assisted the president in the same roles, while the burgomasters performed a similar function in their respective villages (Gasarasi, 1976:71).

Relief supplies during the emergency phase came initially from the government (Gasarasi, 1987:101) and later from donors such as the United States and UNICEF, which sent food supplies, while Oxfam sent non-relief items including clothing and blankets. The government met the cost of transporting these supplies. Responsibility for the distribution of the supplies lay with the settlement officer, assisted by expatriate volunteers and refugee leaders. The British Red Cross and the UN Association provided medical workers while the Roman Catholic Church and the government met the cost of hospital treatment (Gasarasi, 1976:85; Yeld, 1996:30).

There were no organised education services during the emergency phase. But the refugees themselves, under their leader Mr. Kambanda, organised whatever form of school education was possible under the circumstances, both for general morale and to ensure that children would not fall far behind with their studies during their time in exile. Teachers were selected by Kambanda himself and served on a voluntary basis. Kambanda also organised activities for young men and women in order to prevent them from drifting to towns to seek jobs or to engage in immoral activities (Gasarasi, 1976:91–92; Yeld, 1996:33).

## The Resettlement Phase: 1963–1965

With the prospects of the influx of more refugees, the government in 1962 initiated a plan to disperse the refugees within all the districts and sub-chiefdoms of West Lake (now Kagera) region. For a number of reasons the experiment failed, and the refugees were allowed to return to Ngara, from where they would be resettled at their own permanent sites in Tanzania. In September 1962, refugee affairs were transferred from the Ministry of Home Affairs to the Vice President's Office, reflecting the view that the refugees were more an economic/development than a security issue. Having successfully invoked the intervention of Mwami Kigeli, the deposed monarch to whom the refugees still owed overwhelming loyalty to convince reluctant refugees to accept settlement, the government identified two main areas of permanent settlement, namely Kimuli in Karagwe and Bushubi in Ngara districts.

The implementation of the Kimuli settlement scheme began with the demarcation of plots of 10 acres each, to be distributed to refugees upon arrival. Government agricultural extension officers undertook the task of demarcating plots. The local authority built roads with the voluntary contribution of refugee labour. The administration of the resettlements, including distribution of relief supplies, continued to be the responsibility of the settlement officer. There seems to have been minimal involvement of external agencies in the administration of relief supplies. In fact, in 1963, when most of the work of resettling the refugees was done, Kimuli was run by two staff only: a Tanzanian settlement officer and an expatriate volunteer who assisted him (Yeld, 1996:2).

Refugees were also strongly involved in establishing the Kimuli settlement. Under their own leadership, refugees built and ran temporary schools for their children until churches constructed permanent schools. Refugee leaders were involved in arranging exchange of plots in order to ensure that close family and friends lived near to each other and adjudicated disputes over plots. The operation to establish Kimuli settlement was a complete success. Among the reasons cited by Yeld for the Kimuli success was the involvement of refugees in choosing the settlement area, the cohesiveness and unity of the refugees who went to this particular settlement, their viability, community size and the good leadership provided by the refugees themselves. Many of these factors in turn were due to the style of administration adopted by the Tanzanian settlement officer. According to Yeld:

> Here the wise handling of the situation through a policy of laissez faire, by the Tanzanian settlement officer, contributed greatly to the eventual achievement of unity. No pressure was put on them (refugees) to elect a single leader and committee for the whole community and a natural competitive element arose in the common projects (Yeld, 1996:62).

The settlement officer also protected refugees against undue outside interference and accusations by specialist assistants of government departments, particularly the agricultural extension staff who were pressing the refugees to give priority to cultivation even before they had had time to build their houses. Yeld describes the intervention of the settlement officer as follows:

> There was a general tendency to accuse the refugees of lack of effort in particular fields. This is perhaps to be expected in that each department was concerned to report progress and overlooked the work accomplished in other fields. Only the settlement officer could judge which of these specialised activities was the most urgent at that particular phase of settlement. Where each department had direct access to the refugees in demanding certain activities, the refugees became confused and discouraged. At Kimuli the settlement officer insisted that his authority over the refugees vis a vis specialised departments and voluntary agencies was final. At the same time he allowed the refugees to express their priorities and left the organisation of work on community projects entirely to them (Yeld, 1996:65).

The second area designated for permanent settlement of refugees was Bushubi in Ngara district. The decision to establish a settlement at Bushubi was made in 1961 and the intended settlers were refugees settled at Muyenzi camp plus those that had been sent to Bukoba district under the failed refugee dispersal experiment and now wanted to return to Ngara. The local Bushubi council donated land for settlement and the agricultural extension department surveyed it. To clear tsetse fly in the area, Oxfam made available 5,000 pounds sterling.

Unlike in Kimuli settlement project where the relationship between refugees and the administrators was harmonious, relations at the Bushubi settlement were antagonistic from the start. The main problem arose out of a conflict of interest between the relevant authorities and the refugees. The choice of the Bushubi area was dictated by a government desire to clear the bushes that harboured tsetse flies, lions, wild pigs and antelopes, and which had led to serious depopulation and consequent absence of economic activity in the area. The refugees, for their part, did not see any reason why they should be moved from Muyenzi camp where they had built their houses, cultivated the land and through their own voluntary labour built some communal infrastructure such as schools. Muyenzi had also additional infrastructure including medical facilities provided by the Red Cross and permanent schools built by the local Roman Catholic mission at Rulenge with funding from the Vatican (Gasarasi, 1976:94; Yeld, 1996:37). The same agency sponsored training of refugee teachers in Tanzanian teachers' colleges and provided money to pay them salaries. The Diocese of Victoria Nyanza of the Church Missionary Society had built an additional school.

Refugees also objected to being given plots, of 10 acres each, which isolated families from each other, increasing the danger of attack by marauding lions. With such a fundamental disagreement, the expatriate settlement officer, who unlike his local counterpart in Kimuli, wholly supported the Regional Administrative Officer's policies, sought to impose his will at all costs. He withdrew food rations to refugees who refused to relocate to Bushubi, arrested and deported refugee leaders, and deployed field force police. At one point, these actions led to a mass exodus of refugees from Muyenzi and the surrounding areas to Burundi. Most of them were stopped at the border by the Burundi army and returned to Tanzania. But by the time they returned, their huts as well as farms at Muyenzi had been bulldozed at the orders of the settlement officer. This was done to ensure that if the refugees returned, they would be forced to register afresh as new refugees and be sent immediately to the new settlement areas. As it happened, the refugees did return en masse in a bad state of health. However, they were still determined to stay at Muyenzi, pick up the pieces, and rebuild their lives afresh, with or without the support of the settlement officer. At the same time, the settlement officer did not show any inclination to budge on his position.

The impasse made one expatriate volunteer contact the UNHCR representative in Bujumbura to intervene in the situation. (The UNHCR office in Bujumbura, opened in 1962, was the first in Sub-Saharan Africa.) After consultations between UNHCR and the authorities in Dar es Salaam, a decision was reached to hand over the refugee settlement operation at Bushubi to the League of Red Cross Societies. At the time, the League of Red Cross Societies was in charge of refugee settlement operations in Burundi and Kivu Province of Zaire (now Democratic Republic of the Congo). The Red Cross was contacted and agreed to run the settlement operation for six months only. On 1 August 1963, the Red Cross took over the operation and introduced a modified settlement plan, which satisfied both the refugees and the authorities. Refugees were allowed to regroup from isolated areas and to build in village sites near the roads. As a condition for assuming responsibility for the settlement, the Red Cross insisted that there be no political interference from the local authorities throughout the period it would be in charge of the operation (Daley, 1989:215). This marked the beginning of external agencies operating in refugee-affected areas autonomous of government control.

The success of the Kimuli settlement operation and the failure of its counterpart at Bushubi carry a number of lessons relevant to administration of refugee projects. The success of the Kimuli settlement, which was managed by a Tanzanian from the region with ample knowledge of the Rwandese and the local environment, contrasts sharply with the debacle of the Bushubi operation where the settlement officer was a foreign expatriate, with no knowledge of the local environment. This differences support a point made and emphasised by a number of scholars of the importance of knowledge of the local environment in the success of refugee projects. The other lesson is the importance of refugee participation. As Yeld points out, "the lesson which emerged from the success of the Karagwe (Kimuli) settlement relates mainly to the importance of securing voluntary acceptance of settlement and of leaving initiative in the control of community affairs to the refugees themselves" (Yeld, 1996:66). Conversely, the difficulties that were encountered in implementing the settlement operation in Bushubi show the negative consequences of "ignorance and refusal to allow refugee participation in execution of settlement which could have provided the information needed to solve problems without conflict" (Ibid.:83).

## Towards Local Integration: 1965–1970

From the mid-1960s, refugee assistance policies changed from refugee-targeted assistance towards an integration of social services for refugees and the local population. During this period, food rations were completely withdrawn as refugees achieved self-reliance in food production (Gasarasi, 1976:96). As far as medical services were concerned, Tanzanian Christian Refugee Services (TCRS), an affiliate of the Lutheran World Federation, financed the construction of a waiting room for outpatients at Rulenge Hospital in order to enable the hospital to treat more refugees. During the same period, two dispensaries, one at Muyenzi and another at Kanyinya, were built under the supervision of a protestant missionary of the Christian Missionary Society (CMS) (Gasarasi, 1976:116). Another one had been built earlier at Mbuba. These dispensaries provided treatment for both refugees and local populations without discrimination. The TCRS continued to fund medical services for refugees who went to the mission owned Rulenge Hospital. However, refugees were encouraged to attain self-sufficiency and towards the close of the 1960s were required to pay for medical services provided by private clinics including Rulenge Hospital.

As for education, TCRS built schools in settlements to provide primary education to refugee children, but these were open to children from the local communities. According to Gasarasi, the composition of the teaching staff in settlement schools was a mixture of refugee teachers and Tanzanian ones. Refugee teachers were paid by TCRS, while the government paid Tanzanian teachers. TCRS withdrew from running settlement schools at the beginning of 1970 when it invited the government to take them over (Gasarasi, 1976:119). In the late 1960s, refugee pupils begun graduating from primary school but because they were not citizens, they were not eligible to receive free secondary education in Tanzania. Most of them could not afford to pay the fees demanded by private schools, but some donors intervened and provided money, enabling some refugee children to attend secondary school. Other primary school leavers were able to receive vocational training offered by aid agencies and the Tanzanian government. Adult education was also offered in settlements in the form of language classes for Kiswahili, English, as well as skills such as sewing and child-care. Adult education services were offered by TCRS personnel until 1972, when the programme was handed over to the government. (Gasarasi, 1976:120). The withdrawal of the TCRS from providing services to refugees implied that the refugees had become integrated in the local communities with responsibilities for them shifting to the government of Tanzania.

# Phase II. The Era of the Tripartite Partnership Model

The drafting of the Red Cross to run the Bushubi settlement operation marked the emergence of international agencies as critical players in the administration of refugee programmes in Tanzania. When the Red Cross relinquished responsibility for the Bushubi settlement in May 1964, it was succeeded by the TCRS, set up by the Lutheran World Federation in the same year at the behest of the World Council of Churches (Matthews, 1976:97). Although operationally largely independent, TCRS was an integral part of the Lutheran World Federation, which raised funds for core, as well as some programme, costs and provided senior staff.

In the same year (1964), the government entered another tripartite agreement with UNHCR and the TCRS where the latter assumed responsibility for administration of Mwesi settlement, established in the same year for resettlement of Rwandese refugees from other countries in the region. In 1965, the government of Tanzania, UNHCR and LWF/TCRS signed another such agreement, which resulted in the TCRS taking over the responsibility for Mozambican refugees in Mtamba settlement from the local authorities. This approach to administration of refugee assistance came to be known as the "tripartite partnership" model.

## The Theory of Tripartite Partnership Approach

There is ample literature on the theory of the tripartite approach to refugee assistance, a great deal of which draws on what is perceived to have been the practice in Tanzania (Neldner, 1981:161–177; Ayok, 1983; Gasarasi, 1987; Daley, 1989). Typically, the tripartite approach to refugee assistance involves an agreement between the government, UNHCR and an international agency, or a national affiliate or branch of an international agency such as the TCRS. These actors then share the responsibility for various aspects of refugee assistance. Usually, the host government provides land, a settlement officer, basic tools and cooking equipment, community services and the waiver of import duty on goods destined for refugee work; the agency runs the assistance programme including registering refugees, providing staff, educational, medical, social and agricultural services, and the UNHCR provides funds and technical advice

In a paper commissioned for the Conference on the Refugee Problems in Africa which was held in Arusha, Tanzania in May 1979, Brian Neldner, the then Secretary for Services Programmes in the Lutheran World Federation/World Service (LWF) explained how the tripartite partnership approach worked. Drawing from his experience and that of his organisation in various parts of Africa, Neldner, described the process of assistance to rural refugees as involving three phases: emergency phase, self-support phase and integrated settlement phase. During the emergency phase, issues of concern include "immediate action in close cooperation with the appropriate authorities to assess the nature of a refugee situation, the numbers involved, their location and their immediate needs" (Neldner, 1981:167). According to Neldner, once a host government seeks international assistance, a needs assessment is undertaken by the appropriate UN specialised agency(ies) and any voluntary organisation that is eager to assist. Upon being procured, the necessary resources would be distributed to refugees. Neldner does not state by whom this should be done; rather, there appears to be a presumption that the international NGOs involved will undertake the task. The "self-support phase" is described as involving planning for and assisting refugees to become self-sufficient at some point in time, with settlements becoming an integral part of the local society. While international actors would still be key during this phase, the role of the government in relation to settlement planning and administration was also critical:

> ... it is essential that local authorities and the ministries concerned are consulted so that they can plan for the inclusion of running costs for public services at the appropriate time. This will apply more to public services such as health and education than to those aspects which relate to the physical build-up of the settlements such as, e.g. roads, water supply, etc. Also ... adequate consultation with the authorities is needed so that the type of service, e.g. water supply, is consistent with the type of water supply being established and developed in the area as a whole... as an over-sophisticated water supply may cause problems in maintenance and payment for operation costs (Neldner, 1981:168).

The author goes on to describe what ought to be done with respect to the major needs, namely food, clothing, housing, health services, education, vocational training and agricultural development. In delivering these services, the author notes the importance of involving local authorities and wherever possible facilitating the use of local facilities such as schools and dispensaries in meeting the needs of refugees. In the "integrated community" phase, the involvement of the international community was expected to diminish, as refugees would have become self-sufficient at least in non-manufactured goods and would have integrated into the commercial structure of the local community. External actors were expected to leave as refugees participated fully in the administration of their communities, while maintaining contact and consultation with district and other local authorities (Ibid.:174). In the concluding observations, Neldner observed that the approach to refugee assistance he had posited had been tried and tested and had produced results and thus he commended it for adoption in resolving refugee problems elsewhere in Africa. He thanked the governments of the countries which had adopted the model "for providing a very clear framework of refugee policy within which (refugee) assistance has been provided ..." (Ibid.:166).

## The Model in Practice in Tanzania

The manner in which the tripartite model worked in practice in Tanzania may be understood by looking at the administration of assistance to Burundian refugees who arrived during this period and dominated the country's refugee agenda. In the period between the 1970s and the 1980s, the most significant refugee situation involved around 100,000 Burundians who arrived in 1972–1973 as a result of ethnic and political conflicts in their country. After a short period of emergency aid, these refugees were transferred to two settlements: Ulyankulu in Urambo District of Tabora region and Katumba in Mpanda District of Rukwa region. In 1978–1979, some 25,000 refugees were transferred from Ulyankulu to a third settlement, Mishamo, together with approximately 3,000 new refugees. By the mid-1980s, the total population of Burundian refugees in the three settlements was estimated at 132,000 persons (Sterkenburg et al., 1991:198–89).

In contrast to practice in the first phase, as well as the theory of the tripartite partnership approach postulated above, the practice in Tanzania in matters of settlement planning and administration is described by Daley as follows:

> Muyenzi, Rutamba and Mwesi settlements marked the beginning of settlement schemes with the minimum of local government input, and also with direct involvement from national government, firstly the Office of the Second Vice-President in Dar es Salaam and, after 1972, the Ministry of Home Affairs. They also marked the ending of local initiatives through the evolution of

the tripartite agreement, which gave donors virtual control over the settlement (Daley, 1989:214).

Donors were involved in the selection of settlement sites and in most cases carried out feasibility studies. The internal organisation of the settlements became the sole responsibility of the implementing agency, in this case, the TCRS (Daley, 1989:221). Unlike at Kimuli, refugee representatives did not participate in the planning of settlements (UNHCR, 1982:15).

Compared to the practice in the first phase, the internal administration of settlements exhibited three major characteristics: firstly, the structure entailed a hierarchy of subordinate relationships in the following order: donor agencies, implementing agency(ies), the state and then refugees. Secondly, there was unequal division of labour between international agencies and their affiliates and the government representatives. Unlike in the first phase, when the government settlement officer was the highest authority in a settlement, in this phase it was the project co-ordinators, usually expatriates employed by the implementing agencies who took charge of settlements. Where disputes arose between settlement commandants (as settlement officers had now been re-designated under the Refugee Control Act) and the project co-ordinators, the latter insisted on having the final word. Thus in one case revolving around control of expenditure and budgetary accountability, the agency, responding to head office pressure replied:

> ... if TCRS is the executive agency for the whole programme, then its Coordinator must also have the final say in deciding the expenditure within the budget. ... otherwise, we shall have a situation where the government officer may wish to incur expenditure which our project coordinator does not agree with and in relation to the UNHCR we bear the responsibility for the funds spent (quoted in Gasarasi, 1984:30 and reproduced in Daley, 1989:238).

The third feature of the administration of settlements under the tripartite model was lack of refugee participation. Although the settlements were organised in villages, whose chairmen were representatives on the Settlement Development Committees (SDC), this did not afford any meaningful opportunity for refugees to participate in decision-making. The SDCs held their meetings following major decisions having been made by the higher Settlement Development Planning Committees (SDPCs). SDPCs, in turn, implemented decisions made in Dar es Salaam. Consequently, SDCs operated "essentially to pass on directives from government to refugees" (Daley, 1989:240).

In theory (cfr. Neldner above) and in accordance with the provisions of the Tripartite Agreements (UNHCR, Tripartite Agreement, 1973) agencies were supposed to undertake provision of goods and social services "in consultation with the various regional officers and departments". In practice however, international agencies and/ or their affiliates usurped the responsibility of local authorities and the villagers and "little consideration is given to how the services are to be provided and maintained after handover ..." (Daley, 1989:233).

## Reasons for the Adoption of the Tripartite Partnership Model

At the Workshop on Building Local Relief Capacity in Africa held in Nairobi in August 1999 under this project, some participants attributed the ascendancy of the role of international agencies in administering refugee projects in Tanzania to two factors. The first was the emasculation of local authorities and local civic institutions through nationalisation of facilities that had helped refugees, such as schools. The second was the decline of the economic capacity of the central government after it had assumed most of the functions of local government and churches in provision of social services. These propositions contain some truth. In Tanzania, as elsewhere in Africa, the drive to Africanise politics and to create the central government as the undisputed hegemonic power resulted in deliberate measures to weaken local authorities to ensure that they did not become alternative foci of power. In the case of Tanzania, this included the abolition of chiefs, who in the first phase had been instrumental in setting and implementing refugee policies in their respective jurisdictions. Also the drive to establish the state (central government) as the focus of power and the source of all benevolence was manifested in the government's usurping the functions of civic and voluntary organisations (Hyden, 1995:39–42). In the case of Tanzania this went as far as nationalisation of mission-owned schools, a matter which led to demoralisation on the part of the former owners who also had to reconsider their cooperation with the government in the provision of social services (Ishumi, 1995:156). (For the opposite view as far as the Catholic Church is concerned, see Sivalon, 1995:179–191.) As it turned out, the government was in the end unable to maintain the existing services for its own citizens, let alone refugees. This might have made the intervention of external actors in a situation of a mass influx inevitable.

That said, the transition from the first to the second approach in refugee assistance indicates that neither the destruction of local capacity (by the central government), nor the loss of capacity at the central level were key in explaining the emergence and consolidation of the tripartite partnership model. As noted above, the first instance where an international agency was called in to run a refugee assistance operation was when the Red Cross was asked to take over the Bushubi settlement operation. The reason for this was not that the government had no capacity to run this operation. Rather, the project had run into problems due to a conflict of interest between refugees and the settlement officer, an expatriate civil servant, who was religiously implementing a plan designed by the Regional Administrative Officer. This problem could have been resolved by changing the personnel and policy without calling in another agency to manage the operation.

Similarly, the assumption of responsibility for Rutamba settlement by the TCRS was not due to the failure of the local or central government to manage the operation. In fact, the establishment of this settlement for Mozambican refugees had been the initiative of the local authorities, responding to the appalling material conditions of the refugees. The local authorities were in the process of selecting and surveying sites for the settlement when their plans were superseded by a tripartite agreement between the central government, UNHCR and LWF/TCRS (Daley, 1989:216). For this reason, it has been rightly concluded that "the approaches adopted for the settlement of the Banyarwanda (in Bushubi) and Mozambicans reflect the rapid adjustments in the policy of the newly-formed state to accommodate those of international organisations." (Daley, 1989:214). Daley further suggests that even the Refugee (Control) Act of 1965, which among other things required refugees on pain of sanction to remain in camps, was partly intended to accommodate the international agencies, approach which presupposes the populations they work with to be sedentary.

The growing role of international agencies in refugee work in Tanzania is reflected in President Nyerere's speeches to the two international conferences on refugee problems in Africa held in Arusha, Tanzania in 1979 and 1983. In the 1979 speech, Nyerere acknowledged in general terms the role that UNHCR and voluntary agencies were playing in assisting the government to cope with the refugee problem

(Nyerere, 1981:66). In his opening address to the 1983 Conference, Nyerere observed that in view of what had (not) happened since he delivered the 1979 speech, the same speech could still be as true on that day as it was then. However, he added:

> There is only one change I would make if I were to speak for the first time on this subject. I would give even greater emphasis to the tributes, which I then paid to the United Nations High Commissioner for Refugees and the voluntary agencies, which operate in this field. In the last four years these organisations, and especially field workers, have again and again stepped in to alleviate desperate human problems in difficult situations, and then to lay the foundations for human—if not political—recovery (Nyerere, 1983:7).

There appear to be two main reasons why the government adjusted its policy to reflect the preferences and approaches of international aid agencies. First, as Gasarasi points out, "the increasing sophistication of refugee rehabilitation *that resulted from the multiplicity of aid agencies' programs,* coupled with the recognition in 1962 of the permanence of the refugee problem, necessitated a more permanent strategy to handle the refugee question" (Gasarasi, 1987:104, emphasis added). Gasarasi adds that "it was ... in this context that the government thought of having one single organisation coordinate all assistance from voluntary agencies" and successfully appealed to the LWF to establish the TCRS for this purpose (Ibid). In other words, it was the influx of NGOs to deal with refugee problem, which made the government decide to draft in an external agency to co-ordinate refugee work. Critically significant is that the government consented to LWF establishing TRCS as its local affiliate (branch). In effect this was a step towards maintaining local capacity. However, by the 1990s, the role of TRCS was overshadowed by international actors.

The other and related reason for the government adjusting its policy was the increased preference of donor governments to channel their refugee aid through expatriate organisations rather than the host governments (Daley, 1989:234). In this regard, it is worth noting that in the case of Bushubi settlement, the idea of bringing in the Red Cross to administer the settlement as a way of resolving the crisis came from UNHCR, which at that point in time had already spent US$86,000 on the project (Daley, 1989:215). As argued earlier, the problems at this settlement could have been solved by a few simple steps: adjusting the policy, changing the plan designed by the Regional Administrative Officer, or replacing the settlement officer.

The approach of channelling aid through international agencies was consolidated under the ICARA II framework, which saw most of the pledges for refugee projects in Tanzania tied to NGO participation, which in practice meant mostly the internationals. For example, in 1984, the British government decided that all its ICARA aid to Third World countries would be channelled through British-based NGOs (Daley, 1989:256–257).

### The Impact of the Tripartite Partnership Model

With money flowing reasonably freely from donors, the TCRS generally did well in establishing settlements for refugees. However, there were a number of negative features arising directly from the presence of other international agencies operating at field level. First, the use of paid expatriate staff naturally raised the costs of operations. Further, access to easy capital led international agencies to construct unnecessarily expensive infrastructure, which was not easy to administer, inspect or sustain. For example, while local schools in Tabora region (where the Burundi settlements were located) were built at $20,000 per school, some $80,000 was used on a refugee school. (Daley, 1989:232). In Mishamo settlement, staff houses were elaborately designed and upon completion were equipped with wooden furniture imported from Scandinavia (Ibid.:222). The high cost of the infrastructure, and the failure to in-volve local authorities in planning, resulted in many services being discontinued once a settlement was handled over to the local government. There is also some ev-idence that the power, prestige and wealth which international NGO staff enjoyed may have created incentives for them to prolong the assistance period unnecessarily (Daley, 1989:258).

The most important negative impact of the tripartite model was the erosion of the power and position of local government by international aid agencies. For exam-ple

> ... in Mpanda district, TCRS with its fleet of Landrovers, drilling machines, road graders and access to foreign exchange, possess(ed) materials beyond the capacity of the district authorities, which in the 1980s had to rely on TCRS to import four much-needed Landrovers (Daley, 1989:257).

The other victims of the model were local actors, namely the refugees themselves, the local authorities and the churches, which had to compete with international aid agencies for resources but without the same political clout. Eventually they became as ineffective as some government departments (Daley, 1989:257). The demise of lo-cal relief capacity was complete.

## Phase III. Refugee Relief Practices in the 1990s

By Tanzanian standards, the 1980s were relatively uneventful years in relation to the refugee problem, as new refugee arrivals diminished significantly and projects to re-habilitate refugees from the 1970s influxes entered the integration phase. However, the problem of refugees reared its ugly head again in the 1990s, as conflicts in Bu-rundi, Rwanda and later ex-Zaire left many of the citizens of these countries with no other rational choice but to vote with their feet. Peaceful Tanzania became the main destination for the majority of them.

Refugees began trickling into Tanzania from the Great Lakes countries in 1990, but the major influxes were the arrival in 1993 of some 350,000 Burundians after the turmoil that followed the assassination of the first elected president in the coun-try. For months, the international community did not develop interest in the plight of the Burundian refugees who were cared for by the central and local governments with the few resources they could muster. When UNHCR and some international agencies did take an interest in the situation of 1993, it was too late. The refugees had decided to return to Burundi en masse partly because the political situation in their country had improved, and partly because they did not want to be relocated away from the border areas—as UNHCR and NGOs were planning to do—from where they had been able to continue to tend their crops across the border in Burun-di. This section therefore discusses relief administration practices in relation to the post-genocide Rwandese refugees, which has set a pattern that later continued in re-lation to the refugees from the Democratic Republic of the Congo and Burundi.

In early 1994, some 700,000 Rwandese arrived in the Ngara region of Tanzania following the genocide. The arrival of these refugees, if not the size of the influx, was anticipated, and UNHCR had planned for them well as described by Maureen Con-nelly, the first Head of the UNHCR Sub-Office in Ngara District where over 90 per cent of these refugees were settled:

> In mid-April 1994, UNHCR had fielded an emergency officer to prepare a contingency plan for an influx into the Ngara Region. Discussions were held within UNHCR and between UNHCR, the GOT and international agencies already in the country (who had come to deal with the Burundian refugee crisis of 1993). A basic contingency plan, using a figure of 50,000, was drawn up, including standby arrangements of implementing partners (Connelly, 1995:para 3.4).

Thus, as during the tripartite model phase described above the parties that were involved in contingency planning were UNHCR, the central government and external agencies. Implementing partners with whom UNHCR had standby arrangements were external, not local. Local government authorities were not involved to ensure that issues relevant to their people were addressed. A study commissioned by Oxfam in December 1994–January 1995 underscored this marginalisation:

> ... in all villages where UNHCR has selected places as ideal camp sites for refugees, there are no formal contractual agreement with the UNHCR. Therefore the village governments do not know for how long these camps are going to be in their villages, and who should compensate property found on farms of individual Tanzanians destroyed by the construction of camps. (Mwakasege, 1995:12).

In relation to the delivery of humanitarian assistance, this period marked the consolidation of the control of refugee relief work by UNHCR and international agencies and the concomitant marginalisation of local actors. UNHCR's involvement came as a result of being nominated by the government of Tanzania as the coordinating agency for relief operations (Connelly, 1995:para 3.4). The functions of the UNHCR in this capacity were wide and they included resource mobilisation, appointment and supervision of NGOs to implement programmes. In addition to the above functions, UNHCR became involved in other practical assignments on the ground such as reception and registration of refugees upon entry into Tanzania, camp planning and surveying. This marked a shift from the classic tripartite partnership model under which UNHCR was a "non-operational partner" (Gasarasi, 1987:102).

In order to discharge its statutory mandate as well as the additional functions described above, UNHCR had to expand its infrastructure considerably. Thus, from having no office in Tanzania during the first phase and just one in Dar es Salaam for the better part of the second phase, UNHCR established two additional and autonomous sub-offices in Ngara, and Kigoma; a logistics office at Mwanza airport on Lake Victoria; an office at the headquarters of every district in which there were refugees, and field offices in every camp in the country with the exception of Mwisa in Karagwe. Fleets of cars and other heavy equipment were brought in and staff, both expatriates and local, recruited to run various UNHCR programmes.

The actual delivery of humanitarian assistance was handled by international aid agencies that had implementing partnership agreements with UNHCR. Unlike the tripartite agreements of the 1960s and 1970s, parties to these agreements were UNHCR and the individual NGOs concerned. The government was not privy thereto. Over twenty international NGOs were involved in the administration of refugee projects after the genocide in Rwanda. Although this is a very small figure compared to relief operations in Rwanda and ex-Zaire where NGOs numbered in their hundreds, it is still very high in proportion to the numbers of refugees. Refugees at Muyenzi camp in the early1960s were looked after by a handful of staff without NGOs. Likewise the TCRS alone looked after some 150,000 refugees hosted in various settlements before the 1990s.

Like UNHCR, NGOs had to establish an elaborate infrastructure to discharge their responsibilities. Hundreds of people were employed by these agencies, including a significant number of expatriates who occupied virtually all positions of responsibility. Houses had to be constructed for them and funds raised to pay them salaries. As with contingent and camp planning activities, local authorities were marginalised in the execution of refugee projects. In Ngara, where most of the refugees were concentrated, the Chairman of the District Council, as well as his Council were not involved in any way in the management of the refugee programmes. The only time any of these officials entered refugee camps was to collect tax from refugee businessmen (Harrell-Bond and Rutinwa, 1996:24).

Likewise, the rehabilitation of refugee-affected areas was also dominated by UNHCR and international NGOs in near total exclusion of local government structures in those areas. The principal framework for addressing the impact of refugees in Tanzania was the Rehabilitation Programme for Refugee Affected Areas (RPRAA), established with financial support from the EU, the Dutch government, UNDP and UNHCR and jointly overseen by the Prime Minister's Office (PMO) and UNDP. In a study conducted in 1996 by Harrell-Bond and Rutinwa for the Norwegian People's Aid-Tanzania, the authors observed of the RPRAA (quoted in extenso):

> The programme is said to be based on the principles of decentralisation and the use of existing local capacities, particularly those in local government, the private sector and NGOs. Practice on the ground does not seem to conform with this principle. For example, even though the programme emphasizes the involvement of the district authorities, the major complaint we received in all districts we visited was lack of communication between UNDP/PMO offices established under this programme and the existing government planning structures.

> [...] In Ngara, the Chairman of the elected District Council, a former MP and senior civil servant who also happened to have been the first settlement officer in the district in 1962 had never been consulted by any of the actors on the refuge situation ... He has had no contact whatsoever with the RPRAA and his council members have not been consulted on priorities...

> At Bukoba regional headquarters the Planning Officer complained that the RPRAA was establishing a parallel planning structure instead of working through the existing one. Plans were being drawn up without consultation with his office, in contradiction to the declared objective of empowering the region to enable it to carry out its own development programmes. (See Harrell-Bond and Rutinwa, 1996:24.)

Also marginalised in the administration of refugee projects were the refugees themselves. At camp level, there was an arrangement for electing refugee leaders at different levels of camp organisation. However, their functions related much more to maintenance of peace and order in camps and not to wider administration of settlements as had been the case during the early 1960s, when refugee leaders could appoint primary school teachers, supervise plots allocation and exchange, and even participate in discussions as to durable solutions.

A number of reasons may explain why the government appointed UNHCR to coordinate relief operations during this phase. First, for reasons discussed above in relation to phase two of the government's refugee policy, local capacity in relief matters at this point in time was weak and would not have been able to handle the large number of refugees that was streaming into Tanzania. Second, as previously major donors had decided to channel their assistance through UNHCR and large, international NGOs. Although Tanzania is said to have "nominated" UNHCR as the Coordinating Agency for the operation, in reality the government had no choice in this matter after the European Union Humanitarian Office (ECHO) and USAID had taken the step, rightly described by von Bernuth as "unique" of giving all their funds directly to UNHCR (von Bernuth, 1996:288). Although the channelling of relief resources through UNHCR and other international agencies had been standard practice, given the magnitude of the problem, resources channelled through UNHCR and other northern-based agencies in Tanzania were huge. The inability of the government to have an influence on the resource flow was therefore clearly evident. Typically, if a particular project was funded by country X, then the Implementing Agency would, in most cases, be an NGO based in country X.

Tanzania had also just learnt a bitter lesson about attempting to get international actors fund activities without coming in to run it. Following the breakdown in the cease-fire between the forces of the then government of Rwanda and the RPF in 1993, Tanzania, which was the facilitator of the Arusha Peace Process, called the parties to Dar es Salaam. Here, they agreed to restore the cease-fire and to request the OAU to increase the unarmed military observer group from 50 to 500. To effect this measure, the Secretary General of the OAU approached the Secretary-General of the United Nations for financial assistance. Rejecting the request, Boutros-Ghali wrote back informing the OAU that the United Nations cannot fund an operation which is not under its control (UN, 1996, Doc. 11:159). Such communication must have been passed on to the Tanzanian government as a matter of course, in its capacity as the facilitator of the peace process.

In sum, by relinquishing control over relief operations to UNHCR and INGOs during the Rwanda emergency, Tanzania was being pragmatic. The government realised that was the only way to ensure that enough resources would be raised to deal with the situation.

## Implications of the Present Approach

The pattern of relief administration set at the time of the Rwanda emergency, and which has remained, has some serious implication for the humanitarian regime. The first implication is one of costs. There is no doubt that the transformation of UNHCR into a de facto operational agency, the multiplicity of international NGOs and the attendant expansion of bureaucratic superstructures and staff by both UNHCR and the agencies have increased the costs of relief operations quite substantially. Quite often one hears clamours about the un-sustainability of the present relief system because of the high costs involved. This is in turn attributed to the growth of the refugee problem to unmanageable levels. Quite possibly the principal, or at least a major, explanatory factor for the costs is not the size of the problem but the costly nature of the approaches chosen to address it.

The second implication of the internationally dependent approach relates to the increased reliance on expatriate staff in refugee work. As these have to be recruited and brought in from abroad after the emergency has occurred, it is inevitable that this will always delay the commencement of relief operations at the critical phase and many lives will be lost. Explaining why the response to the influx of 300,000 Burundian refugees into Tanzania in 1993 was so slow and ineffective as a consequence of which thousands of refugees died of dysentery and malnutrition, one senior UNHCR official put it down to the absence in the country of adequate implementing partners (Connelly, 1995:para 2.4). The marginalisation of local actors in refugee projects, for its part, may have had the unintended consequence of encouraging the government to renounce its obligations to refugees under international law. For example, in 1979, President Nyerere expressed the policy of the central government with regard to granting asylum to refugees quite clearly: while acknowledging the role of international assistance, he affirmed that "the refugees of Africa are primarily an African problem, and an African responsibility" (Nyerere, 1981:67). Less than twenty years later, the granting of asylum and respect for the non-refoulement norm were contingent upon donors meeting the costs of care and maintenance of the refugees (Government of Tanzania, 1995). At the operational level, the Tanzanian government has shirked some of the responsibilities belonging to host governments, claiming that these are the duties of UNHCR. For example, asked to respond to the charges that Tanzania was harbouring armed elements in Burundian refugee camps in Tanzania, Mr Jakaya Kikwete, the Tanzanian Foreign Minister, replied that Tanzania had no responsibility for whatever transpired in the camps. According to him, refugee camps were "UNHCR islands" in which the Tanzanian government had no role, apart from providing security around them! (The Guardian (T) 17 February 1999).

At the local level, the marginalisation of local authorities has undermined the sense of ownership of refugee related projects, which in turn threatens their sustainability. For example, in Biharamulo district, the district authorities decided to prepare their own comprehensive plan for rehabilitation of refugee affected areas and present it directly to donors after rejecting the plan prepared for the district under the RPRAA, which was not in line with the district's own priorities (Harrell-Bond and Rutinwa, 1996:24).

The problem of securing local ownership and sustaining projects that are planned and implemented by agencies without consulting local populations is exemplified by a case documented in a study commissioned by Oxfam in 1995. This case involved five shallow wells that had been built by Oxfam in Herushingo village in Kasulu district in early 1994. When the study team visited the area in December 1995 only one shallow well was working, two were dried up due to the continuing dry season and over-usage and two were broken down. According to the study:

> The village leaders when asked what they were doing to solve the problem of the 4 wells, which were not being used, said they were waiting for OXFAM to come and see them as they were the ones who constructed them (Mwakasege, 1995:28).

The experience forced Oxfam to reconsider and shift from an approach that "brings" assistance to people to "engaging" local communities in greater participation in planning the amenities to be provided.

## Conclusions

This chapter has examined the decline of local relief capacity and the reasons behind it. It is clear from the study of relief policies and practices in the three phases identified above that the process of decline was gradual. During the first phase, refugee problems were addressed mainly through local initiatives, even though the central government and donor agencies participated. In the second phase, the administration of refugee settlements and delivery of services were undertaken under tripartite agreements between the central government, UNHCR, and large (mainly international) NGOs. Whatever meaning the word "partnership" might connote, the relationship between the three parties, especially in the areas of administration of settlements and relief supplies was such that the NGO was the principal actor, the government a junior participant, and the UNHCR a non-operational, fund-channelling partner.

Contrary to established wisdom, Tanzania did not invite international agencies to administer refugee programmes because it had lost administrative capacity to do so. Rather, the Tanzanian government did so as a response to the approaches preferred by aid agencies and donor states and institutions on whom it depended for its resource capacity to deal with refugee situations. TCRS—a local affiliate of a large INGO—was formed in the early 1960s specifically to assist with co-ordination which had been necessitated by the increasing sophistication of refugee rehabilitation projects that resulted from the multiplicity of aid agency programmes (Gasarasi, 1987:104). One way in which the donors could have boosted the capacity of the government was to pool their resources and channel them through the government and community agencies. During the second phase, Tanzania relinquished responsibility for refugee programmes to UNHCR and international agencies because of the preference of donors to channel resources through such institutions, and not the government itself.

Contrary to the established myth, international NGOs that came to supplant local actors in refugee work did not posses prior greater expertise or resources than their local counterparts. As pointed out above, although its creation in January 1964 was facilitated by the LWF, TCRS was staffed by Tanzanians, and by May of the same year it had signed a tripartite agreement with the government and UNHCR to implement programmes at the Mwese refugee settlement operation. A month later it had taken over the operations at Bushubi from the Red Cross, with many more projects to follow. The reason it was able to do a good job was that it had some prior expertise but also some local knowledge that enabled them to learn on the job.

The massive refugee inflow after the 1994 genocide in Rwanda prompted a total take-over by UNHCR and international NGOs of refugee work in Tanzania. Whatever the merits of this model, the multiplicity of NGOs and the attendant work duplication has been detrimental to efficient and effective delivery of humanitarian assistance (Borton et al., 1996; von Bernuth, 1996:281–290). It has also made the operations more costly. The consequent marginalisation of local actors, moreover, has encouraged the central government to neglect its primary obligation to protect refugees and to make asylum conditional upon a decision by UNHCR and international agencies to provide care and maintenance for them. At the local level, failure to involve the local people and their authorities in planning and executing refugee projects has undermined the long-term sustainability of these projects.

The above shortcomings may account for some of the problems that presently threaten the sustainability of the refugee protection regime in the region. At the international level, the costly nature of the present regime may have played a part in donor despondency that humanitarian situations have grown to unmanageable levels, which in turn has contributed to so-called "donor fatigue". Within Tanzania, the marginalisation of the government and local authorities encouraged avoidance of responsibility at the central government level, and xenophobia at the local level. This dynamic in turn threatens the continued viability of the institution of asylum. Rebuilding local relief capacity could go some way to arrest this situation.

## Policy Implications. Towards Rebuilding Local Relief Capacity

Building local capacity calls for the creation of four conditions. The first is to improve the action environment—in which administration of refugee relief is carried out. This means the development of a sound policy for delivery of humanitarian assistance. The second condition is the creation or improvement of the institutional environment. This entails putting in place sound laws and administrative structures relating to the administration of humanitarian relief. The third measure in creating local relief capacity is to support local voluntary organisations to develop appropriate organisational structures and management capabilities necessary for delivery of humanitarian assistance. The fourth condition is utilisation of local institutions and personnel. This section briefly examines the present situation in Tanzania in relation to the above four aspects of capacity building and makes some suggestions on what needs to be done.

## Improving the Policy Framework

In the specific context of Tanzania, there are two areas that require further policy development. The first is the distribution of refugee responsibilities within the central government itself, and between the central government and the local government. Since independence in 1961, responsibility for refugee matters has shifted from the Ministry of Home Affairs to the Vice-President's Office (1962) and then returned to the Ministry of Home Affairs in 1972 where it has remained since. However, certain aspects of refugee administration, such as rehabilitation of refugee-affected areas are dealt with by the Prime Minister's Office. Meanwhile, the Ministry of Foreign Affairs plays a crucial role in the delicate matter of relations with countries of origin. Although the functions carried out by these different government departments are closely related, there does not seem to be appropriate coordination between the ministries. This may explain the lack of communication noted above between various actors involved in refugee projects at the local level, who are accountable to different departments at the national level. There is therefore a need for review of the applicable policies and administrative structures with a view to improving coordination between the various government departments dealing with refugee matters.

Also in need of review is the allocation of responsibility for refugees between different government levels from national to regional and district level. As noted, during the first phase policy was in theory made at national level, although in practice it was made at regional headquarters level and implemented at district level. In the second phase, policy was made at the national level and implemented by external agencies. In the third phase, national authorities were nominally involved in policy making. Donors effectively formulated and implemented policies. The ongoing restructuring exercise within the government, which aims to transfer responsibilities from the central to the local government, provides an opportunity to re-examine the current situation in relation to refugee protection and assistance. A study is needed to establish what this may imply for refugee protection policies.

An area of policy that requires greater attention is the national policy relating to voluntary organisations. After almost five years of work, the government recently came out with the official national policy on NGOs. However, as noted in the preparatory work for this document, there are many areas that still require more work if the policy is to be translated into action.

## Creating Appropriate Legal and Administrative Framework

Two main areas of law have direct relevance to the administration of refugee relief projects. These are the laws relating to registration and administration of voluntary organisations and labour legislation. In relation to the former, there are three main weaknesses in the present legal framework. First, there is no single piece of legislation that governs matters of NGO legislation in Tanzania. Instead such matters are governed by a myriad of legislation dating from colonial times, about which the National Steering Committee for the National Policy on NGOs had this to say:

> NGOs currently can be registered under three separate ordinances, the Societies Ordinance cap 337 (enacted in 1954), Trustees Incorporation Ordinance (1956), Cap 275 and Companies Ordinance, Cap. 212. The content of the basic structure of the Societies Ordinance together with the Rules made thereunder have remained virtually unaltered since 1954. The same applies to Trustees Incorporation Ordinance. None of the pieces of legislation which are currently used for purposes of formation, operation and coordination of the various activities of the NGOs were enacted with a clear vision of the nature, roles and varieties of activities currently being carried out by NGOs (NSCNPN, 1999:para 5(a)).

Second, registration of NGOs is centralised, with all registries in Dar es Salaam, the capital. This makes the process of registering NGOs costly and time consuming (NSCNPN, 1999:para 5(d), NPA, 1996:9). Third, the legislation mentioned above confers wide and discretionary powers to registrars and ministers, opening space for abuse. For instance, these offices may register and de-register NGOs. Further, there is no provision for redress for the aggrieved NGOs (NSCNPN, 1999:para 5(b)). These problems need to be urgently addressed in order to create a legal environment that is conducive for NGOs to develop and flourish.

In relation to labour legislation, a review is required to see whether and to what extent labour laws could be used to promote the employment and retention of local personnel in refugee related jobs. One issue that should be addressed is the regulation of employment of expatriate personnel to ensure that such staff are recruited only where necessary and that they are utilised in such a manner as to impart skills to local personnel.

Another issue to be looked at within this area of law is the terms of employment for local staff. Presently, contracts of employment for local staff with foreign aid organisations are characterised by, among other things, being short term, having a lack of security of tenure and an undefined basis for establishing the terms and conditions of services. Some of these problems are dictated by the terms on which the organisations get their funding. As a result, there is a high turn-over of local staff in aid organisations resulting from uncertainty about renewal of contracts, or movement of staff to other organisations offering better pay and longer contractual periods. Such a situation is inimical to building the local expertise associated with long-term experience.

Also in need of consideration are the terms of employment for refugees. The current practice is that refugee workers are paid arbitrary sums called "incentives" that are usually below local labour market rates. One study on Kenya proposed that refugees working in refugee camps should, as a matter of human rights relating to equal pay, be paid the same wages as Kenyans with comparable qualifications (Guglielmo, 1998). However, apart from commonality of race, the basis for interpreting this provision of human rights as requiring refugees to be paid the same wages as local staff—but not the same as expatriates with the same qualifications who do the same job—is entirely, both in general and as a matter of legal logic, fallacious. The proper interpretation of the provisions of human rights relating to equal pay would require all persons with similar qualifications and doing the same jobs, including refugees, to be paid the same salary. All these matters need further exploration, taking into account principles of sound employment theories and relevant rules such as human rights standards.

## Enhancing the Competence of Local NGOs

In a report prepared for the Norwegian People's Aid-Tanzania it was noted that NGOs need to have competence in a variety of fields, of which the following are the most important: governance, management practices, human resources, service delivery, external relations, and sustainability. The same report noted that "in general Tanzanian NGOs are deficient in all of these sectors..." (NPA, 1996:8). This situation should be rectified through training programmes for government and NGO personnel aimed at building competence in the above mentioned areas. This training should take a variety of forms including formal training, workshops and conferences, and use relevant local institutions. The other way of building the capacity of local institutions is by having local NGOs work side by side with international and other local NGOs with established expertise and experience in order to gain operational experience. Short-term attachment of Tanzanian graduates to international agencies working with refugees could be another way of building a pool of local expertise in the field of humanitarian assistance.

## Utilisation of Local Institutions and Personnel

As a way of enhancing local capacity, donor countries and agencies should be prepared to channel refugee aid through local institutions, including the government at all levels and local voluntary organisations. The reason often given for channelling donor funding through UN agencies and international NGOs is that they are more effective than government departments. This may or may not be the case. What is certain however, and what is proven by the experience reviewed above, is that "such an approach is directly harmful to the efforts to get Africa back on its feet. It totally overlooks the fact that better domestic resource utilisation will come about only if people are allowed to build on and organise around their own initiatives." (Hyden, 1995:44).

It is important to emphasize that what is advocated here is not that international aid agencies should be excluded from refugee work in Tanzania. Even if the measures proposed above are taken, it would be illusory to expect that Tanzania would acquire sufficient administrative capacity to respond alone to humanitarian situations. Accordingly, international agencies will continue to play a vital role in this regard. The point is, rather, that local institutions should be enabled and given an opportunity to realise and apply their potential to play a meaningful role along with other actors in addressing humanitarian situations occurring on their own territory. International agencies should as far as possible give priority to local personnel in their recruitment policies. It is commonly argued that the recruitment of expatriates is necessary because the local population lacks the required expertise, and there is a need to avoid draining qualified personnel from government services. However, this is not always true in all situations. In relation to the former reason, it has been rightly stressed that, in general, "the institutional crisis in Africa is no longer a crisis of knowledge, or the absence of educated and trained people who can man and lead institutions." (Wohlgemuth et al., 1998:7). On the contrary, the problem is the emigration of well-trained Africans because they are not being fully utilised at home. The failure of international agencies to identify and utilise local skilled people serves to perpetuate this situation. That there was no shortage of well-trained people in Tanzania was confirmed most recently by the Vice Chancellor of the University of Dar es Salaam at the University graduation ceremony on 27 November 1999, where he lamented the ever-growing number of unemployed graduates. Some of these could be targeted and employed in humanitarian assistance programmes. The fact that graduates may not have qualifications relating to delivery of humanitarian assistance as such should not be a barrier to their employment. Indeed many of the expatriate staff occupy positions for which they have no prior training and experience, but they learn on the job. There is no reason to assume local personnel cannot learn equally well on the job as their international counterparts.

This chapter has addressed the situation in Tanzania and the proposals made are based on Tanzania's problems and experience. However, it is submitted that the situation in Tanzania is not markedly different from that in many other refugee hosting countries in Africa. Accordingly, the proposals made above could, and should, be implemented elsewhere. That may go some way towards ending the unsustainable practice of parachuting in international agencies, whenever there is a humanitarian emergency in Africa.

# 6. Strengthening Local Relief Capacity in Kenya

## Challenges and Prospects

*Peter Mwangi Kagwanja*

This chapter argues that Kenya for most of its independence period had evolved a relatively strong local relief capacity. Such capacity was found mainly within religious and secular organisations and, to a lesser extent, state structures. However, the 1990s saw this relief capacity shrink remarkably with the influx and take-over of international agencies and Non-Governmental Organisations (NGOs). Ironically, this was a time when emergencies were multiplying and becoming a permanent feature of Kenya's humanitarian scene. Sitting at the axis of the refugee-producing Horn and Great Lakes regions of Africa, Kenya's refugee population increased dramatically from a high of about 15,000 refugees in the 1963–89 period to an all-time record of 420,000 camp refugees, excluding an estimated 150,000 urban refugee case load. Furthermore, ethnic violence which gripped parts of Kenya in the 1991–98 period produced nearly half a million internally displaced persons (IDPs), mostly in the Rift Valley, Western and Coast provinces. Although nearly half of the refugee population repatriated and a large number of IDPs were resettled by the middle of the decade, the problem lingered on, turning what initially appeared as a temporary problem into a 'permanent emergency'.

These emergencies over-stretched the existing local capacity and attracted a large number of international actors. Following the declaration of an emergency in 1991 and an appeal by the President to the international community to assist Kenya in dealing with this situation, international NGOs flooded the humanitarian arena in Kenya. The need for a swift response coupled with the desire to ensure effectiveness and sustainability of the relief effort translated into dominance of local relief capacity by an international one. This dominance posed two interrelated policy questions. To what extent are international agencies prepared to 'exit' or devolve responsibility to indigenous players? And further, do local agencies have the capacity to assume such responsibility?

While there is an extensive body of literature on the subject of local capacity in Kenya, much of it dwells on development and does not give sufficient attention to the relief sector (see for example, Osodo and Matsvai, 1998; Ndegwa, 1996; Mbogori, 1994). This chapter focuses on this neglected arena by addressing three main areas. First, it explores the development of indigenous relief organisations and state structures within the relief arena, in respect to their capacity and challenges during the 1963–91 period. Secondly, it examines the nature of involvement of international actors in this sector and the impact of this involvement on local capacity and, finally, it delves into the prospects of strengthening local relief capacity. For the purposes of this chapter, the term 'capacity building' is used in reference to the process of institutional building through the acquisition of assets, skills, knowledge, norms and practices which can foster sustainability of operations and effectiveness of organisations. Nonetheless, while the term 'capacity building' is employed in this discussion, the alternative word 'capacity strengthening' seems more appropriate in view of the prior existence of local capacity in the humanitarian sphere in Kenya.

It is the contention of this chapter that, whether intended or not, after intervening, international agencies bypassed, weakened and marginalised indigenous capacity. As these agencies established hegemony, especially in the refugee sector, they justified their failure to devolve responsibility to local actors and phase out on the grounds that local actors are bedevilled with organisational weaknesses, mismanagement, lethargy and corruption. This study argues that this attitude worked against the establishment of genuine partnerships among all stakeholders in the humanitarian arena and proposes ways and means of enhancing equal partnerships.

## A Bird's Eye View of the Humanitarian Crisis in Kenya

As early as the mid-1930s, Kenya was a leading refugee hosting state in Africa. Between 1935 and 1941, it hosted nearly 10,000 refugees, fleeing the Italo-Ethiopian conflict (Wilkin, 1980).[1] During the Second World War, a small number of Polish, Greek and Jewish refugees were brought to Kenya by the British Government (Carlebach, 1962; Lwanga-Lunyiigo, 1998). As Bravo (1999:8–9) and Harris (1987) have argued, the Mau Mau war of independence in Kenya created massive displacement. The historiography of this displacement, which is outside the scope of the present study, is, however, understudied compared to, say, similar events such as the Algerian War of independence (1958). After independence in 1963, Kenya received refugees fleeing ethnic conflicts, civil wars, human rights abuses and famines in the neighbouring countries and wars of liberation and Apartheid in Southern Africa. By 1988, most of these refugees were repatriated following independence in Angola, Zimbabwe and Mozambique and the refugee population stood at between 8,000–15,000. These consisted of a mixed bag of full status refugees, mandate cases, asylum-seekers and de facto refugees who settled in cities as "urban refugees" (Headley, 1988).

Before the massive influx of refugees from Somalia, Ethiopia and Sudan in the 1990s, Ugandans were by far the majority of refugees in Kenya.[2] In the 1990s, Kenya's refugee population increased to unprecedented proportions and surpassed the 400,000 mark, as indicated by Table 1.

**Table 1. Camp Refugee Population in Kenya 1989–1998**

| 1989 | 1990 | 1991 | 1992 | 1993 | 1994 | 1995 | 1996 | 1997 | 1998 |
|---|---|---|---|---|---|---|---|---|---|
| 12,400 | 14,400 | 120,200 | 401,900 | 301,600 | 252,400 | 239,500 | 223,600 | 232,100 | 238,200 |

Source: UNHCR, Country Profile: Kenya Statistical Fact Sheet 1998.

1. These refugees were settled in camps in Northern Kenya near the border with Ethiopia. The UK government and numerous international NGOs, including Save the Children Fund, provided financial support while the colonial state in Kenya managed the camps with the help of some missionaries. It was during this time that the notion of Kenya as a non-refugee hosting state emerged. This position was institutionalised by the enactment of two laws, the "Control of Fugitive Belligerents (Amendment Bill) and the "Ordinance to Regularize the Residence in the Colony of Certain Refugees from Ethiopia", in 1938.
2. Most Rwandese refugees presented themselves as Ugandans in the hope of benefiting from educational opportunities, material assistance from agencies and local hospitality available to Ugandans, thanks to a long history of cultural and political ties between the peoples of Kenya and Uganda.

The new waves of refugees were fleeing internal wars and political repression in Rwanda, the Democratic Republic of the Congo, Burundi, Uganda and more significantly Sudan, Ethiopia and Somalia. Thousands of refugees, especially from Somalia, initially settled in the camps of Utange, Marafa, Swaleh Nguru, Hatimi and Jomvu, which mushroomed along the Coast, near the port city of Mombasa. In pursuance of its camp policy, the Kenya government kept insisting that refugees be confined to camps away from its urban centres. Repatriation of a substantial number of refugees, especially Ethiopians and resettlement in the West, reduced the population to an average of 230,000 by mid-1990s. At the same time, Kenya's urban refugee caseload increased almost tenfold. UNHCR's estimates put the figure of urban refugees in Kenya at between 55,000 and 150,000 by 1998. The real numbers are likely to have increased as more refugees fled Rwanda and Sudan in the mid-1990s and refugees dissatisfied with camp life migrated to towns, where they remained illegally. In addition to the refugee caseload in the 1990s, Kenya saw an unprecedented scale of internal displacement. To be sure, internal displacement is not new in Kenya.[1] Between 1991 and 1998, politically motivated communal violence erupted in the Rift Valley province and quickly spread to Nyanza and Western Provinces[2] catapulting Kenya's problem of internal displacement to heights unknown before. Numbers displaced by November 1993 were estimated at over 300,000 (HRW, 1993a). In 1997, fresh violence in Coast province killed nearly 100 people and displaced more than 100,000 others. In 1998, post-election violence in the Rift Valley province displaced thousands of people. Thus, in the 1991–98 period, over half a million Kenyans were forced to flee their homes. Most of them took refuge in makeshift camps in compounds of churches and mosques or in market centres throughout the affected areas (Kagwanja, 1998b). Together with refugees, this brought the victims of displacement in need of relief in Kenya in the 1990s to nearly a million people.

## The Rise of Indigenous Relief Capacity

By 1963 when Kenya ascended to independence, a relatively strong local non-state relief capacity was in existence. This consisted overwhelmingly of religious/church-based organisations. This partly reflected the strong ecumenical roots of Western-style welfare delivery system in Kenya, as in many other parts of Africa, which is linked to the coming of Christian missionaries in the turn of the century. The Presbyterian Church of East Africa (1891), the Salvation Army (1921), the YMCA (1910), and YWCA (1920) are examples of the earliest church-based organisation participating in relief work in Kenya. As Wilkin (1980) shows, during the 1930s, missionaries and medical personnel affiliated to some of these religious organisations delivered relief to refugees in camps. At independence, the Christian Council of Kenya (CCK), later renamed the National Christian Council of Kenya (NCCK), emerged as the most effective player in the relief sector. Most of these religious organisations started as foreign organisations, but, like the church, they were increas-

---

1. From the early 1960s, the problem of displacement occurred intermittently in parts of Northern Kenya. Before 1990s, cases of internal displacement were linked to non-political factors such as famine, cattle rustling and banditry among pastoral communities. However, the frequent displacement of Kenya's ethnic Somali population in North Eastern province is an exception to this rule. In the 1960s, Somali nationalism, and secessionist intentions precipitated the so-called Shifta (bandit) War (1964–67) involving the Kenyan forces and secessionist forces armed by Somalia, resulting in many Somalis fleeing their homes. In the subsequent decades, the state's often high-handed and brutal response to frequent cases of politically motivated banditry in the province has caused many cases of internal displacement (M'Inoti, 1992; KHRC, 1998).
2. Kenya is divided into eight administrative provinces: Nairobi, Coast, Eastern, North Eastern, Central, Rift Valley, Western and Nyanza.

ingly 'Africanised' and came under local control and leadership. Nonetheless, they continued to draw from their networks and affiliations with sister international organisations.

In addition to religious organisations, secular organisations began to make inroads into Kenya in the period after the Second World War. Such Northern NGOs as OXFAM and CARE extended their charitable activities to Kenya. Their model of delivering relief inspired the formation of local and NGOs along similar lines. Local organisations such as the African Medical and Research Foundation (AMREF), which was oriented towards providing health care, emerged. At independence, forty-five NGOs are reported to have been operating in Kenya, two-thirds of which were local organisations (INTRAC, 1998:59). The number of NGOs increased to 132 by 1978 and to 267 by the end of the 1980s decade. However, during the 1978–88 period—the high noon of the authoritarian one-party state—foreign NGOs grew faster than local organisations. This was because of the state opposition to the formation of independent organisations in the civil society and its continued dominance in delivering relief and development assistance.[1] With the collapse of the one-party system in the 1990s, local NGOs experienced a tremendous growth. For instance, between 1988 and 1996, local NGOs grew by 131 per cent, nearly tripling the rate of growth in numbers of international NGOs. By March 1996, there were a total of 555 registered NGOs.[2] As the following analysis shows, before the 1990s, local organisations had established themselves as formidable actors in the delivery of relief before international actors stepped in, sidelined and marginalised them, reducing their influence in the relief sector to its lowest ebb.

## Local Relief System Prior to 1990

### State Policy and humanitarian Response to Refugees

As I have argued elsewhere, Kenya's refugee policy right from the colonial era oscillated, in a distinctly Machiavellian sense, between 'hospitality' and 'hostility' to refugees and asylum-seekers (Kagwanja, 1998a:53). This policy was forged on the anvil of a fragile agrarian economy, acute shortage of arable land, constraints in the provision of social services, rural and urban poverty, population pressure and mass unemployment. Unsurprisingly, Kenya, unlike Uganda or Tanzania, considered itself a transit state. The state wielded a heavy stick against groups of refugees it considered as a security threat, such as Somali refugees in the 1990s. But whenever refugees did not threaten its interests, it closed its eyes to them and gave a free sway to NGOs to manage refugee affairs.

By 1990, Kenya had evolved three distinct humanitarian systems. To begin with was an elaborate inter-ministerial structure that dealt with drought and famine related emergencies. This was dependent on the provincial administration machinery co-ordinated through the Office of the President. The second tire, consisting of the Kenya National Council of Social Services (KNCSS) based in the Ministry of Culture, brought together state operatives and organisations of the civil society involved

---

1. In the 1978–89 period, the state, like a giant octopus, affiliated existing organisations of the civil society such as the Central Organization of Trade Unions (COTU) and the national women organization, Maendeleo Ya Wanawake and youth movements to the sole political party, the Kenya African National Union (KANU). It further proscribed and emasculated organisations it considered hostile to the party.
2. The source of this data is the National NGO Co-ordination Bureau of the Government of Kenya. It is worth noting that many indigenous NGOs operating in Kenya are not officially registered or recognised. It is estimated that by 1997, between 3000 and 3500 NGOs operating in Kenya had no official recognition.

in relief work. The third tire was the Committee on Refugees, later the Refugee Directorate, located in the Ministry of Home Affairs. Of the three, the machinery for dealing with refugees was the most under-developed partly because the state tended to leave refugee work to the UNHCR and its local and international implementing partners.

The pre-1990 relief system in Kenya can be characterised as hospitable, an attribute explained by a number of historical factors. As indicated earlier, the entire 1963–89 period saw Kenya deal with a relatively small refugee caseload. While a large number of them depended on relief assistance, a critical number of refugees possessed technical skills, education and capital, and became a boon to Kenya's nascent market economy. This category was allowed to practice their professions, run businesses and take gainful employment in the private, public and informal sectors. Those with employable skills and talents were absorbed into the economy as shopkeepers, artisans, professionals and as high school and university teachers. Some became successful entrepreneurs in the informal sector, as the case of Ethiopians and Eritrean de facto refugees in Nairobi shows (Kagwanja, 1998a). Subsequently, these groups contributed to the economic growth of Kenya and tempered hostility against asylum-seekers. Historical and cultural linkages between Kenya and Uganda—including common membership in the then East African Community[1]—also acted in favour of the integration of Ugandan refugees. This generated a level of self-sufficiency among some refugees who became critical social safety nets for their less fortunate relatives and friends. As Tandon (1984) points out, the self-sustaining among refugees supported the unemployed kith and kin, thereby breaking the chain of virtual dependency of refugees on relief aid, which became the bane of Kenya's relief industry in the 1990s. The prevailing thinking in the 1970s and 1980s was that refugees in the urban areas "were a forgotten group as far as international assistance is concerned (Refugees, May 1983). Rather than being forgotten, refugees in Kenya utilised their own capacities, those of local agencies and diaspora networks to empower themselves economically and to reduce dependency on relief aid.

Not surprisingly, the relief system of the pre-1991 era has become a subject of growing nostalgia. "[T]his pre-1991 regime", one researcher reminisces "was characterised by the fact that, other than poverty, which made survival difficult for many refugees in Kenya, there were few formal obstacles to local integration and enjoyment of such basic rights as the right to work, to education, and to freedom of movement" (Verdirame, 1999:57). However, a closer look indicates that with the onset of economic hardship from the mid-1980s, the state grew increasingly hostile to refugees. In September 1982, the Government ordered that Ugandans should obtain work permit, sparking off fear of deportations. This compelled many de facto refugees to seek the protection of the UNHCR and planted the seed for what was to become a strained relationship between the state and humanitarian actors.

### Indigenous Non-State Capacity and Urban Refugees Prior to 1990

Principally, the delivery of relief assistance to urban refugees prior to 1990 was undertaken by church-based groups including the NCCK, the Kenya Catholic Secretariat (KCS), the Church of the Province of Kenya (CPK), and the All African Council of Churches (AACC). Since the late seventies these actors had created co-ordination

---

1. The EAC, which brought together the three East African countries of Kenya, Uganda and Tanzania collapsed in 1977. In 1999 a treaty on East African Community was signed, revitalising this cooperation.

mechanisms such as the Joint Refugee Service of Kenya (JRSK), in an attempt to co-ordinate their work, avoid duplication of programmes and unhealthy competition for funds. JRSK drew its funds from UNHCR and other international agencies such as the International Rescue Committee. It financed assistance (relief), education, health and counselling programs (Pirouet, 1979). However, religious rivalry, power wrangles and absence of a history of collaborative action among church organisa-tions seriously undermined JRSK.[1] In 1983, JRSK broke, splitting into denomina-tional based agencies. Within the Catholic establishment, the Jesuit Refugee Services (JRS) and the Catholic Secretariat assumed the mantle for relief work while the NCCK formed the Refugee Service Unit to run its refugee programmes. Some of its affiliates such as the CPK continued to run their own refugee programs (Pirouet, 1979). These splits led to disintegrated response mechanisms, came with accusations of inefficiency and led to disaffection and restiveness among refugees (Pirouet, 1979; Tandon, 1984).[2]

Of these actors, the NCCK emerged as the most able local actor in the refugee arena. The high-mark of its approach was it conceptualisation of rights as indivisi-ble. It championed justice and human rights as integral components of relief. It not only galvanised its relief machinery towards this objective, but ceaselessly challenged the state on issues of human rights.[3] Further, NCCK promoted economic rights and embraced the 'relief-development continuum' thinking, which aimed at moving ref-ugees from reliance on relief to self-reliance. The hallmark of this initiative was the Refugee Loan Scheme, which supported refugee entrepreneurs. By the end of the 1980s, the NCCK was UNHCR's principal implementing partner, in addition to managing funds from its local and international constituents. Reflecting its capacity at the time, one researcher observes, "through its endorsement and priorities com-mittee approximately US$250,000 has annually supported approximately 40 local self-help projects (Nelson, 1983: 4)." Some of NCCK's programs such as the Urban Community Improvement Programme (UCIR) had as many as 80 employees. Such was the capacity of this actor!

An array of secular NGOs complemented the work of church-based organisa-tions. These included, the Kenya Red Cross Society, the Kenya chapter of the Inter-national Commission of Jurists (ICJ), African Refugee Education Programme (AREP) and African Refugees Training and Education Services (ARTES), Refugee Enterprise Special Programme (RESP), Window Trust and Appropriate Technology (AREP). While these organisations delivered assistance to urban refugees, the Red Cross Society (Kenya) also managed the Transit camp in Thika on behalf of the Ken-ya Government. In the 1990s, these secular local NGOs were overwhelmed by the presence of international actors, which sidelined and eventually eclipsed them in the

---

1.  Right from the colonial period the various religious groups in Kenya always carried out their relief and development work independent of each other. Each group tended to be dominant in different parts of the country, a fact that mitigated inter-agency competition and duplication of work. But the influence of the NCCK and Catholic Church cut across the country and rivalry and competition between them was clearly evident.
2.  The more elitist Ugandan refugees began to agitate for some form of independence from local and interna-tional NGOs, charging that these organisations were not pushing the "development agenda" hard enough. In the early eighties, they eventually formed the Uganda Refugees' Relief Services (URRS). The URRS reflected the "developmentalist" ideology, which was pervasive during the period. This is evident from its campaign slogan: "busy hands are better than out-stretched hands." In addition, the URRS crusaded for self-reliance, and sought to hasten the shift from reliance on relief to sustainable development.
3.  From the late 1970s, the NCCK emerged as a foremost crusader for human rights and democracy in Kenya. Together with like-minded actors such as the Catholic Church and NGOs such as the Law Society of Kenya and the Kenya Greenbelt Movement, they created a momentum for the pro-democracy movement that ush-ered in a multi-party system in the 1990s (for example see, Ndegwa, 1996).

relief sector. By the mid-1990s, none of them was playing any significant role in the refugee sector.

Throughout the 1970s and 1980s, indigenous relief organisations confronted serious challenges, which turned them into battle-hardened veterans in the relief field. As Louis Pirouet (1979) aptly remarks, urban refugees in Nairobi were "small numbers" which presented "large problems." Diverse in their social origins and class orientation, scattered through the towns and their actual numbers largely unknown, urban refugees complicated the process of estimating the volume of relief resources and the number of personnel and organisations needed to deliver relief. Commenting on Ugandan refugees, Professor Yash Tandon, chronicled that:

> There is no large influx; refugees trickle in –singly or in small groups. Secondly, they are not in the camps where one can count. The Thika refugee camp in Kenya is only a temporary shelter for asylum seekers. And finally, while most of those Ugandans who criss-cross the borders at Kitale and Busia are peasants, most of those who reach Nairobi are urban and peri-urban. Most of these disappear, either living in wealthy homes of friends or relatives; or into the squalor of sub-urban Nairobi. They "keep a low profile." Many are shy of officialdom, and do not announce their presence even to the UNHCR; some because of their fear that they might be repatriated, others because of plain ignorance of their rights and obligations as refugees (1984).

Until the early 1990s, partnership with international counterparts seemed to favour the empowerment of local capacity. The UNHCR, for instance, relied almost exclusively on local actors as its implementing partners while other international agencies run programs through local actors. The UNHCR's disbursement policy attests to this. Yefime Zarjevski (1988) informs us that in 1976, UNHCR established an assistance budget of some US$350,000, which was doubled the following year. In 1982, the agency's budget in Kenya stood at 2 million dollars that was used to finance its various types of aid to refugees. Refugees recognised by the UN agency were given a monthly allowance of 350 Kenya shillings ($35) per family and 150 Kenya shillings ($15) for single persons[1] (Tandon, 1984). UNHCR spent a vast amount of this budget through disbursing it to local actors (Zarjevski, 1988:146–147; Nelson, 1983; Headley, 1988).

In the late 1980s, local organisations began exploring the idea of settling refugees in rural camps as an alternative to the urban model. This was against a hostile state policy which defined Kenya as a transit rather than a resettling country. With 85 per cent of its land being arid or semi-arid, Kenya's acute shortage of arable land perpetually undermined the option of relocating refugees to rural agricultural settlements. However, the CPK relocated 70 urban refugee families, mostly Ugandans and settled them on a 100-acre plot of leased land in Bungoma District (Nelson, 1983). NCCK followed suit and opened several rural settlement schemes for refugees on leased land in Badasa (in Marsabit District), Isiolo and Taita. In 1990, the UNHCR provided the NCCK with Kshs. 640,000 (about US$20,000 at the time) towards the purchase of a tractor, building of 10 new houses for refugees, buying farm input and hiring 26 extra acres of land for refugees. The Isiolo camp, conceived together with the UNDP, was meant to be a rural settlement scheme for women refugees. In contrast to the camps that emerged in the 1990s, these refugee rural-based settlements were based on the principle of self-reliance rather than dependence on relief aid.

---

1. Underlying these 'handouts' was the logic that by the end of the six months of support, the refugee recipients would have found something to make them self-reliant.

## Local Capacity in the Refugee Sector in the 1990s

The relief arena in Kenya changed drastically from the opening years of the nineties. The influx of large numbers of refugees not only overwhelmed local relief capacity but attracted severe hostility from the state. The state accused refugees, especially those from Somalia, of smuggling in firearms and escalating crime and insecurity. It also considered the new crop of refugees as a social, economic and environmental reliability largely because most of them were poor and without skills to offer. In December 1992, President Moi threatened to forcibly send back Somali refugees and, in January 1993, he asked the UNHCR to repatriate all Somali, Ethiopian and Sudanese refugees. Refugees, he argued, had "seriously compromised the security of this country [and] greatly outstretched the infrastructure and medical services" (Carver, 1994:53).

In response to these threats, UNHCR for a while put its weight behind the Cross-Border, Cross-Mandate Operations (CBO) 1993, which the UN Secretary-General requested it to initiate.[1] Eventually, this operation collapsed in 1993, after which UNHCR found itself compromised and having to acquiesce with the position of the Kenya Government. The CBO had dire implications for local relief capacity. They paved the way for the hegemony of UNHCR and its international NGO partners and for the marginalisation of local capacity in the refugee arena. In the wake of the CBO, UNHCR embarked on recruiting extra staff and inviting international NGOs as its implementing partners. This period saw a meteoric growth of the UNHCR Branch Office in Kenya, from a staff of 8 to more than 50 officers. The period was also characterised by a reinforcement of the link between UNHCR and international NGOs such as Care International, the Lutheran World Federation (LWF) and the International Rescue Committee (IRC). This relationship manifested in expanding programmes at the NGO level. For instance, Care International implemented some of the largest Quick Impact Projects (QUIPs) during this time. While the UNHCR policy "encouraged" the use of local NGOs in the implementation of quips, no local NGO was a key partner during this period. Instead, evidence indicates that participation of local actors was, if anything, minimal.[2]

In the camps, UNHCR's partnership with international NGOs got a new lease of life. Arguing that these actors had the requisite capacity, experience and flexibility, UNHCR bestowed relief leadership to international actors. However, this taken-for-granted assumption that international actors have relevant capacity has been heavily criticised by some researchers, some of whom have questioned the assumed experienced human resources within international actors. As Kirkby and co-researchers observe, "IRC had little experience of work in pastoral societies, and on

---

1. The CBO along the Kenya-Somali border were conceived within the framework of the "safe havens" created for the Iraqi Kurds or the "zones of tranquility" set up for the returning Afghan refugees. The CBOs were meant to stabilise populations by stemming the inflow of refugees from Somalia into Kenya and to entice those refugees already in Kenya to return home. By investing in the rehabilitation of Southern Somalia the UNHCR hoped to create a situation that would attract an equivalence of "voluntary repatriation." Its Geneva Office launched the Special Emergency Fund for the Horn of Africa (SEFHA) to finance the Operation. The anticipated cost of repatriation was US$5.5 million. With over 320 quips in 1993, and still enjoying favorable response from donors, the CBO seemed to be firmly on the road to success (Kirkby, et. al., 1997). However, the CBO proved an expensive experiment because its future depended on the success of the US-led "Operation Restore Hope" which was replaced by the UN-sponsored UNOSOM. With the failure of the humanitarian intervention in Somalia, the security framework on which the CBO was conceived collapsed. Material incentives—which included a three-month food for each person—proved an irresistible attraction to refugees some of whom made a kill by returning to collect rations more than once. In the end, refugees were neither repatriated nor prevented from streaming into Kenya.
2. Informal and unconfirmed estimates indicated that there were 2,200 local NGOs set up in Somalia of which 150 were engaged in the cross-border zone. None of these was from Kenya.

receipt of core funding from the UNHCR hired enthusiastic, brave and young staff from the International community in Nairobi..." (1997:195).

## The Reduced Role of the State in Camps

Capitulating to international pressure and keen on repairing the breach with external financiers who had suspended aid, the government of Kenya suspended its threat to expel refugees and grudgingly allowed them to settle in the country (Hyndman and Nylund, 1998). However, it imposed conditionality. Refugees would only stay on account of residing in camps located in Northern Kenya. Arguing that the presence of refugees around Mombasa increased insecurity and threatened its tourist industry, the state pressurised UNHCR to transfer refugees who could not repatriate to designated camps, away from the major cities. In January 1995, these camps hosted 97,000 refugees, with Utange alone sheltering more than 45,000 refugees. But by 1997, the Mombasa camps were closed down and nearly 20,000 refugees transferred to Kakuma camp located in Turkana district.

Dadaab and Kakuma camps are located in Kenya's most arid areas, away from major economic developments and in traditional zones of insecurity associated with cattle rustling and banditry. Noting the marginalisation of these areas, and the absence of the state, one Catholic priest noted, "Here, the government is spoken of in past tense, mocking its claim to be in-charge" (Expression Today, No. 2, 1997:2). By settling refugees here the state may have hoped that hardship would force refugees to drift away to their homes.[1] The state might also have planned to take advantage of the massive flow of relief aid to ensure that local population benefited from the spill-over effects of the huge resources and infrastructure meant for refugees. Be that as it may, refugee aid became an integral part of the politics of local development in refugee-settled areas.[2]

Beyond these objectives, the state adopted a remarkably abdicationist policy in regard to refugees. District officers in refugee-hosting divisions interpreted their duties in a strict sense as ensuring the security of the Kenyan citizens while refugees were the responsibilities of UNHCR and partner NGOs. Kathina (1999a) observes that, the DO considered refugees as outside his brief and never entered the camp unless he was invited by the UNHCR when there is a security problem, especially involving refugees and the locals. The feeble presence of the state in camps was accentuated by the inability of the national refugee administration to make its influence felt beyond Nairobi. The refugee Directorate in the Ministry of Home Affairs, for instance, had no representatives in the camps. UNHCR became so powerful that it was brokering land deals with the local population without consulting either the central government or the local administration. For instance, in 1999 the resident officer in Kakuma camp negotiated a deal with Turkana elders to acquire more land to set up a new camp (Author's interview, August 1999).

1. In Kenya's nationalist narrative, the area around the camps, especially Kakuma, is depicted as the symbol of ultimate hardship where the founding father of the nation, President Jomo Kenyatta, was 'exiled' by the British colonial administration.
2. The centrality of refugee aid in local politics became clear to the Nordic-African Dialogue project research team during a visit to Kakuma camp in August 1999. At a meeting held with local government officials, including the local chief, District Officer, Security officer and the area Member of Parliament, who is an Assistance Minister in the Ministry of Labour various issues were discussed. This included refugee-host relations, the development of host communities in the form of sinking boreholes, expanding educational and health facilities to the local Turkana people. For the MP, this was a powerful strategy of consolidating his political power.

The state was even unable to offer adequate security around the camps. This forced UNHCR to subsidise local security personnel and to established police stations, in Dadaab and Kakuma. For instance, between 1992 and 1997, it spent an estimated Ksh. 30m (US$430,000) to establish a police post in Dadaab. In 1999, it upgraded the police station in Kakuma and paid incentives to the police in the station. Inside the camps, lead agencies (CARE in Dadaab and Lutheran World Federation in Kakuma) established separate security machinery. As a result of the state's "abdicationist" position in regard to security, camps provided but a "dangerous refuge" (KHRC, 1999:5). They were easy targets of bandits who killed, maimed refugees and sexually assaulted and raped women refugees (HRW, 1993b; AR, 1993; KHRC, 1999). In response to a question about state obligations to refuges at the height of the of rapes scandal in 1993, a Kenyan official in Dadaab was quoted as saying, "it was not Kenya's responsibility to investigate what happened in the camps..." (Carver, 1994:53).

## NGO Capacity in Refugee Camps

On the whole, relief work and administration is controlled by UNHCR and its international relief partners. In Kakuma, UNHCR works with three main partners, IRC (health), LWF (food distribution, social services and security) Don Bosco (Tertiary education and vocational training). Its principal partners in Dadaab are Care International (lead agency) and MSF-Belgium (Health). These agencies carried out most activities and rationalised their hegemony in camps on the grounds that they, unlike local organisations, possessed huge capacity, experienced personnel, skills, knowledge, and were accountable and transparent. These justifications were starkly contradicted by the reality on the ground. As the head of the UNHCR sub-office in Kakuma, Mr. Saber Azham observed cuttingly: "the main job of UNHCR has become baby-sitting because these agencies (NGOs) keep bringing in new and inexperienced workers". Key to the central position of the international NGOs was their ability to raise funds beyond what they received from UNHCR and their lobbying capacity, which was critical for the retention of their contracts and lead positions.

The Kenya Red Cross Society was the first casualty of the direct involvement of international NGOs in the refugee sector. In 1991, UNHCR closed the Thika transit camp, thus signalling the demise of the role of the agency in the refugee sector. In the 1992–96 period, the KRCS, in partnership with the International Federation of the Red Cross, effectively managed the camps at the coast. In June 1995, the society presided over 1,017 personnel including its own 125 staff, 10 IFRC delegates, 2 federation local staff, 121 casual labourers (Kenyans), 733 refugee staff, and 16 government staff (IRC, 1995). It provided food, water, non-food items, health, and educational services to refugees. Funding came from UNHCR and other international agencies, and foreign governments, including Japan which funded the handicapped programme in the camps. By 1996, this capacity had been whittled down to a skeleton staff and its activities ground to a complete halt in 1997 when the camps at the coast were closed down. By this time, KRCS was effectively sidelined in the refugee sector because, except for an insignificant tracing programme in Kakuma camp, which was aimed at reuniting families which had been separated during flight from Southern Sudan, it had no foothold in the camps. Even then, this programme was an extension of the International Federation of the Red Cross (Kathina Juma, 1999a).

The NCCK was also a victim of international capacity. Its programme kept on shrinking and it was only implementing a small reproductive health awareness campaign in Kakuma and Dadaab by 1998. Although the NCCK drew its funding from the World Council of Churches and NFPA to fund this programme, its activities were subordinated to the medical programs of MSF-B (Dadaab) and IRC (Kakuma), two actors that remained reluctant to support it. Although RH needs have been expanding over time, a fact acknowledged by both UNHCR and UNFPA, funding for this programme remained inadequate. Between 1995 and 1998, the total budget for Kakuma and Dadaab camps was Ksh. 5 million (US$72,000). Compared to the IRC's annual medical budget for Kakuma alone, which stood at some Ksh.7million (US$100,000), in 1997, the NCCK capacity was small. The NCCK has operated under stringent capacity with only two core workers in its RH programme, one each in Kakuma and Dadaab. To optimise operations, it had depended on health workers of other agencies, however, this has affected its programs negatively. In some cases, there were attempts to overstep the NCCK programme altogether, arguing that it lacked capacity. In one such case, UNHCR in conjunction with UNFPA invited an international agency from Addis Ababa to run a course on reproductive health without informing or involving NCCK. In 1997, another incident occurred. When NCCK organised a series of workshops on community RH workers, IRC organised a parallel RH awareness and training workshop for its health workers arguing that the NCCK lacked capacity. At one stage the IRC attempted to take over the programme arguing it should fall under the healthcare programme which it ran (Kathina Juma, 1999a).

Another local NGO, Windle Trust, ran an English language programme authorised by the social services department of LWF. In the aftermath of reports on widespread rapes of Somali refugee women in Dadaab, UNHCR contracted the Kenya section of the International Federation of Women Lawyers to handle the rape cases. Less that two years later, its services were terminated. A local Muslim NGO, Al-Haramain, was restricted to merely conducting burial rites for the largely Muslim Somali refugee population. This running down of local NGOs was related directly to UNHCR's budget cuts. Unable to seek substantial funds from other sources, when UNHCR began to cut down, local actors were the first casualties. Thus, the period between 1993–97 saw a sharper decline in the participation of local NGOs, compared to their international counterparts. By 1997 there were only 4 local NGOs in the camps compared to 14 international NGOs.

For an indication of the local and international NGOs operating in the relief arena by 1998, see Table. 2.

**Table 2. Local and International Relief Agencies in Kenya**

| Local Non-Governmental Organisations | International NGOs and Agencies |
| --- | --- |
| African Medical Research Foundation (AMREF) | Action Aid |
| African Refugee Education Fund (AREF) | All-African Council of Churches (AACC) |
| African Refugee Education Services (ARTES) | Catholic Relief Services |
| Al-Haramain | Care International |
| Appropriate Technology (AREP) | Christian Reformed World Relief Committee |
| Catholic Justice and Peace Commission | Don Bosco |
| Church Parishes and Mosques | International Child Care Trust |
| Church of Province of Kenya (CPK) | International Federation of the Red Cross and Red Crescent of Hope |
| (Kenya) | Crescent Societies |
| Government of Kenya | International Islamic Relief Agency |
| International Commission of Jurist-Kenya (ICJ) | International Rescue Committee (IRC) |
| Kenya Red Cross Society (KRCS). | Jesuit Refugee Services |
| National Council of Churches of Kenya (NCCK) | Lutheran World Federation (LWF) |
| Windle Charitable Trust | Médecins Sans Frontières (MSF)–Belgium |

**Table 2 cont.**

| Local Non-Governmental Organisations | International NGOs and Agencies |
|---|---|
| | Médecins Sans Frontières (MSF)–France |
| | Médecins Sans Frontières–Holland |
| | Mennonite Central Committee |
| | Oxfam–United Kingdom and Ireland |
| | Rädda Barnen–Sweden |
| | Save the Children Fund-United Kingdom |
| | UNDP |
| | UNHCR |
| | UNICEF |
| | World Food Programme (WFP) |
| | World Vision |

Sources: Osodo and Matsvai, 1998; Shaw and Gatheru, 1998:287.

## Local Capacity and Urban Refugees in the 1990s

Power relations between international actors and local organisations in the urban refugee arena also changed radically. While the number of urban refugees trebled, especially after the closure of camps at the coast, the role of local actors declined (JRS, July 1, 1997). Here, UNHCR sidelined state institutions in decision-making. As Verdirame (1999:57) rightly observes:

> [T]he events of the early 1990s marked a significant shift to a new refugee regime in Kenya. On the one hand, the involvement of foreign NGOs and UNHCR guaranteed external resources at a time when the numbers of refugees exceeded Kenya's capacity to absorb them through its generous, if somewhat laissez faire, policy. On the other hand, the emergency nature of the response of the NGOs, and of UNHCR, did not include any effort on their part to preserve the positive aspects of the pre-1991 refugee regime.

The collapse of the Eligibility Committee that determined the status of refugees in Kenya symbolised the marginality of the state in the refugee sector.[1] From 1991, UNHCR assumed complete control over the status determination process, set up a special office in Nairobi for that purpose and commissioned an International NGO, the Jesuit Refugee Service (JRS) to pre-screen asylum claimants and give them 'protection letters' defining their "refugee status". By sidelining state structures, international actors deprived the refugee sector of any skills and experience that government officials had accumulated over the years. Besides, it sowed seeds of mistrust and animosity between the state and humanitarian actors. For instance, the state began to regard refugees as 'UNHCR's problem' and refused to sanction the protection letters accorded to them by the UN agency. Often, refugees carrying UNHCR protection letters are arrested and detained. Realising the protection associated with determining claims as well as pursuing its protection mandate, UNHCR has, since 1995, been persuading the government to resume an active role in status determination.

In regard to its partners, UNHCR has, since the mid-1990s been encouraging some international NGOs to expand their urban refugee programs while at the same

---

1. The committee included representatives from the Ministry of Home Affairs, the Immigration Department and an observer/advisor from UNHCR. Undertaking individual status determination in accordance with the 1951 Convention, the Committee was partly undermined by the increase in the numbers of asylum-seekers that flooded the country in the 1990s.

time, advising the local ones to withdraw. In particular, UNHCR pressurised the NCCK to phase out its urban refugee programme while simultaneously nudging the JRS, which was at the time implementing its refugee-screening project, to expand and take over the NCCK programme (Kathina Juma, 1999b). According to the officials of the NCCK's Refugee Service Unit, UNHCR favoured the JRS because "it is rich and does not rely exclusively on UN support".[1] While the NCCK's urban refugee programme declined, that of JRS grew steadily and diversified. JRS funded education from nursery to secondary level, offered counselling and alternative healing services for the traumatised, and ran a programme on empowerment of women through income generating activities in Kakuma camp. It also ran a large parish outreach programme in Nairobi, an educational and scholarship programme for over 1,000 refugee students, small business management training and sale of refugee products through the Mkono Craft Shop, Kangemi Rehabilitation Centre for those injured in war, especially by landmines, and expanded its Information and Referral Centre. In collaboration with the UNHCR, it was also running a project aimed at assisting recent arrivals, especially Rwandese and Burundians, with food, clothing, housing, medical care and registration procedures (JRS, 1997).

International actors also sidelined local organisations in decision making and policy formulation in refugee affairs. This is succinctly captured by the exclusion of the International Commission of Jurists (Kenya) from the Partnership in Action (PARinAc) Process. Initiated in 1993 as a forum for forging and reinforcing partnerships in response to increasing emergencies, PARinAc was to weaken rather than strengthen local relief capacity. In the 1990s, the ICJ (K) together with other actors in the civil society formed the Ad Hoc Refugee Advocacy Group (ARAG) to co-ordinate the assistance and protection of refugees. Instead of supporting this local initiative, UNHCR deliberately sidelined both the ICJ and ARAG and eventually threw its weight behind one Islamic organisation, effectively shutting the ICJ out of the PARinAc process (Kathina Juma, 1999b). By 1999, indigenous organisations in the urban refugee sector, as in the camps, were fighting to stay afloat in an arena completely controlled by international NGOs and agencies.

## Local Capacity and the Internally Displaced

The outbreak of ethnic violence in the 1990s shattered Kenya's image as a peaceful and stable country. Violence pitted President Moi's Kalenjin ethnic group and its political ally, the Maasai, against the populous Kikuyu, Luhya, Luo and to a lesser extent Kamba and Kisii.[2] Human rights groups put the blame for this humanitarian crisis on the doorstep of the government, which they argued, stirred up and exploited communal differences for political gains (HRW, 1993a, 1997). These organisations contend that state sponsored communal violence aimed to forestall multi-party

---

1. Mr Kamau, Co-ordinator, RSU August, 1997.
2. Kenya has about 42 main ethnic groups. However, since independence from Britain in 1963 political conflict involving contestation for power has revolved around two ethnic blocs. On the one hand are the traditionally pastoral groups, including the Kalenjin, the Maasai, the Turkana and the Samburu. While these groups are demographically weak, less educated or politically mobilized, they lay claim to a vast territory with huge natural resources, including the entire Rift Valley Province, Kenya's breadbasket. In the 1990s, they formed an informal ethnic alliance, which took the acronym KAMATUSA. On the other hand, are the largely agricultural groups, mainly the Kikuyu, Luo, Luhya, Kisii and Kamba, who collectively constitute more than 75 per cent of Kenya's population, who are relatively educated and better mobilized politically. Having come to the former 'White Highlands' as squatters on the farms of British settlers, these groups base their claim to land on 'the sweat and blood' during the colonial period, and the Bill of Rights in the constitution which protects the right to own property, anywhere in the country.

democracy, and when this failed, to derail pluralism or keep genuine democracy in cold storage. On its part, the state blamed its political opponents for instigating the crisis in order to discredit it. Be that as it may, the ethnic clashes occurred against the backdrop of Kenya's return to a multi-party system and the consequent polarisation of national politics along ethnic lines. The conflict thrived on long-standing inter-ethnic competition for diminishing land resources. Hence, the clashes were meant to violently evict "foreign" populations from indigenous territory.

Kenya presented the typical dilemma that confronts humanitarian actors in situations of internal displacement. Foremost in this dilemma is the weak and lukewarm response from the international community to the plight of internally displaced persons. This is in spite of the recognition of the fact that the IDP population far outstrips conventional refugees. Although encouraging steps have been achieved internationally, within the framework of the UN, to facilitate the protection of internally displaced populations, response to their needs remains ad hoc, limited and largely unsatisfactory (Deng, 1993; Cohen, 1996; ICRC, 1996). Primarily, the displaced are within the jurisdiction of their governments, which are responsible for their protection in compliance with international human rights and humanitarian obligations. As was evidenced by the case of Kenya, the predicament of the displaced is complicated further when the government is implicated in the persecution and human rights violations, which trigger such displacement. In such cases, the state does not only fail to take its responsibility to wards the displaced but it sometimes becomes obstructionist and a stumbling block to relief and protection work.

## Kenya: The Obstructionist State

From the outset the state in Kenya was heavily involved in IDP emergencies. As Kathina Juma has cogently argued, "a significant feature…was the pervasive role of the central government in dealing with IDPs" (1999b). The state, however, dealt with the IDP situation from a security rather than a humanitarian standpoint. It relied heavily on the Provincial Administration to keep local actors within the IDP arena under control. This machinery collated figures of victims, determined the extent of destruction and resources needed, and in some cases, provided assistance and facilitated return and rehabilitation.

Legally, the state invoked laws that reinforced its control over the IDP situation. In September 1993, President Moi invoked the infamous Preservation of Public Security Act and declared Molo, Burnt Forest and Londian clash areas "Security Operation Zones". This cast an iron curtain over affected areas and locked out NGOs, human rights groups and the press from these areas. During the application of this emergency declaration, security forces prevented a Red Cross Society's food convoy intended for the clash victims from entering Molo. They also denied a group of Dutch parliamentarians, keen to assess the impact of clashes, passage to clash areas. The state also prevented journalists from gaining access to and making known the atrocities against the displaced in Kenya to the world. In January 1994, the government banned all NGOs, churches, and UNDP officials from visiting the Maela camp near Naivasha following damning local and international exposure of the plight of the displaced population in the camp. And on December 24 1994, government security forces violently dispersed and expelled the displaced from Maela and razed the camp to the ground. Arguing that the victims were not *bona fide* displacees, the government forcibly moved approximately 10,000 of them to "their ancestral land" in Central Province where it dumped them by the roadside.[1]

Besides obstructing relief efforts, the state was slow in mobilising relief to the displaced. Following scathing attacks in parliament on the government's lethargy in providing resources to assist the displaced, it set aside 10 million Kenya shillings (US$125,000) to meet the cost of food and other supplies. This was a drop in the ocean given the enormous relief needs of the victims. With increasing fluidity of the political environment in the country, the state intensified its coercive and obstructionist policy in the IDP arena throughout the 1990s, making relief work a nightmare.

## Undermining Indigenous Capacity in the IDP Sector

Following the eruption of ethnic violence in 1991, a local relief infrastructure developed. Church-based NGOs, particularly the NCCK and the Catholic Church built upon the advantages and grassroots connections offered by the spatial and demographic spread of their ecclesiastical and welfare work since the colonial period. These organisations established nation-wide networks and functional structures whose flexibility and resilience no international capacity could master. The NCCK, Catholic Church and CPK, for instance, operated schools, hospitals and polytechnics on a welfare basis and were the foremost partners of the state in responding to emergencies relating to natural disasters throughout the country (Shaw and Gatheru, 1998). Commenting on this indigenous capacity one international organisation aptly observed that:

> NGOs have developed a wealth of experience...in dealing with displaced populations. Local NGOs are often closer to the ground and have better links and a more thorough grasp of the situation. Local groups also remain longer than international programs... (HRW, 1997a:116).

In response to the crisis, local NGOs mobilised huge resources to receive the displaced most of whom left their farms and sought refuge in church compounds and nearby market places. The NCCK, for example, spent 16 million Kenya shillings [US$200,000] each month in 1993 to feed the displaced in the Rift Valley and Western provinces (HRW, 1993a). In 1997, the Catholic Church in Mombasa mobilised a huge amount of resources to provide shelter, food and medical services to between 4,000 and 5,000 victims of displacement at the coast who took shelter in its Likoni Church and Cathedral in Mombasa. It also offered material support to the neighbouring Baptist Church to administer to the displaced within its compound (Kagwanja, 1998b:57). In the same way, the Catholic Church in Mt Longonot organised service provision to victims displaced within its compound.

Besides relief, local organisations were concerned with the human rights conditions of the displaced. During the 1992 and 1997 election periods, local organisations, in addition to relief, supported the rights of IDPs to vote. The Catholic Church in Mombasa rented houses for over 600 displaced families and encouraged them to exercise their right to vote. This was because government agents were harassing them within the church compound in order to prevent them from taking part in the elections (interview with officials, December, 1997). For its part, the NCCK used its publications to expose human rights abuses by the state against the displaced. Its widely cited monograph, The Cursed Arrow and monthly journal, Clashes Updates shifted opinion in favour of a human rights approach to the resolution of the crisis.

---

1. Only 200 of the Maela victims, most of them Kikuyu who were displaced from Enoosupukia settlement in Narok in October 1993, were recognised by the government and settled on two-acre plots in a different remote and dry settlement (HRW, 1997a).

This widened the rift between the state and local relief (especially church) organisations.

Analysts cited competition and lack of cooperation and coordination as the main drawbacks to the effectiveness of local capacity. Shaw and Gatheru (1998:291) describe the activities of local capacity in the Burnt Forest area in Uasin Gishu District in 1992 as "a veritable beehive of largely uncoordinated activities" that considerably reduced the value of intervention. Here, more than 15 agencies from outside the area intervened in the most uncoordinated manner. A local priest involved in the Burnt Forest saga reminiscences that:

> The value of intervention in Burnt Forest could have been much better with co-ordination. We all rushed in ...UNDP, NCCK, the Catholic Church, MSF, ICT, the local businessmen, everyone and all...targeting one man. At times you found a family that received 5 litres of cooking oil from five different NGOs when it had no blanket. There were no systems, no consistent information sharing...nothing! At the end of all this, the victim was under siege and confused. He/she ended up more impoverished than when he was first displaced... (Shaw and Gatheru, 1998:291).

Corruption, lack of accountability and transparency also undermined the effectiveness and credibility of local secular organisations. Emergency became big business for some actors, who resisted all efforts towards co-ordination of operations. While it is largely true that corruption and lack of accountability occurred in some areas, it is possible that the state and international agencies exaggerated its role in order to denigrate local capacity.

## UNDP's Programme: Undermining Local Capacity and the Protection of Human Rights

The UNDP spearheaded international response to displacement in Kenya. In 1993, almost two years after the clashes began, it launched a $20 million "Displaced Persons Programme", as part of its world-wide initiative to incorporate development, relief assistance, and human rights issues, in its search for durable solutions to the ubiquitous problem of internal displacement. This approach was "indicative of a new trend towards broadening the UNDP's traditional mandate to encompass more emergency-type situations with national development implications" in such diverse areas as Cambodia, Central America, Mozambique and other parts of the Horn of Africa (HRW, 1997a). In Kenya, the programme was inspired by the success of the "Drought Programme" of 1984–85 and 1992–93, which brought together NGOs, international actors, and local government agents. The UNDP envisaged building on the goodwill, methodology, and teamwork that had developed with Provincial Administration, NGOs, community groups, and donor agencies.

Although NGOs were earlier-comers to the humanitarian scene and had already developed systems of working together through joint committees that co-ordinated the various humanitarian activities, they welcomed the UNDP arrival and embraced it. It was hoped that the UN body would build on the main advantages of local actors such as their close proximity to the displaced, functional structures in the clash areas and the trust they had established with the displaced. Furthermore, the UNDP was well positioned to mitigate some negative practices in the NGO sector such as duplication of activities, inflation of the numbers of victims for the purposes of fundraising, corruption and undue emphasis on short-term relief needs at the expense of long-term solution to the crisis. Indeed, indigenous relief actors had come to believe that "the UN was better placed to raise the issue (of the deteriorating state-NGO relations) than others" (HRW, 1997b). Besides, the presence of the UNDP was conceived as a means of enhancing the protection of victims and as providing a major advantage in terms of the clout needed to deal with an otherwise "hostile" government. These expectations were soon dashed. While the UNDP created the National Coordination Committee for Internally Displaced Persons (NCCIDP), as a forum through which actors at all levels could co-ordinate their interventions, it soon became clear that the structure was not adding value to interventions. Its operations failed to tap into structures established by local NGOs, remained centralised, subordinated humanitarian operations to the provincial administration machinery and largely marginalised indigenous actors. At the conceptual level the agenda of UNDP was deeply steeped in development concerns and, therefore, neglected other systemic issues such as human rights violations. Thus its plan stated in part:

> Besides the immediate relief element, projects will be supported which are developmental, promote self-reliance and are ultimately locally sustainable (UNDP, 1994:6, cited in HRW, 1997a).

Further, its bureaucratic approach created "a one-way street" relationship with NGOs, particularly those engaged in advocacy. Instead of allying with NGOs, soon UNDP began to distance itself from its local partners because of their vocal criticism of the government's human rights violations. Instead, it began to draw closer to the government, abandoning the human rights component of the programme in an attempt to avoid accusations of being anti-government. While this shift undermined the trust of the local relief agencies in the leadership role of UNDP, it also had a significant, perhaps unintended, consequence; UNDP operations undermined and sidelined local initiatives.

The fears of local actors were confirmed in an evaluation of the UNDP intervention whose conclusions indicated that it had weakened and, in some cases, destroyed instead of boosting local capacity. In the Western Province, UNDP intervention clearly decimated the capacity of the Western Province Coordinating Committee (WPCC), a local initiative previously lauded as a model for replication in responding to IDP emergencies elsewhere in the country. Lamenting this development, one relief worker observed:

> [B]efore UNDP [came] we had formed a coordinating committee with the local groups. We struggled to get our programs coordinated to better serve the area. By the time the UNDP took over the WPCC in 1994, we had even employed a coordinator. Then the UNDP came in and hijacked the process. They didn't want to work closely with us, the local NGOs, because the government was attacking us for helping the displaced. Instead, they hijacked our structures and distanced themselves from us. All donor funding began to go to UNDP and therefore all projects began to get funding through UNDP. Then, without notice...the UNDP withdrew and closed down its program in 1995. Now, the momentum that local organisations had created is gone, and UNDP is gone, and we have no way financially to sustain the efforts that we had begun before UNDP came. So local efforts have collapsed. Now there is a complete vacuum (HRW, 1997a:118; see also Shaw and Gatheru, 1998:291; Kathina Juma, 1999b).

The UNDP failed to strengthen indigenous institutions and to support grassroots initiatives, which would have in effect enabled these civic organisations to demand accountability from the government and move the entire society towards a human rights regime. Instead the manner in which it implemented its programme undermined the civil society in the relief sector, and expanded space for the government to abuse power. The UNDP itself became victim of government manipulation. In Maela, the government used the funds of the Displaced Persons programme to fuel the trucks used to forcibly transport IDPs from the camp as well as to fund the resettlement of its own supporters in lands left behind by displaced victims (HRW, 1997a).

By the time it abandoned its programme in Kenya in 1995, the UNDP's credibility was badly dented.

## The Future of Indigenous Relief Capacity in Kenya

By the end of the 1990s, local capacity, especially in the refugee sector, had been reduced to a pale shadow of what it was at the beginning of the decade. The mistrust that developed between the local actors and their international counterparts during these hard days has complicated the task of building local capacity. The present study visualises the task of strengthening relief capacity at five inter-related levels. First is the task of rehabilitating and refurbishing indigenous relief organisations, empowering and making them autonomous actors in their own right. Second is the challenge of redefining the terms and dimensions of partnership between local and international actors. Third, there is need to rethink the role of the state and its bureaucratic structures in the emerging humanitarian regime. Fourth, it is imperative to evolve ways and means of empowering victims of emergencies, including refugees and the internally displaced. Finally, there is the necessity of transforming the economic and political environments that generate refugees and IDPs, and within which humanitarian actors, local and international, operate.

### Building Partnerships with Local NGOs

The immediate challenge that confronts international actors is to re-establish meaningful partnerships with their local counterparts aimed at devolution of power to the latter. Such partnerships should be based on the principle of equality. Otherwise 'capacity building' will remain what it evolved into in the 1990s—the subordination of local actors because it is "their" capacity which needs building, by international agencies and NGOs, who presumably have capacity. A valuable partnership would be one where international actors build on local knowledge, experience and capacities. At the local NGO level, it entails vigorous efforts towards performance-related capacity building and working towards the autonomy, financial self-reliance, advancement of skills and knowledge and enhancement of efficiency of local relief organisations. This would require international agencies to act as critical catalysts in advising and facilitating the operations of local partners.

Whereas international capacity is key during the initial phase of the emergency, outside agencies should phase out and ease in local actors, as well as engage in development activities. This would go a long way in reducing the dependency associated with long relief operations. Thus, the link between relief, rehabilitation and development requires to be established and efforts must be made towards engaging in activities that will promote this continuum. As argued elsewhere, "[s]hould they (these agencies) choose to remain, programs should revert to development activities that aim to prevent the recurrence of disasters" (Shaw and Gatheru, 1998:296). This is justified by the argument that a development-oriented mode of intervention has far-reaching positive effects on the economic and political structures that generate emergencies. More importantly, it can be used to generate an enabling environment for peace-building efforts. International actors can also play an important role in supporting human rights advocacy and finding durable solutions to the land, environmental and political problems that generated displacement. They can support the training of victims, including refugees and IDPs in preparation for return and rebuilding the communities they left. This may involve investing in scholarships for higher education and technical skills, financing small-scale businesses among refugees and inculcating peace-building skills.

Intervention by international actors needs to define the period of withdrawal and phasing out. Thus, upon intervening at the height of a crisis when their capacities are required, international actors ought to help boost local capacity, devolve power to local organisations and exit the humanitarian scene. When well executed, phasing out should increase local actor efficiency, preparedness, ensure accountability and sustainability of programs and eliminate long term dependency. During the apprenticeship period, it is also assumed that local NGOs will improve their skills, train staff, accumulate resources, gather information and knowledge relating to the causes of conflicts.

Further international capacity can also support state efforts to establish security in affected areas. Since the serious cases of insecurity in Northern Kenya in which hundreds of female refugees were sexually assaulted and raped by 'bandits', UNHCR has successfully experimented in giving support to the state in the area of security. It has since financed the construction of police stations in the vicinity of refugee camps and subsidises security personnel posted in these highly insecure regions. It has also provided supplementary equipment and training to security personnel, especially on human rights. Finally, international actors can support advocacy work in regard to the human rights of refugees and the internally displaced. They can join hands with local human rights organisations such as the Kenya Human Rights Commission and Commission of International Jurists (Kenya) which run programs on the protection of refugee rights. There is a whole area of litigation on behalf of refugees, which has not been fully explored. The justice system within and around the refugee-settled areas is quite underdeveloped. Moreover, litigation on behalf of refugees has not been a priority of humanitarian agencies in spite of numerous cases of violation of refugee rights.

## Bringing the State Back

There is need to go beyond the rhetoric of 'keeping the state out of business' if a sound legal and policy framework for humanitarian intervention is to develop in Kenya. The bitterest lesson of the 1990s is that a combination of an "abdicationist" stance by the state and the practices of international actors that marginalised it in refugee affairs undermined cooperation between actors, ran down the policy framework, and hurt the client—refugees and IDPs. There is need to bring back the state into the humanitarian arena by encouraging it to take a more central and positive role in the management of refugee affairs. This demands the refurbishing of the legal and policy framework for the management of emergencies. As illustrated in this chapter, by 1991, Kenya had a number of humanitarian systems dealing with famine and drought related emergencies, refugees and IDPs. The capability of these systems declined greatly in the 1990s. This prompted calls for rehabilitation and refashioning of such systems to ensure rapid and effective response to the multiplying complex emergencies. Certainly all structures were weak and operated in an uncoordinated manner with little, if any, cross-fertilisation between them. There is need to establish a comprehensive disaster response system, locate it within the same ministry and have its divisions and departments deal with specific emergency-types. This would ensure synergy and co-ordination in responding to disasters.

After a decade of experiencing and responding to emergencies, the legal and policy framework remains largely un-developed. The refugee sector has to some extent been leading the rest. However, the legislation for a refugee bill, which commenced in 1990, is yet to produce a legal framework for refugee administration. The Refugee Secretariat in Nairobi, which functions as a forum in which government operatives and officials of NGOs and the UNHCR deliberate various issues of concern to refugees is in dire need of adequate skilled personnel and sustained funding. The role of local government machinery, including county councils and provincial administration in refugee-settled areas of Kakuma and Dadaab as well as in areas affected by internal displacement, need to be clearly thought through. These institutions are critical in ensuring an enabling environment for relief work, in facilitating good relations between refugees and the locals, and in the reconciliation, rehabilitation, and healing processes, especially in respect to the internally displaced. Unsurprisingly, the lack of such structures at the onset of the emergencies meant that any existing local capacity was overwhelmed. More significantly intervening actors arrived to find no framework that could direct and/or regulate their activities. No wonder they went on to create the structures which they believed served their interests.

Lastly, regional structures such as the East African Community (EAC) and the Inter-Governmental Agency on Development (IGAD) play a critical role in shaping the wider political geography of emergency and strengthen response to emergencies. It has become increasingly evident that emergencies that produce refugees have a regional dimension, which should be considered in the reconfiguration of the framework for local relief capacity.

## Empowering the Victims

Actors at all levels should endeavour to enhance the capacity of affected communities and peoples to deal with any possible disasters in the future. The process of empowering the victims of emergencies will entail encouraging and supporting local peace initiatives through the establishment of local structures such as councils of elders, youth groups and women, movements. Local and international actors should identify skills, resources and capacities within the local communities that can be mobilised to deal with all aspects of emergencies. Furthermore, they should cultivate and increase their understanding of local perceptions, traditions and structures that trigger conflicts and those that can be exploited to build lasting solutions to conflicts. Communities should be supported to strengthen their capacities to cope with conflicts and disasters through such methods as sponsoring programs, workshops and meetings that strengthen existing structures, especially in areas affected by ethnic clashes. With regard to refugees, building capacity should focus on conflict resolution and arbitration. Refugee education should include inculcation of skills in peacemaking, conflict resolution, civic education, respect for human rights and the rule of law. IDP camps, refugee camps and settlement areas provide an excellent opportunity for training a cadre of peacemakers and arbitrators as a long-term process of preparing for repatriation and rehabilitation.

The system of "councils of elders" which UNHCR has sponsored in refugee camps has come under severe attack because it operates like "kangaroo courts" which violate human rights (Verdirame, 1999:62–63). If they are to serve a useful role, such "councils of elders" should be presided over by knowledgeable people equipped with basic skills in law and human rights. Workshops and/or short-term courses should be organised to train these elders on human rights and basic arbitration skills. Efforts should also be made to establish cordial relations between refugees and host communities by strengthening and utilising local structures such as councils of elders to seek solutions to issues of common concern such as use of water, land, resources, local trade in and around the camps, management of slaughterhouses. Assistance programmes that acknowledge the contribution of host communities and which promote harmony between these two communities create social insurance for the victims by facilitating solidarity. This is useful in terms of lobbying for the rights of victims. With regard to refugees, deliberate efforts towards local integration of refugee camps and the local community can minimise conflicts and ensure the human rights of refugees. As they are today, refugee camps operate like alien enclaves amidst local populations. In areas where the local population is impoverished, refugees appear to be a pampered lot that are a target for attacks by bandits, thieves and even murderers. A comprehensive development-oriented intervention strategy, which targets needs rather than dichotomising hosts and victims, could provide a valuable approach. The UNHCR programme on "refugee-affected areas" has the potential for enhancing the kind of harmony contemplated here.

### Creating an Enabling Environment for Relief Work

A big challenge that confronts actors at all levels is the creation of an enabling environment for the protection of human rights. This issue is even more complex in regard to the internally displaced where the state is said to be responsible for the human rights violation, which caused displacement in the first place. Integration of a human rights component in intervention requires that actors invest in setting up or reinforcing existing structures of human rights monitoring, advocacy and protection. Cooperation and involvement together with human rights agencies such as the Kenya Human Rights Commission, Human Rights Watch and African Rights which have been active in monitoring violations of the human rights of refugee and the IDPs is imperative.

A comprehensive conceptualisation of rights as indivisible is another step in advocating and protecting rights. Such an approach to rights would lead to engaging and promoting development as a preventative measure. Long term strategic development offers an ideal area for cooperation between development policy makers and practitioners at the local and international levels. In other words, links need to be built between relief and development programming, as a matter of right rather than privilege.

## Conclusions

This chapter has examined challenges that have confronted local relief capacity in Kenya, explored its prospects and suggested ways of re-building and strengthening it. Adopting a historical analysis, the study traced the emergence and development of local relief capacity and assessed its capability and limitations by 1991. It further examined the decline of local capacity in the 1990s, focusing on the role of international agencies and NGOs in the refugee and IDP sectors. Finally, it explored the prospects of building a strong local relief capacity with specific reference to the role of the state, local NGOs, international agencies and communities affected by emergencies.

The study argued that before the 1990s, a vibrant local relief capacity existed. This was undermined, sidelined and eventually eclipsed by international capacity in the 1990s. In the refugee sector, international actors sidelined local institutions, including state institutions. For its part, the state followed an abdicationist policy in dealing with the refugee sector, only getting involved when it considered its security interests in danger. In the arena of the internally displaced, international actors effectively undermined local initiatives and weakened existing structures. The situation was complicated by the obstructionist role of the state, which not only frustrated the efforts of local actors but also prevented any effective intervention by international actors. In the area of urban refugees, international agencies deliberately weakened local capacity in favour of international actors.

The study has made recommendations at various levels aimed at strengthening local relief capacity. First, it has suggested the establishment of genuine partnership between local and international actors, which will empower the former in the areas of skills, knowledge, personnel, and resources. At the same time, it suggested roles that international partners can play, including acting as facilitators and advisors to their local counterparts. Second, the study called for serious efforts to bring the state back into the humanitarian arena as a major partner. This is in recognition of its indispensable role in providing the legal and policy framework within which relief work takes place. Bringing the state back entails revitalising institutions that deal with refugees at the local and regional levels. The study strongly argued for the inclusion of the victims of emergencies in the whole process of building local capacity. This involves empowering their institutions such as elders councils in decision-making, equipping refugees and the internally displaced with skills for conflict resolution, peacemaking and administration of justice. Finally, the study proposes the establishment of an enabling environment for humanitarian work. This calls for serious collaborative efforts in human rights advocacy and monitoring. It also entails economic empowerment, especially of the population in refugee-settled areas through well-thought-out development programs by both the state and non-state actors. Ultimately, a strong local capacity will depend on cultivation of an efficient, transparent, sustainable and inclusive system in which the actors reinforce and empower each other.

# 7. Revitalising Relief Capacity as Part of the General Reconstruction Programme in Uganda

*Bertha Kadenyi Amisi and Monica Kathina Juma*

This chapter presents the challenges and prospects of building local relief capacity in Uganda in the 1990s. Aware of the destructive effects of the pathological character of politics in most of independent Uganda, we explore the possibilities of creating a relief capacity as part of the general reconstruction and rehabilitation process that started after the takeover by Yoweri Museveni in 1986.

We argue that three factors shaped attempts to reconstitute local relief capacity in the 1990s. First, there is a history of destroyed disaster response structures. Over time, local communities came to depend on their absorptive capacity to deal with emergencies. However, the 1990s saw the capacity of such communities and local institutions diminish noticeably as emergencies confronting Uganda became complex and widespread. Reconstruction of local capacity calls for the creation of comprehensive policy and administrative frameworks to nurture local capacity. Second, the prospects for capacity building are tied closely to Uganda's domestic politics that weave displacement to the centre of the power game, politicising humanitarian action and shrinking opportunities that would facilitate the assistance and protection of victims of displacement. While there have been efforts to depoliticise this arena since the 1990s, these face challenges posed by the destructive legacy of previous regimes. Finally, the macro-economic framework adopted for the reconstruction of the country does not favour issues of displacement. Focusing chiefly on macro-economic issues, the framework viewed humanitarian and human rights issues as side areas rather than key entry areas for reconstruction. The masterplan therefore does not address the perennial problem of insecurity in the country, particularly in the North, and does not, therefore, consider the creation of local relief capacity as a priority in the reconstruction programme. Thus, a combination of a weak local capacity, the legacy of destruction and the lack of a policy framework combine to pose critical challenges to attempts at revitalising local relief capacity in Uganda.

By the late 1980s when the current emergencies began to build up, local relief capacity was feeble or non-existent, opening up the humanitarian arena to dominance by outside capacity in the form of an overwhelming presence of international actors. While these actors were allowed to operate in responding to the refugee crises, the state refused to cede space for humanitarian action in situations of internal displacement, caused primarily by the insurgency. Arguing that insurgency is a political security matter and falls under the jurisdiction of the state, the government employed its enormous security capacity to control and direct humanitarian activities. Humanitarian actors found themselves faced with two choices: either to act in solidarity with victims, face accusations of supporting a rebel movement and risk expulsion by the state, or gain access and deliver relief assistance without addressing fundamental concerns such as insecurity, protection of victims or creating and enhancing sustainable local relief capacity. The latter option became the favoured one for a variety of reasons, including a large security capacity of the state, favourable international opinion about the Museveni government in the early and mid-1990s, lack of a supportive administrative and legal framework and NGO institutional interests. Thus, while Uganda swarmed with humanitarian actors, particularly international ones, most confined themselves to the refugee arena, avoiding issues of internal displacement and security. Subsequently, their presence was not matched by any growth in local relief capacity.

## History of Responding to Displacement

Uganda has a long history and experience of admitting and hosting refugees and other migrants. This has earned her an image of a humane state, with a positive political will and a readiness to respond to emergencies. With regard to refugees, it is defined as a settling and integrating state, willing to forge good partnerships with non-state actors. This perception has earned Uganda a good reputation internationally and led to major attempts by the international community, in particular, the Office of the United Nations High Commissioner for Refugees (UNHCR) to forge a close partnerships in the 1990s in the name of helping to revitalise the government's response capacity. Within this framework, the problem of internal displacement was seen as an internal insurgency that threatened the government's genuine rehabilitation efforts. In focusing on the needs of the government, international pressure failed to revitalise the capacity of local communities to respond to displacement, a practice associated with Uganda since colonial times.

### Uganda as an Allied Sanctuary 1942–52

By the mid-20th century, Uganda ranked among the main host countries to refugees and other migrants in Africa. As Samwiri Lwanga-Luyiigo (1993) aptly demonstrates, Uganda began to develop an elaborate refugee administrative structure when it was still a British protectorate. Starting in 1942, it was host to more than 7,000 Polish refugees in Masindi and Mukono districts. In addition to refugees, it also hosted civilian internees, prisoners of war and detainees from the allied side and the Axis powers in camps in Jinja, Entebbe and Arapai. Across all these settlements, administration was localised and left to the refugees. Determined to promote self-reliance, the colonial administration encouraged refugees to cultivate their own food and make their own clothing (Pinychwa, 1998). This practice was to become the hallmark of Uganda's refugee policy and forms the genesis of the current definition of Uganda as a model country for settling and integrating refugees.

Besides European refugees, Uganda has a history of hosting large numbers of African migrants and refugees from Sudan, Zaire and Rwanda who have been entering the country since the 1920s. As a nationality, the Sudanese have since colonial times been a critical factor in the security sector of Uganda. As early as the 1890s, they provided Captain Lugard with a reservoir of troops for the British East Africa Company and eventually for British colonial rule in Uganda. Unsurprisingly, they would come to play substantial roles in the politics and the military of Uganda, especially during the reign of Idi Amin Dada (Kabera, 1987:73). A second group of Sudanese constitutes labour migrants who entered Uganda after the 1930s. Following the outbreak of civil war in Sudan in 1955, Sudanese started to enter Uganda as refugees.

By 1956, approximately 5,000 Sudanese refugees were residents in northern Uganda. To cater for the increasing number of asylum seekers the government created the first refugee camp in the North at Acholi Pii in 1960. By 1965, the number of the Sudanese refugees hit a peak, estimated at between 100,000–150,000. The administration of Acholi Pii followed the model used for Polish refugees. Sudanese were encouraged to run their settlement in close partnership with local administration. More than half of these refugees repatriated after the signing of the Addis Ababa Accord in 1972, and later in 1979 following the fall of Idi Amin Dada.

The other nationality of migrants and refugees to enter Uganda were Congolese. Like the Sudanese, Congolese migration was prompted by economic opportunities in the 1930s. From 1931 when an estimated 1,600 Congolese were registered in Uganda, their number rose to 19,700 in 1948 and to 24,300 in 1939 (Kabera, 1987:74). Some 30,000 Congolese asylum seekers entered Uganda between 1960-1961 following the brutal murder of the first Prime Minister, Patrice Lumumba (Pirouet, 1988:240). As they settled among Congolese migrant workers, the government did not create any refugee camps for these refugees. Instead, it allowed them to integrate with their kith and kin and to settle among the local communities, using and boosting local resources and the economy.

Rwandese constituted the third and largest nationality to enter colonial Uganda and arrived in three main groups. They first settled in Bufumbira County in southwestern Uganda at the turn of the century and increased considerably from 76,844 in 1931 to 37,656 in 1859 (Kabera, 1987). The second group consisted of labourers who worked on farms in Buganda and Busoga counties of South Central Uganda. The third group was comprised of political refugees who flocked into Uganda during and after the 1959 political struggles in Rwanda, which culminated in the exile of the Umwami (King) Kigeri VI of Rwanda. After Rwanda gained independence in 1962, ending monarchical rule, an estimated 80,000 Batutsi followed their ex-King into exile in Uganda where he had been granted asylum. Large numbers of Rwandese refugees remained in Uganda to return during the invasion by the Rwanda Patriotic Front (RPF) in 1994.

At independence in 1962, therefore, Uganda was host to a substantial number of foreigners, of whom more than 200,000 were refugees. As its neighbours continued to experience instability, it continued being a destination of choice for asylum seekers. Having practised a generous open door policy, Uganda defined itself as a refugee hosting and integrating state. This policy would, however, be tested in the immediate post-independence politics, which thrust refugees to the centre of the power game as they became pawns in the "spoils politics" that were to characterise Uganda, essentially destroying any capacity that may have accumulated in the pre-independence years.

### Refugees, Relief Capacity and Post-Independence Politics

The influx of Rwandese after the 1959 massacre was followed closely by the Congolese and then Sudanese refugees. In addressing the needs of the expanding number of refugees, the government gazetted several refugee settlements in North and South West Uganda. Again following the earlier models, refugees were encouraged to interact and integrate with local communities, administer themselves and utilise local structures. In sum, they were encouraged to participate in local livelihoods and enhance the capacity of the local environment to absorb them.

While Uganda provided sanctuary, developments in the domestic political sphere were moving refugees into the arena of high politics and making it a refugee generating state. Its capacity to handle refugee and migrant populations was tested soon after independence, when Uganda began to exemplify a pathology associated with the category of failed states (Appe, 1994; Mutimbwa, 1992:71–76; Omara-Otunnu 1992:443–463). It was to witness eight changes of government, all resulting from coups or quasi-coups, within its first 30 years of independence (Omara-Otunnu 1987). Until 1996, Uganda became a theatre of violence, characterised by deepening political, economic and social instability. Institutions degenerated into factional politics and transformed into extreme versions of clientele politics, described elsewhere as "spoils politics" (Appe, 1994:9). This fate was to shape the definition and treatment of refugees and other migrants. As endemic instability prevailed and violence became the norm, institutions as well as citizens were subjected to increased state brutality and repression. Except for churches, which operated with great difficulties, political leadership turned to proscribing and destroying any institutions or actors associated with the "enemy" of the system, in essence destroying existing capacity. Among the victims of state brutality were non-state actors that assisted refugees and other victims of displacement.

There were several defining events along this road of capacity destruction, a number of which are worth recalling. When the armies of the three East African countries mutinied in 1964, Obote's response to the crisis was to bolster the power and status of his military. He raised its pay, bought new equipment and promoted army officers. In addition he took control of vital apparatuses of state power and started to use them for his own benefit, thus politicising the security sector and making it a tool of factional politics. When in 1966, opposition members of the cabinet set up an enquiry into the malfeasance relating to the army's Congo operation, Obote arrested five cabinet ministers, the Commander of the Army, suspended the constitution and assumed the presidency. King Kabaka Mutesa, the Constitutional President of Uganda, appealed to the United Nations as his parliament voted in favour of secession. This confrontation set the stage for the first major assault on citizens by their security forces. On Obote's orders, Idi Amin led troops in the attack on the King's palace, killing an estimated 2,000 people and leading to the flight of the Kabaka into exile. A state of emergency was declared in Buganda and later extended to other parts of the country in 1969. Defining the victims of these events as "enemies", the government refused to assist them and prevented any non-state actor from doing so. Except for the Uganda Red Cross, which provided medical facilities and limited relief assistance, no relief structures were created to respond to the emergency that resulted in large numbers of Ugandans being displaced internally. By the time Idi Amin toppled Obote in 1971, an additional 100,000 Ugandan were in exile.

## Accelerated Exile and Decline of Relief Capacity: Amin Era 1971–1979

Once in power, Amin began purging and expelling his perceived "enemies". First among his victims was Milton Obote and his entourage who, unable to return to Uganda after attending a Commonwealth Heads of State meeting in Singapore, lived in exile during Amin's reign. Acholis and Langis, seen as supporters of Obote were ruthlessly attacked and many killed. These events began to create unease among the population and a steady trickle of members of these communities crossed the border into Kenya. After the murder of Archbishop Jenani Luwum in February 1977, an estimated 15,000 Acholis sought asylum in Kenya (Pirouet, 1988:246). Meanwhile, twenty-six Christian organisations working in Uganda were proscribed, an act that completely blocked any humanitarian assistance programs to victims of state brutality.

Amin then turned on the foreigners, starting with the Israelis, who were involved in a number of sectors, including army and police training, education, health and construction. They were accused of sabotaging the economy and security of the country and expelled. The high point in the destruction of local capacity came with the expulsion of more than 50,000 Asians, whose property was confiscated and assets distributed among his followers. In December 1972, the policy was extended to British interests in Uganda. These were taken over. In retaliation, Britain cancelled all aid to Uganda, leading the world in shaping its opinion of Amin. From then on, Amin was listed among belligerent autocratic leaders and condemned for violations of human rights. The expulsion of foreigners was conducted without any assistance from international organisations, which pulled out of Uganda.

In October 1976, the forces of Amin invaded the Kagera salient in North Tanzania, leaving a trail of rapes, murders and looting. After two months, the Tanzanian Peoples Defence Forces, together with Ugandan opposition groups, amongst whose leaders was Yoweri Museveni, attacked Central and Western Uganda, defeating the heavily armed but ill-trained Ugandan soldiers and toppled Amin. Under Yusuf Lule, the Uganda National Liberation Front (UNLF) came to power. Replacing Lule, between 1979–1980, was Godfrey Binaisa QC, an Obote crony who had drafted the Republican Constitution of 1967. Corrupt and lacking order, Binaisa was overthrown in May 1980 by pro-Obote UNLF forces within the ruling Military Commission. What followed was an orgy of violence by Acholi and Langi soldiers in UNLF, who carried out indiscriminate killings in West Nile, Idi Amin's home area, destroying most of the district to avenge massacres committed upon their people by Amin (Museveni, 1997). According to UNHCR estimates, a quarter of a million people fled the West Nile district into neighbouring Sudan and Zaire during this period.[1] In addition to the absence of humanitarian actors to respond to the humanitarian consequences generated by this massive violence, the capacity of local populations to deal with emergencies had by this time weakened considerably.

### Orgy of Violence, Displacement and Exile: Obote II, 1980–1984

In a stage-managed, heavily rigged election held in 1980, the Military Commission declared Obote the winner. Citing fraudulent elections, the National Resistance Army (NRA) launched an armed struggle and established itself in the Luwero triangle, Central Uganda. This opened the way for a second Obote onslaught and perhaps the gravest violation of the civilian population, resulting in internal displacements on an unprecedented scale. The Obote government's response was brutal. Refusing to adhere to international humanitarian law and targeting civilians, the army arbitrarily detained, tortured, raped and killed. In 1983, it established control of towns and trading centres in the Triangle and began clearing operations in the outlying areas. As part of its strategy, it herded the civilian population into 'protective' camps,[2]

---

1. These estimates are corroborated by various researchers including USCR (1985) and Barbara Harrell-Bond's *Imposing Aid* (1986), which was based on research conducted among more than 200,000 Ugandan refugees in Sudan.
2. Within the African context, 'regroupment' villages for enemy populations were first created during the Algerian civil war in 1957 (UNHCR, 2000). They were also created during the Mozambique civil war, and more recently in Burundi.

which lacked basic facilities (USCR, 1985:11). Conservative estimates put the figure of the dead at 300,000, and more than 500,000 internally displaced, within Buganda alone (USCR, 1985; Matovu and Stewart, 2000). Faced with an international outcry and attempting to woo international legitimacy, the government invited the Uganda Red Cross to provide basic services to the victims, within a limited humanitarian mandate.

Reminiscent of Amin's actions of 1971–72, Obote turned to his arch-enemy in south-western Uganda: the Rwandese, whom he associated with the opposition Democratic Party and accused of supporting Amin's coup and regime. The Rwandese were barred from voting in the 1980 elections and pressured to collect in refugee camps. Faced with political insecurity most Rwandese moved into UNHCR's designated settlements by 1981. However, Obote was not satisfied. He began to make inflammatory speeches against the Rwandese and sanctioned state-sponsored violence against them. Backed by a Special Force Unit, the Uganda People's Congress (UPC) youth wing were issued with orders to evict the Rwandese. Attacks on homes began, people were evicted and homes destroyed and rendered uninhabitable. Among the victims were people that had been settled in Uganda for more than two decades. This operation saw some 35,000 seeking international protection in refugee camps and settlements, over 40,000 crossing the border into Rwanda and another 4,000 trapped inside Uganda when the government of Rwanda finally closed its border in November 1982. Eviction teams intimidated local inhabitants to scare them away from offering assistance to the victims in flight. Without local assistance, the Rwandese were left to God's mercy.

Keen to win favourable international opinion, Obote allowed a few agencies, including churches and the Uganda Red Cross, to work with UNHCR in assisting refugees who were in camps and resettlement areas. In response to growing international pressure he promised to review the citizenship claims made by some and examine the matter of compensation to those who had suffered loss. To relieve overcrowding within settlements, he agreed to provide land for an additional refugee settlement, Kyaka II. While the government gave land, it did not abide by its other agreements or end the conflict. Harassment of Rwandese went on unabated. By the end of 1984, local chiefs and UPC youths in Rakai and Masaka districts evicted up to 19,000 Rwandese, following the earlier pattern. With the border to Rwanda closed, refugees crossed into Tanzania while others fled to refugee camps and settlements. In January 1985, the army began to harass the refugees that had moved to the recently established Kyaka II settlement. As more refugees were forced from their homes, international agency staff left the area.

Aware of the on-going violations, relief workers were faced with the choice of either assisting victims of violence while remaining quiet, or criticising the government and risking physical harm or expulsion from Uganda. Security forces reigned without opposition or deterrence. Weaker than the state, UNHCR, about the only remaining national actor, as well as the Uganda Red Cross defined their work in narrow relief terms. Thus, at the close of the Obote II regime, Uganda had become a significant generator of both refugees and internally displaced persons in the North, Central and South West regions of the country. At the same time, the previous practice of allowing victims of disasters to undertake administrative tasks and the policy of encouraging integration with local communities had fizzled out.

**Table 1. Estimates of Displacement of Ugandans: From Obote I to Obote II**

| Period | Regime | Refugees | Exile Ugandans | Internally Displaced |
|--------|--------|----------|----------------|----------------------|
| 1964 | Obote | 200,000+ | - | - |
| 1966 | Obote | 200,000+ | Approx. 15,000 | 20,000 |
| 1969 | Obote | 177,925 | 50,000+ | |
| 1971–79 | Amin | 200,000+ | 100,000+ | (not recorded) |
| 1979–80 | Military Commission | 200,000+ | 715,000+ | (not recorded) |
| 1980–84 | Obote II | 44,000+ | 500,000+ | 550,000+ |

Sources: Tandon, 1987; Betts, 1968; authors' field survey

## A New Dawn? The Museveni Era, 1986–

When the National Resistance Movement (NRM) assumed power in 1986, it inherited a state that had suffered the consequences of years of bad governance, evidenced by a breakdown in the rule of law, gross violations of human rights, and worrying levels of poverty and political violence. The capacity to respond to the humanitarian consequences that were manifested in a large refugee population, almost half a million internally displaced persons and a significant proportion of exiled citizens was simply non-existent. As under previous regimes, refugees began to flood northern Uganda in 1989. To accommodate some 100,000 to 150, 000 new arrivals the Acholi Pii camp was reactivated, and 23 transit centres and refugee camps were established across the region. By 1998, the number of registered refugees hosted in camps and settlements surpassed the 200,000 mark (Refugee Network, 1998:1). Unlike the pre- and immediate post-independence era, refugees found themselves in environments without any capacity to sustain them. Indeed, delivering assistance and protection posed critical challenges as hosting areas were within the activity areas of insurgent groups. In the same vein, humanitarian programs became targets of insurgent groups, generating a number of dilemmas related to access and security.

Meanwhile, as the government sought to redeem the situation in Luwero triangle and south-western Uganda, the arena of internal displacement switched to the North, specifically to areas associated with support for Obote and Amin. A few months after coming to power, the NRM government was faced with armed opposition, from the remnants of the armies of both Obote and Amin, in the West Nile, and the North and North East regions of the country. The ensuing insurgency was to generate massive internal displacement, comparable only to that witnessed in the Luwero triangle in the 1980s, which together with the refugee crisis turned into a complex humanitarian crisis that eluded solutions throughout the decade of the 1990s.

The search for peace was marked by public distrust of the NRM government, associated with betraying the Nairobi peace talks held to negotiate modalities of power sharing, under a temporary cease-fire in 1986. As the negotiations were in progress, the NRA marched on and captured Kampala. From then on the public opinion viewed Museveni with suspicion, believing that his sole aim was to "finish" them in line with the pathology of 'spoils politics'. After seizing power, Museveni engaged a two-pronged approach in search of peace in the North: a public relations and a military approach. However, both leaned towards resources and frameworks formulated outside of the affected communities and failed the legitimacy test from the beginning. Organised around conciliatory political steps, the public relations approach aimed at winning over the rebels as well as the (hostile) populations in the North. Shortly after coming to power, Museveni signed a peace agreement, which led to the surrender of some UNLA remnants. However, a majority of insurgents rejected the deal, and sporadic attacks on government sites and civilians continued unabated. In 1987, the regime's National Resistance Council enacted a statute providing amnesty for people involved in "warlike" acts. In the meantime, negotiations with the three main factions of the Uganda People's Democratic Army/Movement (UPDA/M) were initiated and led to a peace agreement in 1998. Large numbers of insurgents surrendered and some were integrated into the NRA. However, these measures collapsed within two years of their initiation. Peace became evasive as displacement became the dominant feature of life in the North, providing an opportunity and justification for the second government strategy: military campaigns.

In October, the NRA launched a major offensive against rebels in Gulu district. Employing a scorched earth policy, the military destroyed homes, displaced some 70,000 people and herded others into "protected" villages in the North. In Kumi and Soroti districts similar tactics led to the relocation of another 120,000 to towns and next to NRA posts and detachments. In Kumi and Soroti, these strategies curbed activities and by 1990 a majority of civilians had returned to their homes. Similar success was scored in West Nile district where peace had attracted a large number of humanitarian agencies, regenerating destroyed relief capacity in Koboko and the Arua districts.[1]

However, the situation was markedly different in the North Central Region where rebel activities intensified as one rebel movement, first under Alice Lakwena and later under Joseph Kony, transformed itself from a spiritual and socio-cultural cleansing movement to a militant and extremely violent predatory rebellion—The Lord's Resistance Army (LRA). Even today, this group carries out deliberate and arbitrary attacks and kills both officials and civilian populations, leaving devastating humanitarian consequences in its wake across Gulu, Lira and Apac districts. The NRA has responded with violence against the group as well as civilians associated with it, resulting in untold destruction and dispersal of populations. Faced with pillaging from both the rebel movement and some government forces, populations have tended to agree to be herded into government-created "protected" villages. By the beginning of 1999, UNHCR estimates indicate that more than half a million people were displaced in the North alone (UNHCR, 1999).

The combination of insecurity, displacement and destruction has had a direct negative impact on the ability of the community to cope with distress. Insecurity has prevented people from productive activities, especially agriculture, which is the mainstay of this region. In turn this has led to food shortages and total dependence on the limited relief resources available, supplied mainly by the World Food Programme under conditions of extreme insecurity. By 1999, agricultural production by local communities in Gulu and Kitgum districts had sunk below that of refugees, whose camps and settlements were comparatively more secure. Population vulnerability in northern Uganda is further accentuated by long-term marginalisation and underdevelopment that has been characteristic since colonial times, and which post-independent regimes have failed to redress (Banugire, 1989).

Internal displacement presents a complex picture of forced migration, comprising various categories of displacement occurring either suddenly following news of

---

1.  The capture of Mahagi Town in eastern Zaire by anti-Mobutu Banyamulenge rebels pushed the West Nile Bank Front out of their bases and further north into Sudan, thus limiting their activities in the West Nile Region.

an attack, or gradually over a long period of time (more than a decade of insurgency). The categories of IDPs include those settled in camps near or within towns/trading centres, "protected villages" (by the government, but not always effectively protected), near military barracks, commuters (living in the bush, trading centres, or church/seminary compounds and returning to their homes during the day to work on the farm), and migrants living with friends and relatives within the district or outside it (Global IDP Survey, 1999:2). The commuter phenomenon represents a "half-here-half-there" situation, which allows the affected persons to continue with their normal farm activities during the day, but at night they retire to the towns, which are considered safer than the peri-urban areas. There is also the seemingly amorphous category of persons who have moved to safer areas that are not necessarily towns or trading centres, but allow for continuation of livelihoods (access to land cultivation).

The fluidity of this displacement presents numerous socio-economic challenges. There are gender and generation implications, for instance, caused by the stress placed on the family system and gender relations as families are separated and women or men take on new roles and responsibilities for which they are unprepared. Children are sent away, and men leave to avoid being forcibly recruited or targeted. Women are left behind to head the household with little income because some of the men rarely return or provide for their families. Family conflicts between spouses and also between generations are increasing. The extended family can no longer function adequately as a safety net, leaving the old, sickly and disabled in a most vulnerable and precarious situation. Another problem is the additional requirement for financial and social capital to redress the debilitating effects of internal displacement such as the enforced neglect of infrastructure, services and livelihoods. When populations leave their more productive farmlands and move into camps, they are reduced to living from hand to mouth, often unable to cope. Tremendous stress is placed on limited services and opportunities in the small towns hosting the displaced. In many cases, poor health and other socio-economic problems are created, the most worrying being the rapid spread of HIV/Aids (Republic of Uganda/UNICEF, 1998; Finnström, 1999).

Other visible aspects of the humanitarian crisis include the mutilation of individuals, the increasing number of disabled persons, loss of tens of thousands of lives, large-scale abduction of children, lawlessness, human rights abuse, looting and destruction of infrastructure, and loss of livelihoods. The often neglected, but even more significant, invisible aspects include the breakdown of the family, other socio-cultural institutions and the relationships they represent. The consequences are increasing resentment, violence, fear, despair and a sense of hopelessness. In sum, the humanitarian crisis is much greater than just the large displacement of population into camps. These problems are played out against a background of poverty, a stagnant local economy and breakdown of infrastructure for the delivery of social services. The recurring violence further erodes whatever resources have been saved to tide the community have been crises and renders large sections of the population increasingly vulnerable.

## The Reconstruction Programme

The NRM government introduced a number of political and economic changes aimed at addressing the distressing and complex political and economic problems in the country. However, the economic recovery plan is designed within the framework of the IMF's Structural Adjustment Programme and has a strong emphasis on macro-economic stabilisation and structural reforms. So far, impressive results have been achieved in subduing inflation, controlling public expenditure, liberalising trade, privatising non-performing parastatals and promoting growth in public and private investment. The benefits of the acclaimed economic growth, however, are yet to be distributed equally throughout the country, especially in the North where 71 per cent of the population is said to live below the poverty line (Action Aid, 2000:11–17). Furthermore, the impact of the Northern Uganda Reconstruction Programme (NURP) Phase I, initiated in 1991/92 to supplement already existing national rehabilitation programs, has been insignificant because it does not comprehensively address the perennial insecurity and protection issues. The launch of a Poverty Eradication and Action Plan (PEAP) by the government in 1997, with the support of the World Bank, marked a shift in donor thinking by considering the problem of poverty as a central factor in economic reform and growth policies. Since then social sector policies have been developed for education, the most profound being the Universal Primary School Education Programme. Other proposed sectors are agriculture and health.

The policy shift has implications for the development of local capacity for both relief and development in the North. The new policy may address the economic causes of the insurgency. However, it will need to go further to help create conditions favourable for rebuilding lives and the resource bases of communities that are critical to the development of capacities to respond to emergencies. Had donors and the government earlier pursued a programme more focused on poverty eradication through the stimulation of the local economy, this might have spurred rehabilitation and regeneration of local capacity.

At the political level, the government established the Resistance Council system, sometimes referred to as Local Councils (LCs), to allow for popular participation. Initially set up for political education and mobilisation for security, LC responsibilities broadened over time. When the government in 1990 began to decentralise power and administrative authority, the LCs became the fulcrum of a programme to enhance popular participation from the local to national levels. This gave district level structures some degree of autonomy in planning, deciding, budgeting, resource allocation and development of activities at the district levels. Commendable as this strategy is, decentralisation is taking place without the much-needed revenue, experience and tax base needed for effective programme implementation. This has implications for local capacity to initiate and sustain long-term development initiatives as well as humanitarian action.

## Administering Refugee Assistance and Protection

The post-1986 government has attempted to restructure the framework for responding to refugees. Reflecting the NRM's sympathy and closer ties to refugees during its campaign for political power, and its efforts to utilise the new grassroots Resistance Councils, acclaimed for their anticipated role in integrating refugees into host communities, the government has prioritised refugee assistance and protection. Reflecting the mood towards popular participation, the Refugee Directorate, originally located in the Ministry of Culture and Social Services, was moved to the Ministry of Local Government. Indicating the government's interest in disaster management, the Directorate was elevated to the Prime Minister's Office under the Ministry of Refugees, Rehabilitation and Emergency Response in 1998. Undoubtedly, this centralisation of refugee matters has direct implication for the operations of actors running assistance and protection programs.

The refugee administrative structures include an inter-ministerial committee that advises the operations of the Directorate of Refugee Affairs, which in turn oversees the implementation of programs. This directorate screens non-state actors wishing to operate in refugee-affected areas, recommends them to OPM for permission to operate and remains as the government's focal unit on aspects related to refugee matters. It is represented by Refugee Desk Officers in every refugee-hosting district. Stretching from the national to the local levels, this structure is mandated to guide Uganda's policy of integration of refugees to local communities and enhance the creation of a sustainable capacity for dealing with disasters at the local level. Compared to the two other East African countries, one can safely say, in terms of policy Uganda seems to have a better grip of refugee administration and protection.

However, the implementation of this policy is bedevilled by challenges. In 1996, Parliament outlawed the gazetting of land for refugee settlements, provided for in the Control of Aliens Acts (1964) that had been in operation since then. Since 1996, refugees are allowed to use, but not own, land, which runs counter to the logic of the policy of integration: the hallmark of Uganda's refugee policy since colonial times. The policy shift was justified in politico-security terms: as a necessary step to avert conflicts between the locals and refugees over resources, in particular land. Moreover, the increasing tendency of the government to view refugees from a security angle has led to administrative practices that undermine the capacity of the Directorate of Refugee Affairs (a matter discussed in greater detail in Chapter 9). Suffice it to state here, that decisions concerning refugee settlement, establishment of camps, or how and when repatriation should be organised are handed down as decrees from higher offices in Kampala. In spite of falling within the Prime Minister's Office in terms of security, refugees fall directly under the Resident District Commissioner (RDC), a Presidential appointee who doubles up as the District Security Chief. The RDC answers directly to the President and is not accountable to any office at the district level.

## Creating Relief Capacity in Insecure Environments?

Internal displacement is dealt with as a matter of security and high politics, and hence as the sole prerogative of the state. At the local level, military security officers take the lead in organising the response to IDPs. However, Disaster Response Committees (DDRC) are housed within the Ministry of Local Government. These committees are mandated to plan and design tailor-made strategies for responding to disasters and to provide a framework for partnership between local and international actors engaged in humanitarian action. While these committees have great potential several factors hinder their optimal operations, including the desire of the government to control them, lack of financial resources and experience in managing and monitoring emergency response. Although created more than five years ago, they remain fragile and are yet to develop firm structures and organisational capacity. Their development faces enormous challenges because the committees do not have a budget allocation from either the national or district treasury. Their daily operations depend almost entirely on the support and goodwill of humanitarian agencies operating in the administrative jurisdictions.

Since internal displacement is contextualized with the dynamics of 'spoils politics', the involvement of humanitarian agencies—especially international NGOs—has critical implications for this relationship. While the government invokes a range of sanctions to steer humanitarian activities towards favouring its political status, humanitarian actors are forced to engage in activities that ensure some access to the victims, as well as their presence and survival. This is at the expense of engaging in activities that could build a sustainable relief capacity. To maintain a humanitarian, apolitical non-interfering stance, these actors operate within a restricted scope and engage in band-aid type interventions that do not address issues of protection, human rights and state responsibilities to victims of displacement.

## NGO Interventions and Role in Building Local Relief Capacity

In trying to address problems resulting from insurgency, a number of international and local NGOs together with a range of community-based organisations have launched a mix of initiatives. Activities are oriented towards relief and focus primarily on basic needs such as food, water, health, education, and increasingly on psycho-social interventions. Their distribution is uneven in terms of sectors and geographic scope, and to a large extent their operations are determined by the level of security/insecurity in the areas of focus. The more insecure a place is, the less likely NGOs are to have operations. A majority of NGO agencies are therefore concentrated within or near towns, in IDP or refugee camps and in the infamous "protected" villages. As a result, populations in outlying areas have no access to services of any kind. A few initiatives focus on peace and reconciliation at the community and district levels, particularly in Gulu and Kitgum districts.

On the whole, very few agencies were involved until recently in development activities in the North. Although there is a slightly larger NGO presence in Gulu than in Kitgum district, NGOs, whether international or local, are new actors in northern Uganda. Only one Italian NGO has been involved in the rehabilitation of health, education and water facilities. Yet, the opening of the North to humanitarian agencies is happening at the expense of protection. Without exception, all NGOs in the North veer away from protection issues arguing that it is the responsibility of the state to deal with insecurity. INGOs, in particular, confine their operations to emergency interventions, ostensibly as a basis for shifting to development work when prospects for peace are certain. Gulu district has comparatively more NGO activity than Kitgum, where a number of international NGOs have began to venture in and are trying to establish partnerships with local actors. This difference is attributed to the chronic insecurity in Kitgum, which lies on the path of rebel incursions from southern Sudan. On the whole, humanitarian operations are continually disrupted by the chronic insecurity that characterises this region.

Direct intervention to secure peace is left to the government, which is seen as the principle agency for responding to insecurity through use of the army or the Office of the Resident District Commissioner. NGO interventions aim at helping communities to mitigate and cope with insecurity. Through activities such as the provision of relief, reconstruction of destroyed infrastructure and training on peace and reconciliation issues, local residents acquire skills and knowledge necessary to nurture peace, reconciliation and to deal with violence. More recently, education about the Geneva Conventions and human rights is encouraged as a means to regulate the use of force. However, most training does not integrate existing indigenous laws on the conduct of war and protection of civilians, a matter whose value is emphasised in the chapter by Mutoy Mubiala in this book.

In the absence of protection, communities in the North are trying to invoke traditional ways of peace and reconciliation as a means to address violence. Among the most laudable initiatives by local communities is the Acholi Religious Leaders' Initiative (ARLI), which engages in the revival and use of traditional peace building mechanisms. ARLI has grown in stature and usefulness to the extent of becoming an interlocutor between the rebels and the community, and increasingly between the rebels and the government. While it began as a localised effort by religious leaders, ARLI has forged links at district, regional, national and international levels, particularly with the Acholi diaspora.[1] Such organisations are creating focal units that act as entry points for empowering the communities and offer opportunities for partnership with international NGOs and other actors.

The extent to which these efforts can be boosted needs examination. Where outside initiatives are limited in outreach or ineffective, communities have come up with their own ways of enhancing mutual protection. This they achieve through being more vigilant, mobilising support for each other and sharing information on the location, sighting and movement of rebel groups. Clearly, there is a marked desire for peace in the North. Unfortunately, well intentioned as these initiatives are, their success is often severely affected by the inability of communities to prevent or mitigate brutal surprise attacks by the well-armed rebels. The success of the emerging peace initiatives in the last three years is also curtailed because of the exclusion of rebels and the military from peace training. Until such training targets these critical actors in the insecurity landscape of northern Uganda, local capacity for securing peace will remain a job half done.

## Humanitarian Action as Life Saving Operations

Relief assistance is administered directly by NGOs, with minimal community participation. Organisations are often required to work closely with the administrative and security mechanisms at the local level, in which case they draw on the support of the local councils for co-ordination of relief distribution and registration of internally displaced persons. Inter-agency forums are held regularly to share information on the security and emergency situation, and to give an update on planned or ongoing interventions. Most relief assistance targets IDPs, refugee camps and protected villages. While both state and non-state actors claim that these interventions occur within the framework of the Northern Uganda Reconstruction Programme (NURP), there is a glaring lack of synergy between relief programmes and general reconstruction. Indeed, the impact of the relief programme in terms of jumpstarting development is, to say the least, minimal. Further, the relief-development continuum is threatened by pervasive insecurity. No relief programme in northern Uganda has escaped the wrath of rebels. In the most dramatic attack in 1996, the UNHCR Sub-Office and compound in Adjumani was razed to the ground, an act that saw all agencies, except the Italian NGO, withdraw from the area for nearly six months. In the following year, Ikafe camp in Arua district was attacked, its hospital looted and some people killed, including the Assistant Refugee Desk Officer in the district. The

---

1. ARLI is playing an increasingly important role as a buffer between the abducted children who return and their communities, between the children and government forces, and in rehabilitating the children generally. See Kathina Juma and Mengistu, 2001.

World Food Programme food convoy is a favourite target for rebels and has suffered attacks regularly since the operation began. Each time a rebel attack occurs, humanitarian organisations withdraw and scale down their operations until the security situation stabilises. This has a negative impact on programme sustainability.

A further consequence of insecurity comes in the form of fluidity of populations as they move in search of secure places. This presents a critical challenge because conventional assistance programs operate on the presumption of populations located in fixed geographic areas. Attempts to promote food security in displaced persons camps have largely failed to promote self-sufficiency. Community coping mechanisms have been severely weakened because people displaced into "peace" villages have been effectively cut off from their farms, are hesitant to venture long distances from the safety of the camps, and when they grow crops, often these are harvested by others or destroyed. In a peaceful environment, traditional food security safety nets would perhaps have provided a base from which to strengthen local relief capacity. Communities would attempt to survive by resorting to petty trade and selling labour. However, among the displaced in the northern region, the numbers absorbed by such activities are few, the income they generate is small and they also suffer the constraints of insecurity. NURP I has never achieved its anticipated role in rehabilitating and reconstructing agriculture as well as other sectors to levels that could support livelihoods and build sufficient reserves to tide the population over emergencies.

An area where a measure of capacity has emerged is in dealing with mental health and trauma issues. Although working against many odds, a considerable number of traditional healers, birth attendants and community volunteer counsellors have emerged to deal with the effects of emergencies in northern Uganda. Perhaps the most touching case in the struggle is that of local communities to ensure continuity in the education sector. Parents in some areas pool together the resources available to them and purchase construction materials for schools, run existing schools through Parent Teacher Associations (PTAs) or even establish private schools in camp situations. However, these activities occur during the periods of lull in the violence and are marked by significant enthusiasm on the part of community members to engage in reconstruction activities. This reality challenges NGOs to adopt programmatic shifts from relief to rehabilitation and development if they are to play a catalytic role in making the promise of peace signalled by such periods real.

## Rebuilding Community and the Lives of Children and the Youth

A peculiar challenge facing northern Uganda is rebel abduction of children. Child abduction assumed crisis proportions between 1993 and 1996 when the rate of abductions by the Lord's Resistance Army rose dramatically. At the same time an increasing number of those abducted managed to escape from the hands of the LRA, raising the questions of how the communities as well as the government should address their reintegration (Human Rights Watch, 1997; Okwe and Amisi, 1997). The marked rise in the incidence of mental health and psychological problems caused by the general insecurity has overstretched and overwhelmed the local medical capacity to provide psychiatric treatment and mental health care. A growing number of volunteer counsellors are emerging from the communities, attempting to address outreach gaps created by the limited non-governmental sponsored counselling services and government health capacity. Yet, these supplementary and complementary efforts fall far short of the need on the ground.

Formerly abducted children pose a particular challenge in northern Uganda. The community's way of dealing with former abductees was to send them away from areas of rebel activities to stay with relatives in other districts not affected by war. Over the years, however, a number of NGOs, mainly internationally based ones, have come to northern Uganda to address the needs of formerly abducted children and youth. These agencies borrow from community traditions in dealing with an otherwise painful and traumatic experience. However, attempts by NGOs to adapt and integrate local knowledge and capacity are recent developments. The first NGOs to deal with trauma healing employed a Harvard-developed Post Traumatic Stress Disorder model, which did not have significant results. Alongside this emerged community organisations to deal with trauma, one in Gulu, and later another in Kitgum. Both the Gulu Save the Children Organisation (GUSCO) and Kitgum Concerned Women's Association (KICWA) have adopted an innovative approach that integrates local knowledge and practices on trauma healing, forgiveness and reconciliation with western models. KICWA runs a centre that draws on traditional cleansing rituals and reconciliation for abductees. Involving the participation of parents, the extended family and neighbours, this model has produced significant results in re-integrating formerly abducted children back into the community. Considered as locally initiated, both organisations enjoy a high level of confidence and trust from the community, a fact that has seen their relative success compared to programs initiated from outside.

These two organisations receive significant support from outside actors. KICWA is supported financially by the International Rescue Committee, which does not interfere with its modalities of operations. It is a good example of how a valuable partnership between local and international actors could be instituted in a manner that complements rather than weakens one or the other. Its main target group is formerly abducted children and their families, but it also considers other vulnerable groups such as victims of rape and other forms of sexual abuse, communities in distress and individuals who have been affected by continuing violence. More recently, the ARLI has become a critical actor in integrating former abductees back into the society, as noted above.

It seems the scale of problems facing the youth and the former abductees in particular have proven to be a challenge to purely Western or traditional approaches, demanding instead an innovative blend of traditional and non-traditional approaches to address the problems. Whereas international agencies are able to provide technical expertise in this area in the form of expatriates, very little is done to develop or train equally competent local human resources, knowledgeable in traditional rituals and capable of adapting them innovatively as the situation demands.

## Limitation of Developing Local Relief Capacity in Conflict Situations

The humanitarian situation in northern Uganda highlights several challenges relating to the development of local relief capacity in a situation of ongoing emergency.

Foremost, insecurity inhibits the creation and nurturing of local relief capacity. It destroys and limits opportunities for the creating of such capacity. For instance, several traditional healers and elders have been targets of abduction by rebels forcing them to flee their communities ahead of everyone else. With them go their services. District officials and local council members are also targets for attack, thus discouraging any support for government efforts to quell the insurgence.

Secondly, displacement affects a people's mode of production, weakens their ability to sustain their livelihood, turning them into complete dependants of relief aid. While this has a deep psychological impact on the individual, it also affects the capacity of a community to withstand disasters. For instance, movement as well as raiding of Acholi animals has reduced their livestock dramatically, even wiping out entire herds in some areas. This translates into loss of livelihoods or means of survival, and in turn the ability to withstand a disaster or mitigate its consequences. In the face of both the insurgency and Karamajong raids, it is pointless to invest in large herds of cattle, a traditional "insurance" that the Acholi have always resorted to in times of distress. Without a strategic reserve, the Acholi community's vulnerability has been accentuated many-fold.

The inability of actors to venture into insecure areas means relief and development activities are concentrated within the safety of camps, in and around urban centres. This act of exclusion raises several dilemmas for actors. Is safety for humanitarian agencies primary to that of victims of disasters? Insecurity has also forced agencies to focus on small-scale, targeted assistance, which does not go beyond the immediate needs in an ad hoc manner. By extension, assistance hardly promotes any sustainable capacity, which leads to a second question: Is such targeting of assistance justifiable?

Even though there is some partnership with local NGOs and organisations, on the whole, very little community participation is encouraged or cultivated. As a result there is a loss in terms of drawing on local knowledge and ownership of the intervention. This has much to do with the limited time frame of the projects and limited financial resources, both of which inhibit a process-based intervention that is necessary for the development of local capacity. The band-aid type intervention many save lives but cannot strengthen the capacity of the community through recovery of livelihoods.

## Conclusion

The complex situation in northern Uganda presents real challenges and dilemmas for the creation of local capacity. The most difficult is that of the highly uncertain security environment and the devastating consequences it has had on the lives of the population. The development of local capacity for relief presupposes an enabling socio-economic environment and positive political will, ready to facilitate the building of an asset-base that can tide a community through crises. The assumption is that there are periods during which this has been possible. For North Central Uganda, these periods have been few in the last decade, due to the emergency, and not enough to allow for recovery of livelihoods through the exploitation of the area's high agricultural potential. Even if enough resources were to be mobilised for the regeneration of livelihoods, these are useless if there is no certainty as to whether the insurgency will end once and for all. Developing local capacity in a highly unpredictable and uncertain environment is no mean feat, especially when investors and also planners are discouraged by the fact that long-term implementation cannot be guaranteed. The dilemma is how to stimulate recovery of livelihoods and savings when the targets of the insurgency are these very assets. In fluid situations such as the one in northern Uganda, the challenge is to develop new asset bases or (local) economies that are beyond the reach of insurgents and which communities can fall back on in times of crisis.

The "spiritual" nature of the insurgency (in the memory of the residents) and the insecure environment it has birthed have shaken the once familiar local cosmology, putting to the test existing knowledge systems on responding to war and crises of this nature (Finnström, 1999). Traditional mechanisms per se would be rendered ineffective by the socio-cultural, economic and political transformation that the insurgency has wrought unless there is a replacement of the social capital lost with one able to address the new life challenges. Years of neglect in developing human resources, in terms of skills and expertise, coupled with migration out of the region have created a lost generation.

The second dilemma is that ensuring peace in northern Uganda is closely tied to a cease-fire in southern Sudan. The challenge here is to move local initiatives beyond the borders. In particular, there is a critical need to initiate peace activities in southern Sudan, in a type of a movement that complements government initiatives in Uganda. The recent effort by the ARLI to involve their counterparts in southern Sudan in the search for peace is a step in the right direction. This effort needs to be multiplied in other sectors, among women groups, youth groups and government actors. Where peace is concerned, the government and Western donor community (both governmental and non-governmental) approaches have been found wanting. The challenge is whether these different knowledge systems and the different political wills are capable of finding creative ways of working together towards sustainable peace. A peaceful northern Uganda is a first step towards fostering an environment critical to the sustainability of other factors necessary to ensure local capacity for relief. It goes beyond just bringing the current insurgency to an end; it means addressing the years of economic marginalisation and neglect that characterise a region with the potential for producing food for the entire country. Such a rational proposition requires international humanitarian actors to move beyond the conventional dichotomy between assistance and protection, which they seem stuck on in dealing with North Central Uganda.

**Table 2. Government Response to the Humanitarian Problem in the North**

| Government Actor/Programme | Type of Intervention | Target | District Coverage |
|---|---|---|---|
| District Security Committee | Ensure security | Local population and refugees | Adjumani, Apac, Arua, Gulu, Kitgum, Lira, Masindi, Lira, Masindi, Moyo |
| District Disaster Manage-ement Committee | Relief: non-food and food items | IDPs | Apac, Kitgum, Gulu |
| Ministry of Local Government | Relief: non-food and food items | IDPs, refugees | Adjumani |
| Uganda People's Defence Forces | Rescue of abductees, debriefing of abductees, protecting the community | Child abductees | Kitgum, Gulu |
| District Hospitals Arua, Gulu, Lira, Adjumani, Moyo | Mental health treatment and education | Mentally affected | Arua, Lira, Gulu, Adjumani, Moyo |
| District Medical Officer | Health care | Residents, refugees, IDPs | Adjumani, Apac, Arua, Gulu, Lira, Masindi, Moyo |
| Gulu/Lacor Hospitals | | IDPs, refugees | Gulu |
| Kalongo/St Joseph's Hospitals | | IDPs, refugees | Kitgum |
| Ministry of Education | Universal primary school education | IDPs, refugees, communities | Gulu, Kitgum, Lira, Masindi, Moyo |
| Community Action Programme (CAP) | School construction, temporary shelters Credit scheme and agricultural implements | Children in refugee and IDP camps, veterans, rape victims, camp residents | Adjumani, MoyoPo |
| Poverty Alleviation Programme (PAPSCA) | School construction, temporary shelters, credit scheme | Children in refugee and IDP camps | Kitgum, Lira |
| Poverty Alleviation Programme (PAP) | Credit scheme and agricultural implements | | Apac, Gulu, Masindi, Moyo Gulu |
| Northern Uganda Reconstruction Programme (NURP) | Credit scheme and agricultural implements | Veterans, camp followers, peasants volunteers | |

Source: Republic of Uganda/UNICEF, 1998.

# 8. Humanitarianism and Spoils Politics in Somalia

*Joakim Gundel*

This chapter considers international humanitarian assistance to Somalia in the context of political changes of Somali society brought on by the conflict in the first half of the 1990s. In contrast to the local capacity issues raised in the other case studies, the analysis of humanitarian action in Somalia focuses on the linkages between the practice of humanitarian agencies and the political transformations in Somalia after the state collapsed. These interactions are examined in the context of the growing debate about the possible negative impact of humanitarian assistance in situations of civil strife. Local capacity issues are raised more indirectly in terms of the interactions between foreign aid agencies and Somali structures of power and authority.

The problems of delivering humanitarian assistance in armed conflicts are now widely acknowledged in the literature and by practitioners (Cremer, 1998; Gundel, 1999; Prendergast, 1997; Fennell, 1998; Maren, 1997). As indicated in Chapter 1, the discussion is reasonably advanced in terms of exploring the moral and practical implications of rendering humanitarian assistance in a conflict situation, particularly with respect to unintended, negative consequences. Yet many studies are founded on inadequate knowledge of the historical and socio-political dynamic of the situation. As a result, conclusions tend to be rhetorical and unhelpful, such as acknowledging that assistance may do harm, but that doing nothing will do greater harm (Pirotte, Husson and Grunewald, 1999). Better understanding would improve both analysis and practice. One important reason why humanitarian aid may actually exacerbate the conflict whose victims it is designed to assist, is that aid actors are ignorant about the origins and dynamic of the strife (African Rights, 1997). It is increasingly recognised that understanding the links between the political dynamic of a complex political emergency, on the one hand, and humanitarian aid interventions, on the other, is necessary to developing effective aid strategies and guidelines for conducting relief operations (Cremer, 1998; Cliffe and Luckham, 1999). Until now, few empirical studies have sought to document these linkages by analysing how humanitarian assistance figures in the political economy of the local conflict. While individual links admittedly are difficult to trace, the general pattern of aid and conflict interaction can more readily be established.

Many of the dilemmas in what amounts to an ethical and moral crisis of international humanitarianism are found in the Somali experience in the early 1990s. The Somalia case reflects the conjuncture of several factors: the simultaneous collapse of the state and the economy, the prevalence of spoils politics, and a massive injection of international humanitarian assistance. As a result, massive resources were fed into a conflict area, producing numerous negative effects as well as some positive ones.

This chapter argues that while there were significant achievements in terms of saving lives, the same assistance contributed to the evolution of political structures of violence (warlordism). In effect, a system of structural violence emerged, characterised by institutionalised inequalities of status, rights and power. As noted in other situations of structural violence, the system was largely the result of coercive actions undertaken by the more powerful groups in society (Uvin, 1998:104). It served to block changes in Somali politics and society that could foster a stable connection between society and whatever political authorities the Somalis seem to need. Central to this blocking process is the relationship between the aid-conflict dynamic and the international structure of state-sovereignty.

Four dimensions seem particularly significant in the aid–conflict dynamic. The externalities of food and other aid distributions with conflict potentials clearly played into the system of Somali "spoils politics". The establishment of local security arrangements and the phenomena of "clan-ownership" further legitimated certain faction leaders and marginalising other actors with different agendas, hence supporting a political structure of violence. The policies of partnership and the use of sub-contracting to local NGOs undermined local sovereignty while encouraging patronisation and disempowerment. Finally, peace and governance building efforts reinforced the context of "extreme localisation of politics".

To examine how the agencies and the resources they brought into the conflict worked in the Somali political context, it is useful to distinguish analytically between traditional humanitarian assistance (the provision of emergency relief such as food, shelter, health and water) and political assistance called "peacemaking" such as reconciliation, reconstruction of governance structures and the reestablishment of civil security. Protection of relief supplies may be seen as an auxiliary to these activities, necessitated by a high level of insecurity. "Peacemaking" involves an explicit political engagement and often the deployment of police and military forces. All of the above activities were undertaken within the framework of UNOSOM from 1992 until 1995, when the last contingents left Somalia.

## Somali Politics: Clannism and Spoils Politics

Somaliland departs from the acknowledgment that clannism is a fact
(Mohammed Gees, Ministry of Planning, Government of the Republic of Somaliland).

One of the difficulties in understanding Somali (and African) politics for a Western mind is the artificiality of our conceptual separation between the state and society when applied to a non-Western context such as Somalia (Doornbos and Markakis, 1994). The defining characteristic of the modern state is based on the Weberian idea of it being separate from the economy and civil society. But, as in many other African countries, the Somali post-colonial state construction embodied a duality. Formal state institutions were created to reflect the specific modern relationship between state and society, in particular the assumed emancipation of the modern institutions from the social processes of the wider society (Chabal and Daloz, 1998). In practice, as elsewhere in Africa, Somali communities established their own informal ways of tying state and society together (Gundel, 1995:19–22). Thus, instead of emancipating the state from society, exclusive client networks with their own logic of exchange were brought into the functioning of government and state institutions. Instead of the state becoming emancipated, it became an exclusive arena of political competition restricted to the newly educated national and urbanized elites. These elites were themselves bound by their clan affiliations and related obligations, but could manipulate clan ties as well to support their own political ambitions. Hence, the political game in Somalia became one of competing client networks with a social basis in the various clan families.

## The Segmented Political Nature of Clannism

Clannism is seen as the most important constituent social factor in Somali politics, and is generally believed to be at the core of any explanation of Somali political dynamics. I. M. Lewis wrote in 1961 that "the segmented clan system remains the bedrock foundation of pastoral Somali society and 'clannishness'—the primacy of clan interests—is its natural divisive reflection on the political level" (Lewis, 1961). In this sense the rationality of clannism is also the most important basis for the logic and dynamics of the Somali polity (or polities). While clannishness pervades the political system in Somalia, its segmented nature has the potential of creating instability (Menkhaus and Prendergast, 1995). Thus, the social context of politics in Somalia cannot be understood without reference to clannism (UNDP, 1998:36).

Somalia is often regarded as an ethnically homogenous society. While reflecting the commonality of language, culture, religion and ethnic genealogical descent, the notion disregards the differences among clans. The Somali clan structure is often depicted as in Diagram 1 below, which shows the six main clan "families", or "societies" (Simons, 1998). The homogeneity might be true for the main nomadic clan families of Darod, Hawiye, Isaaq and Issa, but not so much for the groups found in the inter-riverine area of Somalia known today as the Rahanwein, or Digil and Mirifle communities. In a different category, the so-called Bantu groups, like the Gosha, who historically have been placed in a slave-like relationship in Somali society, do not share the genealogical history of the nomadic Somali clans. The Bantus is the name the Somali nomads give the Africans who were imported as slaves a few centuries ago. Other groups which fall out of the homogeneous picture of Somalis are the Bajunis and Barawanis and other coastal peoples who are historically and genealogically connected to their Swahili cousins further south on the Eastern African coast and in the Arabic sultanate of Oman.

**Diagram 1: The Somali clan system with the six main families and some sub-clans**

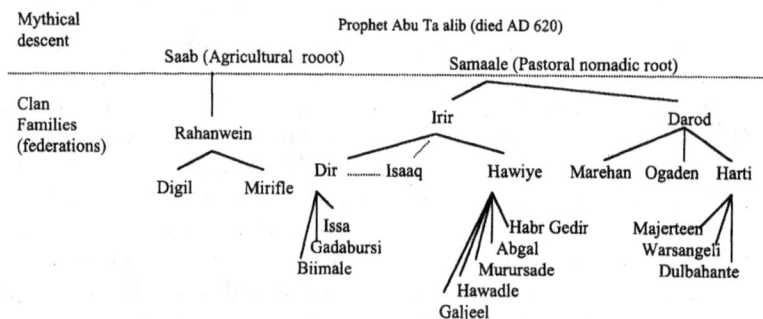

Note: The mentioned clan families are only the main and dominant ones. The diagram should not be taken as complete or factual, as the Somali clan structure is highly potential and contentious and any grafical attempts to describe it tends to be subject to political dispute.

To understand the transformation of Somali polities, it is necessary at the outset to set aside the notion that the original structures of Somali society survived the imperialist period intact (Doornbos and Markakis, 1994). Rather, traditional society should be seen as being constituted historically as a social construction resulting from the interaction between colonialism and the reaction of pre-colonial societies.

By establishing patron-client networks and relations with local chiefs, elders or other authorities, the colonial state facilitated and legitimized its administrations. In British Somaliland, this involved the level of clan-based chiefs like the "Ugaas" and the "Aqiil". These are at a lower level in the Somali clan system, but are extremely important because they control the diya paying groups (diya means blood payment, which is the compensation paid by one family to another family for an offence committed). In this perspective, modern clannism appears as an elite creation based on the most manipulable clan entities. Such clannism emerges out of the competition between elite groups in their efforts to build a social foundation for a conservative modernization process (Berman, 1998). Clannism is thus only primordial in the sense of reflecting kinship relations, language and common cultural traditions, which in turn are based on the communal mode of production. Clan life is governed by cultural and political norms and institutions such as the reer (the smallest clan family unit) and xeer (a social contract between the reer outlining the size of diya to settle a compensation issue), which regulate intra- and inter-clan relations and conflicts. But, clans (and sub-clans, sub-sub-clans etc.) are only instrumental as long as they serve specific individual and/or group interests. A positive element of the clan institution is that it maintains the traditional nomadic values of equity and balance (SCPD, 1999). When sharp asymmetries in inter-clan relations occur, as during the Siad Barre regime, a struggle to re-establish a new balance ensues.

Clannism alone, however, cannot explain recent Somali political history, including the implosion of the state in the early 1990s. Elite manipulation of the clans is one factor for the assertion of clannism, but not its only cause (Adam, 1992). Whether the dynamic of clannism originated in traditional nomadic Somali society, or arose during the colonial period, it is generally agreed that clannism matured with the imposition and evolution of the modern and fundamentally alien western state form. Its recent manifestations must therefore be understood in relation to other political mechanisms, particularly "spoils politics". According to Menkhaus, the Somali clan system is inherently centrifugal, easily fragmenting into sub-clans and sub-sub-clans (cited in Prendergast, 1997:93). When combining with spoils politics, its ultimate form was the total fragmentation of the state and perpetual instability of society.

## The Notion of Spoils Politics

Chris Allen's (1995) notion of spoils politics seems to fit recent Somali history quite well. As elsewhere in Africa, clientelism, understood as personal networks of political dependants built up by politicians, underpinned the relationship between state and society in Somalia. Patron-client networks became ever more profound during the economic crisis of the 1980s as the general sense of insecurity that left people with no option other than relying on their kin (clans) and the patron-client networks for survival as well as enrichment. The result was the production of unstable political regimes characterized by their personalized, materialistic and opportunistic nature (Chazan et al., 1999).

The combination of clientelism and clannism in Somalia generated corruption, which underscored the necessity of being part of the right network (Marchal, 1996:26). Elite networks used and abused the state. When Siad Barre no longer could feed his client-networks through the management of central-bureaucratic policies, spoils politics appeared in full force (Allen, 1995). The crisis of clientelism in Somalia broke out into open conflict when those excluded from power tried to avoid permanent exclusion by utilizing existing or potential communal divisions. Local differences between, for instance, clan-based groups became politicized and could turn into communal conflicts. An increase in repression and violence followed.

The clientelist crisis was first solved by the seizure of power by Siad Barre in 1969. By centralizing power in the hands of an executive president, he briefly resolved the political crisis caused by the clannist proliferation of political parties that had taken place during the 1960's. Using the office of president Barre effected a centralized regulation of clientelist competition. In the exclusive clannist context of Somalia, this only proved possible as long as the president had the resources enabling him to control the game. When external support ceased, it became apparent that the clientelist crisis in Somalia had remained unsolved, and a raw form of spoils politics surfaced (Marchal, 1996:24–32). In 1991, Barre's reign came to an end.

In the words of Chris Allen, "spoils politics can be seen as an extreme version of clientelist crisis, going as far as the complete breakdown of the system, and the abandonment of all restraint" (Allen, 1995). In Somalia, the unresolved clientelist crisis took the form of state collapse, crude military repression, counter-insurgencies, and decentralized, clan-based violence. The mentality, or social-psychology, of spoils politics may continue in its ultimate form after total state collapse such as in the case of Southern and Central Somalia, where it continues to be part of the conflict.

## The Political Dynamics of the Somali Conflict

When Siad Barre came to power in 1969 he claimed that the new socialist system would do away political clannism and construct a modern Somalia. In reality, however, Siad Barre entrenched his power on an increasingly narrow clan-base, that of his father's Marehan group and his mother's Ogaden clan. Others were increasingly marginalised from power, especially the Isaaq who had felt cheated by the Southern clans ever since the unification of Somaliland and Somalia right after independence in 1961, and the Majerteen and Hawiye clan groups which predominantly inhabited some of the most arid parts of the country. The economic crisis and political uncertainty in the late 1970's and throughout the 1980's exacerbated these divisions. People turned to their kin for support and internal trust while searching for new external alliances. That put enormous pressure on the traditional norms and rules that formerly regulated intra and inter-group relations. When the regime and government of Siad Barre finally collapsed in 1991, Somalia, as a nation, was cast into a seemingly indefinite process of political, social and economic disintegration, in the process revealing how Barre had sown new seeds for clan-based conflict (Prendergast, 1997:93).

The resulting political-administrative vacuum combined with clan-based political fragmentation to produce chaotic and violent conflicts between clans, clan-factions and their armed militia. Almost all government and local government institutions literally ceased to exist and their material forms were physically demolished. Somali politics and social authority have since been described as shifting and highly fluid (UNDP, 1998:36). A variety and shifting sets of actors moved into the sudden institutional vacuum of governing institutions. Most noticeable were the main factions in Mogadishu under the leadership of General Aideed and Ali Mahdi respectively. Other principal political forces were various political (clan-based) factions, traditional elders, militias (clan, factional, "free-lance" and bandits), Islamic groups and movements, business people, professional associations, intellectuals, leaders of local non-governmental organizations, "civil-society" associations, and women's groups. It was indeed a mosaic of political actors, traditional and ad hoc institutions that emerged in the void left by the collapse of the state. In this new situation, people had to rely entirely on their local and traditional forms of governance and political interaction for survival. In 1991–92, that applied above all to those places where there was little or no fighting; elsewhere, some measure of ad hoc stability and security was established based on various combinations of traditional authorities, clan-based militias, local governors elected during the UNOSOM period and Islamic courts (Gundel, 2000).

The "structural impediments to the resuscitation of central authority" were formidable (Prendergast, 1997:93). The centrifugal forces became dominating and perpetuated themselves. Spoils politics appeared to complement the phenomenon of clannism. The context in which large amounts of humanitarian assistance were introduced was thus shaped by several important dynamics, which had taken an extreme form during the Barre period:

— "The winner takes all" principle implies that the winning and dominant political faction tries to deny access to resources to all other factions. Sharing of political leadership is nearly unthinkable, as evidenced by the numerous, failed peace agreements. The principle also clashes with a traditional Somali sense of equity, producing a deadly combination of antagonistic conflicts.

— Corruption—understood as the use of public office for private (personal or sectional) gain—was visible in the gross abuse of state resources, and of international assistance and food aid that was used to buy up land (Marchal, 1996). This kind of economy continued during the conflict when UNOSOM and the humanitarian agencies were targeted. Looting of everything perceived to be "public" during the conflict is a derivation of this phenomenon.

— Growing competition within the political elite for access to/sharing in spoils undermines economic development. There is no public dynamic, only private interest in maintaining the status quo.

— Spoils politics does not possess any effective means of preventing mass discontent, or of mediating between discontented groups. In the absence of modern institutions to function as mediators, the traditional authorities are legitimate and in Somalia offer perhaps the only means of re-establishing political institutions for mediation and conflict resolution.

— Clannism is the primary basis for political mobilization of factional activities, equivalent to communalism in other societies.

The dynamic of Somali politics is further shaped by the relationship between clan members and their "politicians", as the Somalis usually call the people of their group who are engaged in politics for personal or clan gain. It is further necessary to distinguish between the "political clan"—the politically organized clan-based faction, which may be led by a businessman or warlord—and the clan-family in itself, as well as between the traditional leaders (religious and so-called famous clan elders) and the "politicians" who may call themselves elders, but in reality do not enjoy that status.

The skills and attributes attached to these persons are central both to their success and to our understanding of Somali politics. For instance, a strong political individual may create an opposition against an incumbent faction leader, or group of political clan leaders, by manipulating their sub-clans. The nature of the relationship between the "political leaders" of the political clans and the clan-families is difficult to determine. It seems, however, that the clans very rarely can defy their traditional leaders, presumably due to the weight of traditions and inherited norms. On the other hand, all leaders seem to aspire to the fullest possible power, probably reflecting the rules of spoils politics. The differences between clan-leaderships are mostly of personality, and to a lesser extent of the nature and history of the specific clans they represent.

The humanitarian emergency in Somalia developed with the new factions seemingly paying little attention to meeting the increasingly desperate needs of the people. Humanitarian concerns seemed overshadowed by their primary ambition to capture the Somali state, rather than to transform and develop it. As Bryden and Steiner have written: "For Somalia's emergent warlords, government meant little more than access to state resources—principally those associated with international recognition and foreign aid" (Bryden and Steiner, 1998:15).

## Humanitarian Assistance in the Somali Conflict

The final war against Siad Barre commenced in 1990 when Mohammed Farah Aideed led the United Somali Congress (USC) militias from Ethiopia down along the Shabelle River and the Belet Weine–Mogadishu highway towards the capital. After the ousting of Siad Barre on 27 January 1991, the war moved after him along the Mogadishu–Baidoa highway, across the Bay region, and through Middle Juba and Gedo regions. From that point on the war moved back and forth from the Kenyan border and Kismayo, across the Juba and Bay regions to Mogadishu and back several times. Each time the mainly "Bantu" agriculturalists and the Rahanwein agropastoralists were assaulted, plundered, raped and displaced. These groups had no defences and no militias. As a result, their harvest and storage rooms were plundered, and new crops could not be planted. Thus the seeds of the coming famine were sown. This movement of warfare and pillaging up and down the fertile riverine areas along the Shabelle and Juba rivers, as well as between them, was to be repeated several times throughout the 1990s.

The ensuing complex political emergency is often divided into three distinct phases, distinguished by the character, magnitude and approaches of the international humanitarian responses. If the conflict were to be divided with reference to internal political and military phases it would probably be a different periodisation. However, the impact of the United Nations was so immense that in retrospect its role is seen as the main demarcation factor.

The conflict shifted in intensity and was punctuated by long periods of relative stability. 1991 and 1992 were the major emergency years, after that only the El Niño flooding in 1997–1998 produced a countrywide emergency. As the conflict changed, so did the approaches of international agencies to providing assistance (Yannis, 1999). A brief discussion of the conflict according to the three periods customarily used is therefore useful at the outset.

### Three Phases of the Conflict

*January 1991–December 1992: Civil War and Humanitarian Emergency*
The first phase from January 1991 to December 1992 was characterised by high intensity fighting resulting in mass displacements and famine, mainly in the inter-riverine area. The international response was dominated by a few international NGOs

that stayed on despite the difficult circumstances. Because of the extremely volatile and insecure conditions, the international community disengaged entirely from Somalia in 1991 except for a few international non-governmental organisations (INGOs) (Refugee Policy Group 1994:14–15). All international UN and NGO staffs as well as diplomatic missions were evacuated between 7 and 9 January 1991. Only Médecins Sans Frontières (MSF) and the International Committee of the Red Cross (ICRC) returned to Mogadishu. The United Nations Children's Fund (UNICEF) was not authorised to reopen its office in Mogadishu until December 1991. However, UNICEF, UNHCR, ICRC and a few NGO relief agencies such as CARE International, International Medical Corps (IMC), Save the Children Fund (SCF) and German Emergency Doctors (GED) continued to work in Northern Somalia and a few other places. These agencies contributed considerable assistance under very difficult conditions throughout 1991 and 1992.

The United Nations Development Office for Somalia UNDOS) estimated that about 350,000 Somalis died from the combination of civil war and famine in the 1991–92 period. Clan conflicts and banditry contributed to the difficulties faced by the humanitarian agencies. The humanitarian agencies contributed to the difficulties themselves as well, for example. by negotiating to get relief supplies through military checkpoints, and hiring "technicals" (heavily armed pick-up trucks) to accompany relief convoys.

The pictures of war and starvation in Somalia did not attract much international attention until well into 1992. Intense lobbying by humanitarian workers was necessary to get journalists to go to Somalia. As a result, the United Nations established in April the United Nations Operation in Somalia UNOSOM). This was a humanitarian intervention limited to relief aid. Insecurity and other difficulties in distributing assistance persisted in 1992, forcing the agencies to employ alternative ways of delivering aid, including cross-border channels, small ports and beach landings.

When the assistance intervention was finally undertaken, it was inappropriate because of two policy-related reasons. First, fluctuating needs assessments, which ranged from "thousands" of starving Somalis to 4.5 million, hampered appropriate and timely assistance. As a result, appeals were formulated and aid donated on the basis of wide speculations, but aid was justified anyway on the assumption that the needs would exceed any possible emergency aid no matter what (Tin, 1999:8–9). The second problem was related to a fundamental error in determining the cause of the famine. The famine was often attributed to drought rather than the conflict, and frequent references to the Ethiopian famine gave misleading suggestions for the reasons for starvation (Tin, 1999:10–11; Netherlands Development Cooperation, 1994:72, 93). The international community consequently focused on providing relief to the starving Somalis, especially through food supplies, rather than addressing the violent conflict. This incorrect analysis also influenced the military intervention in December 1992. Rather than addressing the conflict itself, for instance. by disarming the militias, the intervention was initially designed as a "humanitarian operation" to ensure the relief supplies reached the victims. Eventually the intervention became embroiled in the conflict nevertheless.

*December 1992–March 1995: A Complex Political Emergency*
In 1991 and 1992 the international community was focusing on the Gulf War and its aftermath. A change in United States internal politics led to an initiative in Somalia in late 1992, and UNOSOM was replaced in December 1992 with a humanitarian military intervention under UN auspices—the United Nations Task Force (UNITAF) and the US-led Operation Restore Hope. This second phase lasted from

December 1992 until March 1995. UNITAF was replaced by UNOSOM II in May 1993, which was given the responsibility of establishing a transitional government for Somalia and facilitating humanitarian assistance. Instead, a military confrontation developed between the US military contingents and Somalia warlord factions, the situation worsened, and the crisis took on the shape of a "complex political emergency". On 31 March 1995 UNOSOM II was called off due to the high economic costs of the operation and lack of political success.

*March 1995– : Post-Intervention Amnesia*

The third phase may be called the post-intervention or non-intervention period and has lasted since March 1995. The frustrations of the 1992–1995 international intervention led to a sharp reduction in aid (UNDP, 1998:13–14). The role of humanitarian assistance in this phase must be understood in this context of "donor fatigue". When the last UNOSOM staff finally left Mogadishu in March 1995, all the international operations in Somalia was basically run from the new headquarters in Nairobi. A new body was set up with the promising goal of promoting a humanitarian assistance programme that was more responsive to Somali needs and concerns. However, the new Somali Aid Coordination Body (SACB) gave a prominent role to the donor community, especially the European Union. As a result, the SACB has been characterised by donor fatigue with Somalia and a debilitating bureaucratic competition among donors.

## The Approaches of Humanitarian Actors and Their Interaction with Local Actors

In the first phase, the INGOs focused only on relief activities that could alleviate the effects of the civil war and the ensuing famine; that is, they were only concerned with the humanitarian imperative of helping the innocent victims of the conflict. This has been called the "mandate blinders" approach (Yannis, 1999; Anderson, 1995). The advantage of this approach is a high degree of efficiency insofar as agencies work with a clear ideological commitment to humanitarianism, unconcerned with any side-effects of their activities. However, as Alexandros Yannis argues, the immediate saving of lives can produce negative side-effects that later can endanger the lives of those it intended to save (Yannis, 1999). While the success of the INGOs in terms of saving lives in the initial stages of the conflict can be attributed to the "mandate blinders" approach, it simultaneously created problematic relationships with the Somalis which were to trouble future humanitarian assistance.

During the second phase, when humanitarian intervention acquired a military and an explicit political dimension, the main focus was on securing the delivery of relief aid and, secondly, on peace-building. At this stage the INGOs appeared far more critical towards the international response, above all with respect to the humanitarian military intervention, but also towards the conduct and ethics of their own activities. The timing and the magnitude of the military intervention in December 1992 also proved inappropriate. As some INGOS and human rights organisations documented at the time, the famine had already peaked in September that year and the death rate had fallen dramatically by November to about one fifth of the September level (African Rights, 1992).

While some INGOs continued on a "mandate blinders" approach, several of the more experienced ones began to realise the negative impact of their strategies in the first phase and started searching for new approaches. Later called the "do no harm" doctrine, the new thinking acknowledged that humanitarian action can have negative side effects and called on the agencies to develop a code of conduct that continuously assesses the impact of their actions and seeks to minimise the negative effects. Efforts in this direction were largely neutralised, however, by UNITAF and UNOSOM II. The military intervention exacerbated the negative effects of the previous approaches and added more problems. The only positive result of the reassessment in the humanitarian aid community was to advance the critical self-awareness of the organisations as well as some of the donor countries, which became increasingly concerned about the impact of their assistance (Netherlands Development Corporation,1994:2).

While the military intervention preventing meaningful application of new approaches, an innovative process took form at a late stage of UNOSOM II. Jointly undertaken by the donors, UN agencies and the INGOs, it led to the first deliberate and formulated approach for the third phase, called the "peace dividend" approach. This contrasted with previous approaches, which had largely been based on separate agency initiatives rather than joint efforts to formulate a new strategy. The peace dividend approach was elevated into an official strategy by the newly established (1994) Somali Aid Coordination Body (SACB) and incorporation in its "Strategy of the International Aid Community on Humanitarian, Rehabilitation and Development Assistance to Somalia" at its fourth meeting in Rome in May 1997 (SACB, 1999). The approach was based on the idea that international assistance for rehabilitation should be grounded in local initiatives, and that it should be relevant for peace-building. A code of conduct was applied in 1995, which stipulated conditionality of international aid to Somalia to this effect. Problems soon became evident, however. The peace-dividend strategy required, for a start, a sustained commitment by both donors and humanitarian agencies, which was not demonstrated. Somalis were deeply sceptical about the new co-ordinating body, seeing SACB as nothing but a political instrument of the donors.

## The Externalities and Magnitude of Humanitarian Assistance

Borrowed from economics, the term "externalities" here refers to local advantages from a humanitarian presence such as jobs, cars, compounds, guards, rentals etc. The problem of negative externalities exploded in Somalia as the military intervention massively inflated prices for labour, housing, vehicle hire and other local services, paving the way for numerous security incidents and, eventually, serious problems of disengagement caused by dependency on international aid agencies (Yannis, 1999).

Augelli and Murphy, 1995:346 found that by the time multilateral assistance was provided (April 1992), local fighting groups had already appropriated everything. "The war continued to be funded, in part, by rich local traders and by Somalis living abroad, though the former were no longer in a position to support the various militias as much as they had been at the beginning of the conflict. New resources were needed, and they were provided by the international relief agencies." The militias extracted resources from the agencies as bribes or direct payments for letting them operate in their areas of control. This happened in several ways: offices and houses were rented at high prices; armed escorts were hired for protection; relief transports had to pay militias to ensure protection from their own men; food was transported by trucks rented from those who had stolen them from the agencies in the first place; personnel were hired in greater numbers than needed and were overpaid. Augelli and Murphy suggest that fighting groups appropriated "some hundreds of thousands of dollars a month in Mogadishu alone" (1995:347). In the UNOSOM period, rented houses cost 10–12,000 dollars a month, an additional 2,000 dollars was paid per month for each security guard. An armed car, a so-called "technical" cost 300 dollars per day. Considering that at least 100 houses were rented, and about 380 "technicals" were used by the UN agencies and INGOs each day in Mogadishu, business was good. In addition, duties and fees were put on everything including landing fees on planes, cargo, ships entering the port etc. Numerous service contracts were concluded with local Somalis. In one notorious case, a Somali became a millionaire from disposing of the garbage from the UNOSOM compounds. Last, but not least, an estimated 40–80 per cent of all food aid was looted. A paradox of the intervention was found in the distribution of benefits among Somali leaders. While Ali Mahdi was supported politically by UNOSOM, Aideed benefited economically even though US General Howe put a reward on his head. Minutes from a meeting between Ali Mahdi and UNOSOM officials are revealing: Ali Mahdi angrily complains that Aideed is benefiting financially, and is in effect claiming his share of the spoils. UNOSOM responds with a reference to bureaucratic procedures (according to a record of a meeting between Ali Mahdi and Robin Kinloch of UNOSOM, 17 January 1994).

Even in the post-intervention phase, the externalities of aid represent the most direct type of spoils that can be obtained from the international agencies. Action Contre la Faim (ACF) in Mogadishu for instance estimates that they support 5–10,000 people through the infrastructure of their programme in terms of local hiring of people, security guards, cars etc. (ACF, October 1999).

There are no reliable figures on overall aid given to Somalia in the period under consideration, and no systematic data on the externalities of relief aid. Even the Somali Aid Co-ordination Body (SACB) in Nairobi does not have reliable statistics over the aggregate aid flowing into Somalia, citing the problem of collecting comparable data from both donors and implementing agencies. The following figures are the best estimates available, but must be understood as indicative only (DHA, OCHA, 1998, Bradbury and Coultan 1998, Refugee Policy Group 1994). International assistance to Somalia clearly was at its highest level in 1992. There was a sharp increase from 1991 to 1992, as suggested by the leap in US aid. From a modest 29.6 million US$ in humanitarian aid in 1991, official US transfers increased to 95.1 million the following year (Refugee Policy Group, 1994). Aid tapers off rapidly: by 1993 the famine was in reality over and the total amount of aid was 215.4 million, sharply down from the 410.6 million in 1992. By 1994 "normality" had returned and aid levelled at 55.5 million. Since 1994, international assistance to Somalia seems to have stabilised around 50 million dollars annually.[1] It should be noted that not all this money reaches Somalia. A significant proportion is used for Nairobi-based headquarters expenses, salaries to expatriates, external consultancy work and expensive transportation (flights to and from Somalia). Some would estimate that of the resources going to Somaliland, air transportation absorbs more funds than what is allocated for projects (interview with "Jamac" at LPI Hargeysa, May 1999).

By the late 1900s, Somaliland and Puntland received most of the allocated funds to Somalia. A little bit of the peace-dividend was after all benefiting the most deserving. The difference was that Somaliland in fact had a government, and the district

1. The total amount of international aid should be compared with the Human Development Report's estimates on the annual remittances from Somalis abroad, which amount to 300 million US$ annually, livestock exports at 70–80 million US$ annually and finally a rough estimate of the GDP of Somalia as 1,000 million US$ annually.

councils seemed to work. The further implication is that because Somaliland already had in place a political structure that enjoyed a relatively high level of legitimacy and could constrain the international agencies, the latter played a smaller role in the generating of social change here than in the South.

## How the Externalities of Relief Aid Fed into Somali Spoils Politics

The ICRC was the main food provider from early 1991 and onwards. A few other INGOs such as CARE International contributed as well. The Lutheran World Federation (LWF) airlift was started in May 1992 and ran until November 1993. The airlift operation did not interact directly with Somalis on the ground, but mainly transported food and other relief items to the agencies operating in Somalia. ICRC differed from the UN and the other INGOs by basing their distribution on the existing Red Crescent organisation in Somalia, the Somali Red Crescent Society (SRCS). Their interaction with Somalis was primarily through this organisation. ICRC pulled out soon after UNOSOM II came in because they realised that by this time they had accomplished their mission (Netherlands Development Corporation,1994:111–128).

The INGOs were more efficient than the UN agencies, and their efforts contributed significantly to the humanitarian improvements in the famine stricken areas, mainly in the inter riverine area between the Shabelle and Juba rivers, as early as November 1992 (African Rights, 1992:9). By comparison, the UN agencies did poorly, and, except for UNICEF, did not even maintain offices in Somalia. The World Food Programme had by mid-July delivered less than one third of the amount of food they had pledged to do (Sahnoun, 1994). ICRC delivered three times as much in the same period. This was one of the main points of criticism that the UN Special Representative, Mohamed Sahnoun, launched against the UN system, and which eventually led to his resignation. Nevertheless, Sahnoun did facilitate a meeting on October 12, 1992, between the donors, UN Agencies, ICRC and INGOs in Geneva where a new 100-day plan for accelerated relief to Somalia was adopted to replace the former and less successful 90-day plan of April 1992.

The extreme insecurity that followed the civil war and the collapse of the Somali state created major problems for the NGOs operating in the area. They were deliberately targeted by all militia factions as well as by gangs, who in the absence of public security forces could loot them without risk. The INGOs, of course, constituted highly valued prey because of the resources they brought into Somalia in the form of money, cars, expensive equipment and scarce goods such as medicine and food.

As usual, the ICRC perceived its role to be impartial and neutral, which meant a right and an obligation to collaborate with all local power structures. This included negotiating directly with the various warlords, which by some was seen to jeopardise their impartiality. It also caused some friction between the UN and ICRC, raising issues about who had a mandate to negotiate deals with the warlords, and the circumstances of how such talks were conducted.

The lack of security compelled the INGOs to hire armed guards to protect themselves, their cars and the relief items. ICRC hired armed protection for the first time in the history of the organisation. The hired protection at times included heavily armed vehicles known as "technicals", a four-wheel drive size car with an anti-aircraft gun mounted on top. Often most of the INGO budgets went to securing relief supplies and paying for safe access to the people in need, which had to be negotiated with the various factions (Yannis, 1999). The Somalis were not slow to exploit a sit-

uation where the collapse of the state left the INGOs bewildered as to which authorities to interact with. Quickly, systems of payment for security as well as for landing
fees and other forms of fees to be paid by the agencies were invented by those with
the armed power to do so (interviews in Hiran, May 1999).

Payments for privatised security arrangements were in the form of sacks of food,
thus diverting the relief supplies from their intended beneficiaries. Other diversion
techniques existed as well; some had developed before the civil war and blossomed
into complete business operations (Maren, 1997). During the war, such techniques
were utilised by people with a vested interest in perpetuating the conflict to build or
maintain the military capacity of the warring factions. Using the power of the gun,
new gunmen and warring factions filled the vacuum left by the collapsed state and
took over the negotiating positions with INGOs and UN agencies for the modalities
of aid delivery. This power could simultaneously be used to enhance their influence
over the civilian populations in their areas of control. In this way the militia could
achieve two things simultaneously: gaining legitimacy by positioning themselves as
guarantors of relief aid, and obtaining resources for continued warfare.

Another major problem with food aid was the methods of distribution. Because
of the insecurity, food could not be delivered directly to the beneficiaries. It was either distributed by the militias who had looted it, or directly from the gate of the
agencies or through soup kitchens. The poorest people often did not benefit from the
food aid because they lacked the resources and organisation to collect the food at
the gates of the agencies. Nor did they have access to weapons to acquire food directly. It is therefore doubtful how much food actually reached those at the bottom
of the socio-economic hierarchy (interviews in Hargeysa, May 1999, and with ICRC
in Nairobi, October 1999).

In an effort to prevent food aid from ending up with the warlords, ICRC began
to set up soup kitchens. Looting was immediately reduced since it was not so prof-
itable to steal prepared food. Some observers claimed, however, that this strategy
had disastrous effects on local agriculture by making people relocate to the immediate vicinity of the kitchens (Natsios, 1997:88). Most of the kitchens were located in
the area controlled by General Aideed, giving his faction a distinct advantage by ex-
tending its control over additional populations and denying recruits to the other
warlords.

While food aid was not the underlying cause of the Somali conflict, it did result
in additional conflict insofar as supplies became a central object of the fighting. During the big famine and during UNOSOM period, the massive influx of food aid
caused more than localised fighting. The security problems surrounding the distribution of food and relief items were briefly solved by UNITAF, however, and security outside Mogadishu did improve noticeably (interviews in Jowhar, October
1999).

Somali humanitarian workers who worked both in the South and in the North
during the early first phase of the emergency gave fascinating accounts of their experiences in 1990–91 (interviews with SORRA (Somaliland Relief and Rehabilitation Association), IRC and ICD in Hargeysa, May 1999). They told of problems of
delivering food aid in the Northwest (Somaliland) that seems broadly representative
of agency experience in the South as well. Throughout 1990 and 1991, food aid entered Somalia through the port of Berbera, or at a small, old port near Erigavo in the
Sanaag region. Most of that food either never left the region, or was completely looted by local clan militias claiming that what they found was their fair share. However, the Somaliland experience differed from the southern pattern in 1991, after a

shipment of emergency food came to Berbera for distribution by the German Emergency Doctors. All the food destined for Hargeysa was looted by militias from Hargeysa itself, prompting most of the local humanitarian agencies to terminate food aid. This was reinforced by the decision in May 1991 by the government of the newly declared, independent Somaliland that the aid agencies should stop food aid and begin rehabilitation instead. At that time, local merchants brought food in as well but were never targeted by the militias and private food contributions were not looted. The local businessmen were part of the local clan-structure and protected by the norms regulating inter-clan relations—notably the reer and xeer. Militias knew that looting would trigger a serious conflict. At the very least, the responsible clan families had to pay compensation (allowing for a distinction in this connection between clan-militias and the outlaw youngsters or free-lance militias). International aid by contrast was seen as public and thus "free to loot" as it would not trigger inter-clan feuds and lay outside traditional jurisprudence.

International food aid had a very destabilising influence precisely because it was outside the local traditional jurisprudence, the Minister of Planning in Somaliland emphasised (communication with author, May 1999). Food aid was the immediate cause for re-igniting the war in Somaliland. The fighting in 1992–1993 around Berbera was often about food aid. When people had returned to their homes in Somaliland after the SNM (Somali National Movement) victory, very little was left. Businesses and houses had been destroyed, and there were few opportunities for earning an income. When food aid suddenly began to flow in questions arose about who was responsible for the distribution at the local level. The struggle for access to the "public" food aid, in which everyone wanted a share, thus basically led to the war in 1992–1993.

The difference between the North and the South in this respect was that the bonds between the traditional elders in the North, the SNM army, and their mujahid clan-based militias were stronger than the militarised warlord factions in the South, which, however, were richer and relied on the free-lance militias (mooryan) in their quest for power. Furthermore, in the North the free-lance militias (dey dey) were very costly for their clans in terms of compensation payments (diya), producing a genuine interest in controlling them. This factor, combined with the stronger position of tradition and the role of SNM and the mujahid militias in the Somaliland liberation struggle, made it possible to control the emerging warlords in the North.

The lesson of Northern Somalia spread to the international agencies, which by the second half of the 1990s had switched to sub-contracting private Somali merchants for food transportation. In this system, the contractor deposits an amount equivalent to the value of the food, and gets it back together with the payment for the transportation when the food is delivered. The contractor is totally responsible for security and delivery. Contractors use the traditional Somali nomadic means of communicating and securing a convoy into the countryside (Marchal, 1996). The debilitating "public dimension" of the food aid thus is removed, and WFP, CARE International and other agencies do not have to take responsibility when a security incident disturbs a convoy.

Initially the system seemed to work. However, the context in the South is different from the North. Traditional authority and practice is not as strong, and the competition among fragmented business-groups, sub-clans and factions is intense. Security incidents, killing and fighting over food transportation, were on the increase during 1999. One of the reasons is that the transports become the focal element in the ongoing feuds between the factions and business groups, and between their sub-clans. This reveals a mismatch between the sensible principle of tendering the contracts, and the real conditions on the ground. The contractor may be good, cheap and reliable. But he may be a Warsangeli sub-clan of the Hawiye clan group, and the Warsangeli are feuding with the Abgal, and the transport has to pass Abgal land. Similarly, most of the contracts go to Hawiye business people in Mogadishu or Merca. But the Rahanwein recipients find it difficult to accept that the transport of food meant for them has to be contracted out to their enemies.

Another reason for the different patterns of food aid in the North and the South relates to the need for assistance. As the need was less in the North than in the South, it was easier for the authorities to reject inappropriate food aid. By the end of the decade, the general opinion in the North is that free food is no good when it is not really needed (Interview with SORRA, 1999). The best solution is that the clans can support their members who are forced to flee, utilising traditional coping mechanisms. The difference between North and South in this respect is again instructive. The North is predominantly nomadic, which means that the people can cope more easily during drought and conflict than the predominantly agro-pastoralist populations in Southern Somalia. In the South, far more people want food aid, which reflects their more insecure position relative to the North and, importantly, the fact that food aid in the harsh economic conditions of the South represents a major business opportunity.

Nevertheless, the experience of humanitarians with delivering food aid in Somaliland was that it did create immediate instability because it occurred in the absence of conditions of law and order. This suggests that in the initial stage of a complex political emergency it is more important to establish some kind of stable security regime than to provide food. Security in Somaliland slowly improved after the consolidation of the new Somaliland Republic and its law enforcement mechanisms took effect following the Borama conference in 1993 (IRC, May 1999). Today EU-food is transported safely through Somaliland to Ethiopia.

Aid workers in Northern Somalia interviewed by this author in May 1999, showed that most found food subsidies to be undesirable because they create dependency structures. Yet, they conceded that food aid in acute emergencies and for a very short term may be necessary. Somali aid workers are very aware about the dilemmas of emergencies. In the midst of violent conflict, there are only two options: not to give food, or to give food with all the negative implications of doing that. Not giving food to displaced populations threatened by famine will conflict with a basic humanitarian imperative, even though the likely negative consequences are known. To react only when the emergency is ongoing, however, is too late. Dumping food in such a situation in Somalia only made things worse. An important lesson here is the need to have good early warning systems in place, and to react in good time.

The dilemmas of delivering food aid apply to other areas of assistance as well. For instance the Sheikh Hospital in Somaliland was completely looted by militias for "monetisation" (interviews, IRC May 1999). Food and seeds in the food sector, "sexy drugs" in the health sector, and motorised pumps in the water and sanitation sector were looted. The looting contributed to a culture of bribery and extortion and was silently accepted by the INGOs at large (interviews, IFRC Nairobi September 1999). The militias were selling looted food at low prices. There was a trade-off for security, which continued in the South: food, fuel and vehicles created more insecurity in the context of extreme conflict, according to local NGO staff (interviews, Candle Light, Hargeysa, 1999).

Drugs and other health-service equipment have a very high local social value since more than money is required to utilise such goods. Expertise and knowledge in using the equipment are necessary. Politically, providing health assistance generates support and legitimacy. Merca hospital is a case in point, where the power of the NGO IIDA/COSV proved stronger than the "warlord" Hussein Aideed, according to Merca staff. If a warlord or a "politician" can attract assistance of vital importance for survival, it can be used as leverage for political ambitions. An important consequence of this—which also was encouraged by the emphasis in the international NGO community on using local capacity and local civil society—was that warlords, politicians and businessmen became very active in establishing NGOs. The strategy had many advantages. NGOs became a means of channelling aid money to their own factions, and could be used to increase the popularity and legitimacy of particular persons who at the same time were part of the clientelist network of a faction or a warlord.

An unfair distribution of resources may generate conflict, especially in the Somali context where highly egalitarian norms concerning what is perceived as public goods prevail. Transparency is important as well, and applies to authorities, communities, NGOs as well as the donors, foreign NGO staff in the area point out. During the emergency, suspicions often focused on the international aid agencies because they were believed to engage in unfair distribution. Lack of transparency contributed to rumours and suspicion. UN volunteers were often young and inexperienced, which could be disastrous in a conflict. In Mogadishu, for instance, numerous foreign aid staff were quite young. Local professionals, by contrast, were not given a sufficient role to play by the international agencies.

It is clear from the Somalia experience that the distribution of the externalities of assistance can cause a lot of trouble. Most communities expect a very careful distribution of such assets. If not, problems may arise, and—under certain local conditions—may trigger an armed conflict. That is why a former aid worker says: "Don't bring food, cars and fuel." At some point INGOs did stop bringing in their own cars etc. and started renting local cars and security arrangements. This required careful negotiations and knowledge about local clan relations and balances. Knowledge about clan-arithmetic becomes particularly important when armies and militias have few, if any, sources of income other than humanitarian assistance.

## Local Security Arrangements and "Clan-Ownership"

While no longer a problem in the North, security is a fundamental issue in Southern and Central Somalia. During the emergency, local security arrangements with international agencies reinforced community dependence on the militias for security and income and became an integral part of the vicious cycle of socio-political instability. Foreign NGO staff noted important differences in local security arrangements depending upon who were hired: clan militias or the freelance *mooryan* or *dey dey* militias. By just accepting the pressure of local communities to hire security packages and the conditions laid out (usually a package of four guards with a car), the agencies contributed to the structures of violence. One of the reasons is that the militias were not members of any organised force or company that controlled them when they were out of contract. Another is that the agencies seldom committed themselves in a region on a long-term basis, and thus did not invest in long term solutions. That is in fact a bi-product of the international community's categorisation of Somalia as a complex emergency. The implication is that the agencies think and work as if they are in an emergency, even when they are not (interviews, ICD May 1999, Merca October 1999).

UNITAF did create a secure space for humanitarian assistance during the three months the operation lasted. However, it was criticised for being an inappropriate intervention and for not immediately disarming the Somalis, as most Somalis actually expected (Refugee Policy Group, 1994). Security conditions gradually worsened after UNOSOM II took over from UNITAF. This was partly was due to unclear mandates and unclear command structures. UNITAF was under the sole leadership of the United States, while UNOSOM II was a multinational force without a clear leadership. The Americans insisted on having a say in UNOSOM II, which antagonised several of the European contingents (Clarke and Herbst, 1997:239–250). Furthermore, the humanitarian approaches of the INGOs, and to a lesser extent the humanitarian UN agencies as well, clashed with the ethics of military intervention and the military wing of UNOSOM II. For instance the military intervention in Kismayo only made security problems worse for MSF-Belgium, which was running the local hospital, and led to further deterioration in relations between the local population and the humanitarian agencies working there.

Nevertheless, UNOSOM II had provided the humanitarian agencies with some general security structures, which disappeared when the mission was terminated in 1995. The most common solution seemed to be to fall back to the pre-UNOSOM kind of security arrangements with local Somali militias. The agencies either hired their own guards with cars etc., or they found a local NGO partner which was on good terms with the local de facto authorities, that is, the traditional elders and/or the warlord who happened to dominate at the time. Either way, the combined dynamics of clannism and factional spoils politics meant that the INGOs had to respect these authorities and co-operate with them. Under the prevailing security conditions, project managers felt compelled to give in to the pressure from clans to hire their people, contractors, security arrangements, compounds, cars etc. This played into the system of spoils politics and contributed to extreme competition in this field as well. Inevitably, the INGOs were was shattered by the reality on the ground. For one thing, an INGO could not work in neighbouring districts or regions if these were perceived to be controlled by an enemy clan. Rumours started to circulate suggesting that the only reason why the INGOs chose to come and operate in a hostile Somali environment was economic self-interest. Why else would they want to be in a hostile environment?

The INGOs themselves would not admit to clan ownership. There were good reasons for concentrating in one area. All INGOs could not operate throughout Somalia, and there was an efficiency rationale in focusing on one area. Working in a conflict where one side would not like the organisation to work on the other side creates strong incentives to comply. Nevertheless, a belligerent that perceives the adversary receives more support from a given humanitarian agency than itself may decide to target and attack the agency. By working on only one side of a conflict, the agency will definitely be associated with that faction or that clan.

Many humanitarian agencies did not use traditional authorities as partners, despite the many good reasons for doing so. It is, in fact, wise to address the local elders on all matters of doubt concerning rentals, hiring and any aspect of operations. The elders can give advice so as to prevent conflict, misunderstandings and other trouble. It is especially important that the security arrangements are clarified with them because security arrangements usually play into the hands of the militias. If the elders do not have full control over them, which is the case in many places of Southern and

Central Somalia where they have lost such authority, security arrangements may contribute to keeping the local communities under the domination of the militias. Care also has to be taken with elders, because not all of them are elders by virtue of their specific position in the traditional clan system, but are younger individuals who because of other attributes such as education, money or trade have acquired status as an elder. Substantial knowledge about the local relations is a precondition for identifying and nurturing relations with traditional authorities. Only few of the INGOs had this, usually in the form of the experience of particular individuals who were suddenly transferred to trouble spots elsewhere in the world.

### Sub-Contracting to Local NGOs, Patronisation and Disempowerment

A major problem for external humanitarian agencies operating in a collapsed state is to find relevant and reliable local partners. In the absence of central and local governmental institutions, the agencies in Somalia had to search for alternatives. Different kinds of alternatives appeared. The ICRC could use the existing network of local Red Crescent societies and thus found the issue to be less problematic than other agencies and organisations. The UN agencies had the largest problem because they were used to dealing primarily with governmental institutions. The international NGOs had more experience in working with local partners. As the notion of civil society and local participatory approaches took hold in the early 1990's, local NGO's seemed to be a preferred type of counterpart and an alternative to working with the government. The UN embraced this idea by sub-contracting international NGOs and local NGOs to carry out the relief tasks. Local NGOs mushroomed as a result. They sprang up throughout Somalia, literally by the thousands. It was excellent business. After UNOSOM left and the assistance decreased to less than a quarter of its previous level, the agencies became more critical in choosing partners. They had also more knowledge of the Somali NGO scene and the business aspects. As a result, many Somali NGOs closed down, or went on "stand-by".

The vast amount of money spent during the UNOSOM period combined with the civil-society approach and an emphasis on local partnerships thus led to the proliferation of local NGOs (Abdillahi, 1998). For many of the local NGOs, this was merely business and nothing else. One result was to make the "genuine" local NGOs seem suspect to international agencies, which had insufficient local knowledge to distinguish the good ones from the bad ones. When UNOSOM departed, many excellent local NGOs consequently could not get funding. The funds were instead channelled to the international NGOs, which in turn subcontracted to local organisations in varying degrees. An underlying suspicion towards the Somali NGO scene has lingered in the international aid community, and manifests itself in the tendency to employ Africans other than Somalis for projects in Somalia.

Nevertheless, the principle of strengthening civil-society and using local NGO capacity stayed on, and by the late 1990s was observed to a considerable extent. In Hiran, the major social-service provider in the water and sanitation sector, an international NGO, ADRA, was working closely together with a local NGO, East-West NGO. East-West NGO may be considered as a "nominal" NGO only. Most of the leadership of the East-West NGO is also employed now directly by ADRA.

In the case of Hiran, the socio-political structure on which this practice rests is one where formal authority is vested in the regional and district council. Its members are in reality little more than agents of the local warlords, politicians and supreme elders, who maintain real power in the military and political sphere respectively. The social service and welfare providers are the international NGOs and their implementing partners. Thus, both the local power holders and the international agencies undermine the governing role of the district and regional councils. The councils are maintained only because they are seen as required by the international community.

A situation where governing power in reality is vested in a combination of warlords or politicians, certain elders, and the employees in local and international NGOs may not necessarily be bad, depending in part on the quality of the people involved. The problem is the dependence on external resources, which reduces the sense of responsibility of the Somali leaders and keeps alive the logic of spoils politics. The involvement of international NGO, in other words, undercuts the establishment of a local polity where the balance of power reflects, and is sustained by, local sources of income.

In sum, the general pattern was that during the first phase the INGOs tended to carry out all the operations themselves. Conditions on the ground were not conducive to finding appropriate partners. The urgency of life-saving tasks and a "mandate blinders approach" reinforced this tendency. As foreign agency personnel concentrated decision-making control in their own hands, they were often perceived as patronising by Somali aid workers who wanted to contribute. By taking over the delivery of humanitarian assistance, the INGOs deepened the dependency syndrome. Nor did they build local capacity to deliver assistance, which would have been important in a longer-term perspective of reconstruction (Anderson, 1999). The bottom line was that relief items were coming in, but the Somalis were not asked to take any responsibility for them, and as a result they did not feel any ownership over the process. Fundamentally, it was a process of local disempowerment (Natsios, 1997:86).

## Peace Building and the Fragmentation of the Somali Polity

The intervention by the international community in the Somali conflict in 1992 was initially about protecting the delivery of humanitarian assistance. An element of diplomatic activity designed to promote peace and reconciliation was present from the beginning as well. For a number of several historical reasons, these initial objectives turned into a large scale international intervention to provide humanitarian assistance and build peace. To understand the socio-political impact of humanitarian assistance to Somalia, then, it is necessary to examine the UNOSOM operation.[1] The main impact of UNOSOM was basically that it both legitimised and funded the warlords. UNOSOM "created" them (Heinrich, 1997). When UNOSOM pulled out, the income and externalities from humanitarian assistance were replaced to some extent by an increase in the trade of khat (a mild drug) and bananas, which flourished under the Lomé IV Convention.

### Building Peace from Below: Establishing Structures of Local Governance

At the Addis Ababa conference in 1993, UNOSOM was mandated to facilitate the formation of district and regional councils. This was the core of the peace building

---

1. The literature on UNOSOM is voluminous and critical. This chapter draws on findings regarding the impact of non-military humanitarian assistance on the socio-political transformation in Somalia. This is supplemented with data on Somali perceptions of the UNOSOM period, collected by the author during field research in Northern, and South and Central Somalia in 1999.

approach to Somalia, which was to run on two tracks: bottom-up and top-down. UNOSOM soon found that it lacked both funds and expertise for this task, and involved a Swedish NGO, the Life and Peace Institute (LPI), in the process. Thus, LPI was involved in humanitarian assistance in the form of peace building. Their approaches, however, soon proved to be delimited by the timeframe and lack of expertise of UNOSOM.

The regional and district councils were largely UNOSOM creations and never really seen as legitimate (Heinrich, 1997). In most of them the governors, councillors etc. were people who managed to gain a position for themselves rather than being locally elected, or were designated by the various warlord factions. This happened even though UNOSOM claimed to monitor the process to prevent just that (Heinrich 1997). UNOSOM nevertheless recognised most of the new local authorities. A main problem was the inexperience of the UNOSOM staff. The Justice Division consisted of young lawyers who had little or no African or Somali experience (UNOSOM archive at UNDOS Documentation Centre, Nairobi). UNOSOM, moreover, was working with tight timeframes that left little room for the time-consuming traditional Somali practices of political legitimisation (Heinrich, 1997:104–151).

Many of the UNOSOM-sponsored authorities are still in place, although without a generally renewed mandate. Councillors who retired or died were replaced through appointments made by the clan of the incumbent. Many of the UNOSOM-sponsored councils consisted of people with military and intelligence background from the Siad Barre era. My own observation from Southern and Central Somalia suggests that this remains the general practice.

In Middle Shabelle, the councils gradually became defunct over time as the UNOSOM flow of money dried up, leaving the councils with no structure of taxation and thus no resources to pay for the police force. Moreover, UNOSOM had paid the police very high salaries, generating expectations that the councils were unable to meet. Without a police force, the council had no means to enforce tax collection. Furthermore, there was no real commitment to solving the problem, since the allocation of taxes would then have to be decided upon. Who had the authority to control that income? The regional council, which was perceived as being controlled by the Ali Mahdi faction in Mogadishu? That option was unacceptable to the community. Instead, a group of "businessmen" representing all segments of the local community, i.e. all the sub-clans in Jowhar district, established a private company— The Farjano Company (members of the Farjano Company). UNICEF, which had rehabilitated the water system in Jowhar, then handed over the management of the new water system to the Farjano Company instead of the district council. Water is an important source of income in Somalia. The money which Farjano Company generated was used to support projects such as the new school, as well as traditional conflict resolution mechanisms by providing the elders with transportation, security guards and "technicals" (four wheel drive cars with a machine gun mounted on top) to the venue for deliberations. This method of financing local government is a unique construction in Southern Somalia. It came into being through the UNICEF water rehabilitation project. The councils, however, are largely ignored by both UNICEF and the community. Sub-clan feuding has been increasing in Middle Shabelle since 1998, which undoubtedly is a symptom of the problematic structures.

In Hiran, the governor and the district council were by the late 1990s still largely the same as during the UNOSOM period. There have been no elections, and changes of councillors have been by appointment by the retiring councillors' clan so as not to disturb the existing clan-balance. The councils are virtually non-functioning except for energetic district commissioners, who may be strongly engaged in developing their communities. The councils have buildings but no furniture or equipment. The governor is a former military officer who was teaching at the military academy in Mogadishu during the Siad Barre era. Hiran seems to be dominated by the Xawaadle clan of the Hawiye group. The main function of the regional council seems to be its role as interlocutor for the international assistance community in Nairobi. The restructuring of the district council from only a handful of districts into 13, reflects the current clan-balance in the region and the desire of each to have a forum for dealing directly with the international agencies. The UN deals directly with the formal authorities in Hiran, while the INGOs seemed to be addressing community elders more directly, avoiding the councils. However, one INGO seems to have very strong connections to the most powerful group of politicians and elders in Hiran, confirming the suspicion of other clan-groups in Hiran that this particular organisation is "owned" by a political clan constellation.

In Bay region, where the Rahanwein people regained power over their regional capital Baidoa in mid-1999, the international agencies—especially UNICEF and WFP, but also CARE International, World Vision and IMC—were demanding basic security structures and a reliable, official counterpart in the administration. The structures of the Rahanwein administration (established by the Rahanwein Resistance Army) reflected their perception of what the international agencies wanted and simultaneously accommodated the competing interests of the various Rahanwein clans receiving their part of the assistance spoils.

It appears that neither the UNOSOM nor the post-UNOSOM approaches involved processes of building political governance structures from below. Whether the approach was to deal with a faction leadership as in the Bay region, or to deal with regional and district councils as in Hiran, or to circumvent the formal councils, the end result was usually that the agency dealt with someone from the top of the local hierarchies and used the security arrangements they offered. However, the international agencies cannot always see which political factions really control a given area. The political clan networks operate within the genealogical clan framework which only persons with intimate knowledge about specific clan and family relations can discern. Expatriates rarely have knowledge about such relations, which can be hidden even for local Somalis. In the South, a direct relationship with the elders does not necessarily mean that the political factions and warlord networks are circumvented. The traditional systems were weakened in the South during the colonial period, and the civil war shattered much of the remaining respect for the elders as the young boys entering the militias found power through the barrel of their guns.

The vast resources and relative stability brought by UNOSOM made life materially so much better for most people in Southern Somalia that they prefer the UNOSOM period to present conditions. Yet the attempts by UNOSOM to buy political agreements through direct payments to local Somali leaders strengthened Somali perceptions of international assistance as a source of competition that undermined the peace process it was supposed to promote (Bryden, 1995).

## Conclusions: Creation of a Complex Political Emergency

Before and during the UNSOM intervention period, humanitarian assistance was a strategic resource and the Somali factions sought to obtain it either directly, especially the food aid, or to exploit the externalities of aid. After UNOSOM, the external resource flow shrank. Nevertheless, when aid agencies move in, and money and resources start flowing, the chase for the spoils resumes and trouble erupts. In areas with no assistance, and no other external interference, life seems to proceed more smoothly and peacefully.

In the context of highly fragmented local polities in the South, international assistance has a greater impact on formal political structures. Whether they are district councils, regional councils or development management groups (Gedo region), all function fundamentally as interlocutors to the international community. The foreign aid co-ordinating board, SACB, specifically used the term interlocutor when discussing their policy towards establishing such local political structures (SACB, 1999). The councils therefore become the main arena for political competition for the spoils of social and welfare services (Gundel, 1999b).

## Aid and Conflict: The Short Run

The significance of humanitarian assistance should not only be seen in terms of its magnitude or in terms of saving lives, but as much in terms of the role it plays in the dynamics of the socio-political processes that are at stake. In such a perspective the impact of humanitarian assistance varies depending on the type of assistance and the issues at stake among the belligerents.

In Somalia humanitarian assistance is business and becomes a significant element in "low politics" partly as a function of the extreme localisation of politics. Yet, low-level competition can escalate into significant conflict. For instance food transports through areas where there is intra sub-clan conflict can cause it to escalate, and possibly spread to all the places where the sub-clans are found. Contracting food to one sub-clan in the conflict may have repercussions whether it actually strengthens the sub-clan economically relative to the others, or is just perceived to. Fighting can be triggered by the egalitarian clan ethic which holds that no one should get more than their neighbouring sub-clan. As Andrew Natsios writes "saving lives over the short term may increase deaths over the longer term and increase damage to civil society" (1997:93).

## Longer term structural impediments

Local security regimes allowing for peaceful conflict resolution are a pre-condition for moving towards rebuilding war-torn societies. Humanitarian assistance, however, has the capacity of entrenching the structures of endemic conflict. The potentials of creating structures of endemic conflict;. While getting relief supplies out and significantly mitigating the humanitarian crisis, the practice of agencies in Somalia had the effect of supporting structures of violence based on warlordism. By negotiating with faction leaders as the "legitimate" authorities, they reinforced a political structure that effectively excluded other Somalis pursuing a different agenda than the warlords. These other groups were left to compete for junior positions with the humanitarian agencies operating in Somalia.

Similarly, because UNOSOM focused on the personalised faction-polities, there was little room for alternative political forces. Consequently, these were largely ignored in practice. If one of the troubling features of the Somali socio-political culture is spoils politics, then the continuance of humanitarian assistance in the present form is not contributing to a different direction. External humanitarian assistance fuels spoils politics whether the agencies try to avoid local governmental control or are subject to it. In this situation, assistance will inevitably keep Somalia in the role of a client in a global patron-client network. At the same time, conditions in Somalia are such that western humanitarians readily can argue it would be heartless to deny assistance.

Somalis are very capable people who do not need empowerment in a general sense. However, they need to discover their own powers, as they did in the regional capital Burco in Somaliland where they lost patience with the international community and began to rehabilitate the town by themselves. Contrary to much rhetoric, external humanitarian assistance structurally serves to prevent such empowerment. The main reason lies in the fundamental asymmetry of the relationship, which confines the Somalis, even well-educated ones, to the role of "recipients"—never the givers. As the Minister of Foreign Affairs, Government of the Republic of Somaliland said when the talk came round to humanitarian assistance: "Well, we are not in a position to choose". Economic conditions compel many to receive whatever assistance arrives, no matter how mediocre the providing agencies are. The tendency of expatriates to patronise recipients and local employees reflects, and also sharpens, this asymmetry.

Another important impact of the presence of international humanitarian agencies is the local tendency to emulate the organisational forms and norms of interaction that the international agencies understand and prefer. This includes the western type of governance institutions, even in cases where it is not demanded or when alternate forms are promoted by international NGOs. As we have noted, the formal political institutions set up by Somalis, like those inherited from the UNOSOM period, are only nominal organisations. They do not reflect local power realities and their principal function is to be interlocutors to the international community.

Leaving aside Somaliland and Puntland, the combined humanitarian assistance interventions since 1991 have significantly contributed to building up warlords and giving free-lance bandit militias something to loot. It has supported a diversified mosaic of local political institutions where traditional authorities, local governmental institutions (district and regional levels) functioning as interlocutors to the international donor community, and militarised faction-leaders co-exist in different combinations of strength. While significantly contributing to saving lives, the same assistance supported the evolution of political structures of violence based on warlordism. A transformation of Somali politics and society that could establish a stable connection between society, and whatever political authorities the Somalis need, was in reality impeded.

To sum up: in the beginning, lack of understanding of the conflict among the agencies combined with "the mandate blinders approach" to constitute a major factor in fuelling the conflict. The two elements tended to reinforce each other as the rationale of a minimalist humanitarian approach downgraded the need for local knowledge. In the second phase, the political evolution of the UNOSOM intervention, with all its mistakes, served to strengthen and legitimise the Southern and Mogadishu based warlords. After UNOSOM, donor attention flagged, and the SACB became a playground for internal rivalries among donor officials and the UN Somalia officials. Despite its intentions, the "peace dividend approach" did not help bring peace to Somalia once the warlord syndrome had been created.

# III

# Conclusions

# 9. The Political Economy of Building Local Relief Capacity in Africa

*Monica Kathina Juma*

> Refugee work remains, perhaps, the last bastion of the ultra-paternalistic approach to aid and development. It is hard to think of another area where the blinkered nonsense of the 'we know what's best for them' approach survives so unchallenged ( Malloch-Brown, 1984).

This chapter landscapes the contradictions and challenges that relate to the conceptualisation, definition and processes of building local relief capacity in Africa. The chapter submits that as currently organised, the humanitarian industry creates a political economy whose key feature—namely the relationship between actors—is structured in ways that inhibit the building and nurturing of sustainable local relief capacity. This conclusion is built on three key arguments.

First, methodologies employed in the attempt to create or build local relief capacity stem from the wrong premise and are, therefore, unlikely to nurture sustainable capacity. Frameworks seeking to build capacity borrow wholesale from the development paradigm whose aim was to "modernise", (in the Western sense) and control the environment (including actors and beneficiaries) as well as the outcome of processes (types of capacities built). Driven by an ideology of superiority, the development project was inherently contemptuous of, and at best indifferent to, the experiences, abilities and aspirations of local actors and beneficiaries. It failed the organic test and remains, to borrow the terminology of one development writer, "hanging" beyond the reach of beneficiaries (Hyden, 1980).

In the relief arena this framework translates into hegemonic tendencies that generate patronage structures that are reinforced by two fallacies. First, is a forced dichotomy between the zones of calm and peace, which "produce" interveners, and the zones of conflict and disaster, for which intervention is designed. A second fallacy, born of this distinction, is the assumption that areas of intervention lack any capacity for remedial action, and as a result, such capacity can only be created and directed from outside, by international "experts". Within this framework, international agencies are the agents of (positive) change and subsequently position themselves in the seat of power and authority as capacity builders and intermediaries between capacity and recipients. As in the development enterprise, local agencies, whether governmental or non-governmental, are perceived as fundamentally incapacitated. The designing and execution of capacity building, therefore, become the preserve of international actors. Such a model ignores local knowledge and experiences and fails to appreciate and harness local expertise, a prerequisite for boosting local capacity. Instead of building on existing capacities, models for capacity building are conceived away from areas of need and attempt to transform local environments in the pursuit of certain types of capacities. This translates into training packages that address the needs of "outsider" actors such as imbibing expertise in procedures for fund-raising and fulfilling donor-reporting procedures. As in the development arena, capacity building becomes a means of reproducing a certain way of doing things that does not necessarily address the needs on the ground.

The second broad argument on which this chapter rests stems from the patrimonial nature of aid (be it developmental or relief) that inhibits meaningful capacity building. Conceiving capacity building from outside the affected areas, with minimal if any consultation with beneficiaries, inevitably leads to paternalistic tendencies, which undermine and destroy rather than nurture or enhance local capacities. This is because implementation of aid is done in ways that overwhelm, play down or reduce the ability of affected communities to respond to disasters in the future. The end result is a vicious circle of greater vulnerability that increases victim dependency on relief aid, which is in turn used to justify the entrenchment of relief agencies. It is this pattern of intervention that explains, in part, the inability of "perennial" disaster areas to recover to normalcy. Generally, interventions throughout the 1990s in Africa, especially in the Greater Horn of Africa region (Somalia, Kenya, Uganda, Sudan, Rwanda, Burundi and the Democratic Republic of the Congo) considerably reduced the capacity of affected areas to deal with the after-effects of emergencies (see for example, Gundel, Chapter 8; Kathina Juma, 2000; Kathina Juma and Masika, 1997; de Waal, 1997; Maren, 1997).

Finally, the chapter submits that wrapping the discussion of capacity building in a humanitarian "techno-speak" avoids addressing power and control, the central issues to any capacity building enterprise. Humanitarian assistance has for a long time been defined and defended as a non-political activity. The humanitarian techno-speak camouflages the interrogation of issues and relations that are intensely political in an environment where political stakes, i.e. power and control, are much sought after. As has become well known, humanitarian actions are not necessarily guided by philanthropy and altruism. Often broader political and economic interests are involved (Kathina Juma, 2000). Even when assistance is driven by good intentions, these are moderated on the ground by power, competition and manipulation. Thus, attempts to deal with capacity building that are guided by an apolitical framework miss a critical point in the process of empowering people. They obscure the critical issue of where and with whom power rests. The experience of the Partnership in Action (PARinAc) process in Kenya is a striking illustration of how imbalances in power and control can cripple the enterprise of capacity building, and is recounted in some detail below.

Capacity building is determined to a large extent by the operations and relationships of actors. I explore these relationships with the guidance of several interrelated questions: How is capacity building defined and pursued within the humanitarian arena? Is there synergy between local and international actors that leads to a win-win situation for all actors, or do structural and institutional requirements associated with capacity building serve to exclude some actors, particularly the local ones? In other words, to what extent is the notion of building capacity rhetoric only? How does it relate to issues of technology transfer, human resource development and general enhancement of emergency response capacity in the south? In terms of scope and illustrative material, the chapter draws from experiences in East Africa, a region that hosted large numbers of refugees and internally displaced persons (IDPs) throughout the 1990s, and one that is the subject of three of the four case studies presented in this volume.

## Defining Capacity Building

Capacity building is a slippery term that is caught up in a means and end confusion. As an end, it is sought by organisations to enable them to pursue and achieve their objectives. In this sense, capacity building becomes a process of institution building that involves a range of activities designed to attain internal cohesion and to strengthen organisational service delivery. From this perspective, capacity building constitutes changes within the organisation aimed to improve its performance. At another level, capacity building is external to the organisation: it is a transferable asset to the environment. In this sense, it consists of a myriad of activities engaged in by actors to support people or other organisations in taking control of their lives more effectively. Capacity builders, therefore, play a catalytic role of transforming other actors and the environment external to themselves. Although slightly different in emphasis, the first is centred around the organisation, while the second focuses on its environment. Central to both definitions, however, is the intrinsic intent of capacity building to empower and strengthen institutions and the ability of people to take control of activities that affect their lives. In this broader sense, capacity building is not an end in itself but a broader strategy for maximising and sustaining the positive impact of both development and relief work (Eade and Williams, 1995:12, 341). This chapter is based on the premise that empowerment is the primary objective of any capacity building activity, and that it seeks to enhance the ability of affected populations and local institutions in ways that reduce their vulnerability to disasters.

If capacity building means strengthening institutions, boosting the ability of individuals and communities affected by disasters to cope with adversities, then it is safe to argue that efforts at building capacity in East Africa were elusive and limited throughout the 1990s. A range of systemic factors became disincentives to, and hindered, capacity building processes. While the presence of large numbers of well-funded international actors presented a unique opportunity to nurture and boost local relief capacity in East Africa, this was sadly missed as the politics of institutional survival dominated the humanitarian arena throughout the decade. At the close of the 1990s limited, if any, local relief capacity had been created, and where it existed prior to the 1990s, or was built during this period, it failed the sustainability test and was quickly destroyed or overwhelmed within short periods of time. At the dawn of the new millennium, the humanitarian arena in East Africa was the preserve of large international humanitarian actors.

## Contextualising Capacity Building in the Relief Arena

As development theorists and practitioners wrestled to define the fluid notion of capacity building, some humanitarian actors deemed this debate irrelevant. For a long time, charity and philanthropic predisposition remained a sufficient condition for humanitarian action, equated to (swift) voluntary action that is driven by compassion. A compassionate "heart" was enough justification to help. This concept long remained unquestioned or critiqued. However, as capacity building became an increasingly central concept in development thinking, it stimulated critique of the conventional notion of humanitarianism as charity. Emerging analysis began to portray capacity building as a critical bridge in the transition from relief to development, as well as a means for people to cope with extreme circumstances. As Astri Suhrke indicates in Chapter 2 of this volume, the underlying assumption was that capacity building produces greater effectiveness, efficiency and overall professionalism, further ensures beneficiary ownership of the response process, and promotes sustainability, which is key to future response to emergencies. Unsurprisingly, the impetus for building capacity in relief situations coincides with increasing criticism of the distinction between relief and development interventions in favour of the so-called relief-development continuum. (See for example, Chambers, 1979:381–392; Gorman, 1993; Cuenod, 1989:219–253.)

The 1990s were particularly critical in this policy shift. A consensus coalesced among donors, states and non-states that capacity building was crucial in a world that was becoming increasingly volatile. With this, international actors set the mood and pace by creating frameworks to promote capacity building in the South. While capacity encompasses material, organisational and human resources, a key aspect to all of them is the relationship between actors. Reflecting this emphasis, the Joint NGOs/INGOs/UN meeting held on January 24–28 1993 discussed policies, rules and guidelines for twinning and operational partnerships. Emphasising the need to built local capacity, the draft agreement from this meeting read in part: "The building and strengthening of local and national capacity, enhancing effectiveness and efficiency are fundamental objectives for INGOs operating in the south. This implies that collaboration and co-operation with governmental and non-governmental partners is both a policy and a goal". This mood was to dominate policy debates and operational guidelines throughout the 1990s.

Within the relief arena, this momentum led to the launching of the Partnership in Action (PARinAc) process in 1993. Aimed at improving and enriching the relationship between UNHCR, NGOs and states, PARinAc was structured in regional consultations that culminated in a global meeting held in Oslo in June 1994. Out of the PARinAc experience and in recognition of the significance of relationships between actors, UNHCR produced a Management Handbook for Promoting Partnership between itself and its partners, in which it outlines procedures for choosing implementing actors during emergencies, delegating responsibilities to local actors and methodologies for building partnership. Further, it urges synergy of action, mutual respect and complementarity among actors (UNHCR, 1996: section 1.6). Two years later, UNHCR reinforced its position by producing a draft document on UNHCR-NGO Partnership Effectiveness. Among its stated objectives was support for national NGOs to ensure that UNHCR can adequately meet international protection standards and humanitarian assistance needs of refugees. Another was to build national NGO capacity to work beyond the needs of a UNHCR operation and contribute to longer-term rehabilitation and development, including the development of civil society and dissemination of basic human rights principles as part of the prevention strategy (UNHCR, 1998). In other words, the aim was sustainable peace that could stave off future conflicts and refugee flows.

These developments follow similar approaches in the non-state sector, which had embraced the notion of capacity building much earlier. A leader in this was the Red Cross movement, whose Code of Conduct includes as one of its principles the "attempt to build response by local capacities". It further urges the use of local actors in responding to emergencies. This approach was seen as key to institutionalising a sense of ownership and responsibility among recipients of assistance and victims of emergencies as well as entrenching development through focused intervention efforts—in short, building local capacity.

## Translating Policy into Action

Translating this intention into action is a major challenge within the relief sector. As in the development enterprise, the key players are 'outside' interveners while the beneficiaries/recipients of capacity are local actors and populations. In a context of increasing state marginalisation and weakening public institutions, recipients remain without an effective interlocutor to mediate what are clearly power relations between foreign humanitarian actors, local organisations and beneficiaries. Once celebrated as the vehicle for development, the state in Africa is fracturing under deepening balance of payment and fiscal problems, rapid population increases, slackening agricultural production and declining institutional ability. These conditions are worsened by the failure of structural adjustment programmes whose effects became more manifest in the 1990s. Within the humanitarian arena, state marginalisation has taken a particular form. Since the 1970s and 1980s a large number of Western donors have started using NGOs as their preferred channels for delivering aid resources to Africa. Arguing that NGOs were more flexible, grassroots-based, sensitive to the needs of beneficiaries, effective and accountable, donors sponsored NGO formation and expansion (see for example, Bratton, 1987; Fowler, and James, 1994). As a result, the operational space for NGOs expanded rapidly at the expense of the state (Borton, 1993).

By the mid-1980s, starting with BandAid, large-scale relief delivery became a growth area for NGOs, especially international ones. As complex emergencies multiplied in the 1990s, the role of NGOs expanded remarkably. However, donor enthusiasm to fund large-scale complex operations soon waned in the face of heavy costs and the danger such operations entailed for aid workers. Besides, such operations throw up a number of dilemmas, as discussed by Gundel in Chapter 8. While the expansion of NGOs' activities "liberated" them from operating within strict government frameworks, it hastened debate on the dichotomy imposed for a long time between relief and development, and forced NGOs to reflect on the root causes of emergencies as well as rehabilitation and prevention activities. This expansion led to another fundamental change: it exposed NGOs to critical scrutiny and raised a series of questions about their identity, legitimacy and accountability. In essence, NGO expansion at the expense of the state was plunging the process of building (transferring) capacity into an "agency" crisis. Over time, the once assumed role and capacity of NGOs to act as an alternative path of development came under intense criticism as doubts arose about their role in the South. In attempts to deal with this crisis, the notion of partnership is promoted as a means of enhancing the comparative advantage of actors at various levels.

As doubts about the ability of NGOs to succeed where governments 'failed' have taken root, and the debate on harnessing genuine local participation have intensified, questions about how to ensure real development remain unanswered. However, there is a curious aspect to these debates: without exception, all are formulated outside of the scenes of intervention, with little if any input from the perceived beneficiaries. Following the pattern from the development and conventional relief interventions, INGOs are cutting a wide niche for themselves in the process and are positioning themselves as the key advocates for partnership and capacity building programs. This position was especially noticeable in the relief sector in East African during the 1990s.

Without exception, all international actors operating in East Africa in the 1990s professed the objective of building local capacity. Although the means by which this objective was sought varied among actors, its practice was driven by one basic assumption: international actors had capacity and were, therefore, the capacity builders, while local actors were recipients of capacity. This categorisation had an immediate impact on the manner in which building capacity was conceived. Typically, the starting point was an assumption that there was no relevant aid capacity in countries prior to the emergencies. Therefore, when international capacity moved in, no effort was made to draw lessons or build on existing capacity. Instead, local aid structures were overwhelmed, diminished or destroyed. In unveiling the manner in which this happened, the following analysis focuses on relationships at three levels:

(i) Relations between host states and international actors (national level);
(ii) Relations between humanitarian agencies and donors (funding/resource issues); and
(iii) Relations between local and international NGOs (operational/field level).

## Relations between Host States and International Agencies

Emergency intervention is premised on the principle of delegation. While the conventions of sovereignty give a government authority and responsibility over the population within its territory, when an emergency overwhelms its capacity to cope, the government can, and typically does, invite other actors to help. Operationally, this involves delegating the responsibility of providing services and protection to victims of disasters. More importantly, it is based on the assumption that invited actors have the requisite capacity to undertake humanitarian action. While delegation means surrendering some responsibilities, it also presupposes a capacity within host states to monitor and supervise the quality of interventions by invited actors. This was not the case in East African countries during the 1990s.

The presence of international actors correlated with the state's inability or unwillingness to implement or regulate humanitarian activities. International aid actors overshadowed host governments in the humanitarian arena, a situation that over time further impaired the state's ability to monitor or supervise relief activities. The overall effect of this was a progressive marginalisation of the state. This was effected by multiple processes, three of which are crucial for our purposes: these are: (i) the disregard for, and failure by international actors to learn from, previous experiences, (ii) the renunciation and bypassing of existing policy-making and implementation structures, and (iii) the creation of parallel structures that competed against local and national institutions.

### Disregard for, and Failure to Learn from, Previous Experiences

East Africa has a long history of dealing with both natural and man-made disasters (Wilkins, 1988; Daley, 1989; Kathina Juma, 2000). Even Kenya, whose restrictive policies and definition of itself as a transit state has earned it the reputation of being most hostile in the region, has attracted large numbers of refugees over the years. Its location on the axis of refugee producing states and its relative stability in the region makes it an attractive destination for asylum seekers. Thus when the Horn of Africa plunged into conflicts in the 1990s, Kenya became a natural flight destination. Until then, the government practised a hands-off, "no camp" policy, treating refugees largely as migrant workers. By defining itself as a no-asylum state and not developing policies in the refugee sector, the state effectively divested itself and the relevant line ministries of humanitarian activities. The resultant vacuum was filled by local non-state actors, which over time developed substantial relief capacity. Agencies such as the Kenya Red Cross Society (KRCS), the National Council of Churches of Kenya (NCCK), the Catholic Refugee Secretariat (CRS) and the All African Conference of Churches (AACC) operated in conjunction with local churches, communities and institutions in assisting refugees. This partnership was critical during the initial response to the emergencies related to internal displacement in the 1990s.

In contrast to Kenya, Uganda encouraged self-reliance and de facto refugee integration among local communities. Starting in the 1940s with the Polish refugees, the colonial government gazetted refugee settlement areas and practised an open door policy. After independence Uganda remained a significant country for hosting and settling refugees even during the difficult eras of Idi Amin Dada and Milton Obote. Although many challenges, particularly xenophobia in the 1990s, Uganda remained a major country of refugee settlement in East Africa. Uganda has also had to deal with emergencies related to internal displacement caused by insurgency. Since 1986, close to half a million Ugandans have been displaced in the North, West and East of the country. In addition, North Eastern Uganda is a zone that is constantly afflicted by drought and famine-related disasters. These conditions have transformed large parts of the country into major emergency zones.

Compared to Kenya and Uganda, Tanzania, particularly under Dr Julius Nyerere, had by far the most sophisticated framework for refugee settlement and integration. Driven by the African Socialism and Pan-Africanism ideologies, Tanzania adopted a landmark policy that was to earn it international repute in refugee administration. Supportive of liberation wars, it established training camps for refugees from colonised territories and facilitated their struggles. Besides practising an open-door policy and encouraging refugee integration, the government offered refugees the option of naturalisation as a durable solution. As illustrated in the Tanzanian case study, local communities and government structures were principle actors in this administration. They established refugee settlement areas and ran assistance programmes until the early 1990s.

Rich as these experiences are, they were largely unacknowledged or viewed as irrelevant or non-instructive by the international actors that flooded the humanitarian arena in the 1990s. On the whole, there was failure to draw from or build upon them in all three countries. Instead, local structures were marginalised and over time pushed out of the humanitarian arena. Even when local NGOs expressed interest to participate fully in the humanitarian operation, opportunities remained limited. For instance, although the Kenya Red Cross and Red Crescent Societies (KRCCS) had accumulated impressive experience working with Ugandan refugees since the 1970s, it played a limited role in the emergencies of the 1990s. For most of the decade, it was a junior partner to its international counterparts, the International Federation of the Red Cross and Red Crescent Societies and the International Committee of the Red Cross, which remained the preferred choice for UNHCR. Uganda Red Cross owed its role as partner of UNHCR to government leverage and insistence that at least one local NGO remain as a major implementer of services to refugees. However, this did not guarantee it considerable programme activities. Between 1996 and 1997, Uganda Red Cross was relieved of its lead agency status in the West Nile district, then the largest refugee operation in Uganda, leaving it with a small refugee caseload in Nakivale settlement, South West Uganda. Local actors in Tanzania, particularly local administration and churches, also experienced a shrinking of programme activities with the influx of international actors. In the few cases when international actors acknowledged local capacity, this capacity was deemed insufficient and therefore inconsequential for handling the emergencies of the 1990s. Reflecting this opinion, a high-ranking staff member of the International Federation of the Red Cross and Crescent Societies observed of the contribution of Uganda Red Cross, in the West Nile operation:

> It would have been simply impossible to run the West Nile operation without the involvement of the International Federation of the Red Cross and Crescent Societies (IFRC). The Uganda Red Cross simply had no capacity to deal with it. (Communication with author, Kampala. February 1997.)

While staff of international agencies claimed that there was no local capacity, they made no effort to create it or to augment the limited capacity that existed. Instead, the horde of international agencies overwhelmed the local scene and went about their activities in disregard of any prior experience or knowledge about emergency response. By 1996, top international humanitarians were admitting that their presence had not contributed to local capacity. Asked whether the presence of international actors had facilitated the creation of capacity capable of responding to future emergencies, the Deputy Resident Representative of UNHCR in Kenya responded:

> I am afraid if we faced another emergency now, we would have to depend on international NGOs to respond. Because, there is no local capacity that can respond... We [international actors] have created no local capacity (Communication with author, Nairobi 1995).

### Renunciation and By-passing of Existing Policy and Implementation Structures

The impact of the failure to build on or enhance previous experiences was accentuated by a corresponding disregard for existing policy and implementation structures. The latter practice led to the rejection and/or by-passing of government structures, further weakening the capacity of the state to supervise or monitor humanitarian activities. By the close of the 1990s, planning for and implementation of humanitarian programmes took place away from government structures. The effects of these practices were accentuated by state acquiescence to its marginalisation, particularly in regard to its line ministries in the humanitarian arena. Faced with economic decline, calls for political reforms and breakdown of social structures, emergencies associated with forced displacement presented critical challenges. Claiming to be overwhelmed, all three governments called on the international community to help deal with the emergencies relating to forced displacement, in particular with refugees. Viewing refugees as presenting a lesser risk to state security, the governments adopted a lukewarm approach and left them to international actors. Refugees were perceived to be the responsibility of UNHCR and the international community, or the governments acted in ways that suggested they were simply glad to turn over responsibilities for refugees to foreign agencies. The case of internally displaced populations in Kenya and Uganda was slightly different. Viewing internal displacement as a state security issue, both governments remained reluctant to allow foreign actors free access to these populations.

At the start of the 1990s when the emergencies were brewing, none of the three countries had a comprehensive administrative and legal framework for refugees, and that remained the case for most of the decade. While Uganda and Tanzania instituted refugee bills in 1998 and 2000, respectively, attempts by Kenya to have a bill were met with distrust by humanitarian actors who suspected government ill-intention and desire to control humanitarian activities. For instance, humanitarian actors have remained uneasy about Kenya's de facto practice of treating refugees like other immigrants. Although this policy accorded refugees freedom of movement and involvement in economic activities, it also made them invisible and vulnerable. Over the years, UNHCR consistently argued that by this policy Kenya had refused to allocate land for refugee settlements (camps), an argument that led to its exclusion from access to funds allocated to refugee hosting states within the Lomé IV Convention.

In dealing with the lacunae created by lack of policy or structures considered 'unfriendly', international humanitarian actors cultivated patrons and clients in powerful sectors within the political system. These powerful individuals gave them access to power brokers and ensured political support within the state. Such social networks had the immediate effect of marginalising line agencies and other units with administrative responsibility for humanitarian affairs. In the refugee sector, Refugee Secretariats in all three countries were first line victims. Arguing that these structures were weak and lacking in political clout to "make things happen", humanitarian agencies in Kenya sought intervention from the Office of the President and usually with the President personally. In Uganda and Tanzania, the Prime Minister's Office became the most heavily lobbied. Effectively, this practice of circumventing the responsible line agency structures took policy-making away from the institutions designated as the lead units within governments. In environments where the culture of higher orders overshadows bureaucracy, lobbying of higher offices impairs the ability of the Secretariats to engage meaningfully in policy formulation or implementation. Refugee Secretariats were reduced to low-level implementers of directives handed down to them from "above." In contrast, UNHCR was perceived as the most powerful intervener. One top official in the Refugee Secretariat in Kenya told this author in 1999 that "UNHCR has reduced our function to minor consultations during the signing of agreement documents." Marginalisation of these structures took place even at the most basic level: information sharing. No humanitarian agency, including UNHCR was obliged to provide the Refugee Secretariats with information about their operations, and when they did so, it was at their discretion. Consequently, the government unit that should be the focal point in refugee assistance and protection remained the weakest link in the chain of actors.

Snubbing of administrative line agencies by humanitarian agencies is not confined to East Africa. The experience of Sudan is particularly instructive. In 1967, the Government of Sudan created the Office of the Commissioner for Refugees (COR) as an attempt to have a say in refugee assistance programmes. COR was charged with the duty to direct intervention, including determining the nature of assistance being delivered, mitigating agency competition, redressing the imbalance between wasteful duplication of services in some areas to the neglect of others and establishing and demanding some standards of competency from agency personnel. When this structure attempted to implement its objectives, humanitarian agencies responded by accusing it of being militaristic. When COR persisted, UNHCR adopted a non-intervention strategy towards Sudan and remained passive without operating between 1975 and 1980. The impasse came to an end when, among other political developments, there were changes in staffing at the office of COR that enabled UNHCR to cajole staff, influence COR's direction and have its way (Karadawi, 1983).

In other cases, staff of international agencies intimidated government officials when the latter demanded accountability. In one such case in August 1997, at a meeting of agencies called for a briefing on rehabilitating populations affected by clashes in Western Kenya, the head of an international NGO threatened the District Commissioner with leaving the country. When asked to account for the work of his

NGO against the background of alleged misappropriation of resources (including a Government forest donated as a contribution to the reconstruction project), he threatened to withdraw his organisation,"… should the DC attempt to do to his NGO what the Kenya Government is known best for, being aggressive towards non-state actors." The agency withdrew from the area shortly after this confrontation without constructing a single shelter, responding to accusations of fraud against it or accounting for material resources under its administration. Reacting to this behaviour, a government official observed, "… well, INGOs have money and money is power. So they do what they want."[1]

In defence of by passing government line agencies, INGOs argue that emergency needs are pressing and call for quick action, hence they cannot follow slow-moving bureaucratic procedures. They also lament restrictive mandates that do not allow time and resources to build local structures of delivery. This does not address one of the negative impacts of this manner of operation: the hegemony of international actors that generates suspicion and which works against nurturing partnerships. As Ahmed Karadawi (1983) argues, it would sometimes appear that host governments, like refugees, are expected to accept assistance without questioning the suitability of the gift, the competence of the giver or the method of giving. Though rarely addressed, this hegemony of aid institutions is a source of immense frustration to African institutions and citizens.

## Creation of Parallel Structures

Failure to borrow from or build on local capacity and the practice of bypassing government structures typically translated into two relief operations. On the one hand a better-funded international humanitarian actor dominated the emergency system and, on the other, a state-led response system that by the internationals was seen as, and accused of, following an ethos that inhibited humanitarian activities and programs. Rather than complement one another, the co-existence of these systems was marked by intense competition and distrust that saw them work to undo each other. On the ground, the two systems translated into parallel structures.

Citing lack of functional systems, international humanitarian actors created delivery systems that excluded most of the local actors, and to which they invited government participation when deemed necessary. Meanwhile, the governments continued to use their own relief structures, with minimum if any participation by international agencies. For instance, although the Museveni government created an elaborate disaster management structure in the early 1990s that comprised numerous tiers of disaster and relief response committees—spanning from the national to the local levels—humanitarian programs were organised and implemented largely outside this framework. By the mid-1990s Kenya had at least three discernible humanitarian systems, which exhibited little if any synergy, as Kagwanja shows in Chapter 6. When in 1996 Tanzania formulated a framework for the affected area approach, designed to integrate assistance to refugees with development in the host areas, this became another system rather than an integrative framework for humanitarian action.

In theory, partnerships between experts and non-experts are supposed to provide opportunities for strengthening capacities to manage programs after international actors phase out. However, as discussed above, rather than empower public

---

1.  These and other non-referenced citations in the text are from the author's research notes based on fieldwork in Kenya at various times during the second half of the 1990s. For further details, see Kathina Juma, 2000.

administration for relief, the international capacity marginalised it. This led to several adverse effects on the state, four of which are key to the issue of building local capacity.

First, marginalisation of line agencies and official responsibilities for particular humanitarian functions erodes their capacity to perform related duties for the citizenry. The result is a further weakening of state legitimacy. This was the case in Turkana district where refugees are concentrated in an ecologically fragile area that experiences repeated drought-related emergencies. The government's response to a recent famine was undercut by the presence of a large humanitarian operation for refugees. In 1997, competition between the two reached a peak when the government was responding to the needs of the famine-stricken Turkana district at the same time as UNHCR was relocating some 20,000 refugees from Mombasa to Kakuma camp. Few in number, transport and haulage companies found themselves under pressure that pushed transport prices up. Without consulting, and indeed to undercut, the government, UN agencies paid between Kshs. 20–30 per tonne per kilometre of food hauled, between 100 and 200 per cent more than the government rates of Kshs. 10 per tonne per kilometre. The impact of this was instantaneous—government relief operations ground to a halt. For the local population, dying next to the relatively better-fed refugees was interpreted as the failure of the government to assist them and seen as the height of discrimination by a humanitarian system that targeted and favoured "foreigners" in their midst. Out of this experience grew animosity between the local administration and UN agencies, in particular UNHCR which was accused of undermining state operations, and between the locals and refugees because the former felt that strangers were being offered preferential treatment. So deep did the acrimony between the locals and refugees grow that the latter subsequently could not venture beyond the camp in search of local resources such as wood-fuel or local vegetables without being attacked. On their part refugees look down upon the locals with scorn because they are materially worse off.

Second, the creation of parallel humanitarian structures that are "independent" of the state shifts accountability for humanitarian action from the realm of the host state to that of the headquarters of northern-based NGOs or donors in foreign capitals (Gariyo, 1992). This practice solidifies links between humanitarian actors on the ground and their donors, in clear disregard of host states, and leads to skewed partnerships that work to marginalise the state. In this framework, both the state and local community are unable to benefit from the positive aspects of emergency assistance and international expertise that they can neither monitor nor hold accountable. This trend is unlikely to create effective local capacity.

Third, failure to utilise local structures results in programme unsustainability, especially when international actors leave. A case is point is the Marsabit refugee hospital, built and run by UNHCR in conjunction with AMREF (a Kenyan registered international NGO), to cater for Ethiopian refugees that fled into Kenya after the fall of Mengistu in 1989. When the Ethiopians repatriated and UNHCR proposed to hand the hospital over to the Ministry of Health, the latter declined to take it over, arguing that its construction and running was conceived outside its own development strategy. After three years of disputes, the hospital fell into disuse. In Northern Uganda, UNHCR through Oxfam constructed an elaborate infrastructure in Ikafe refugee settlement area that targeted refugees exclusively. When refugees unexpectedly left the camp en masse in April 1996, these facilities were left unused. In an evaluation of the Oxfam programme, Barbara Harrell-Bond criticised the failure of the agency to integrate refugee assistance with national and local programming. This,

she argues, is a major cause of resource wastage and non-sustainability of programmes after refugees repatriate or external agencies withdraw (Harrell-Bond,
1996). In Southern Uganda, the government was locked in disagreement with
UNHCR for more than three years over the agency's attempt to withdraw from and
hand over Kiryandogo settlement to the government. As in Kenya, Uganda's argument was that the settlement was planned and administered outside government
strategy, to the exclusion of relevant departments. Consequently, it had no capacity
to manage or sustain it.

Finally, when humanitarian actors usurp government obligations, the latter's reaction turns negative. In Kenya, the government has institutionalised a laissez faire
attitude towards refugees and views them as the responsibility of UNHCR. This in-
difference has left UNHCR with no alternative but to take over what is in effect a
state responsibility. For instance, UNHCR started determining asylum claims after
Kenya in 1991–92 froze status determination procedures. In addition to generating
dilemmas for UNHCR, this role contradicts its protection mandate. More importantly, it provides the government with an excuse to accuse the agency of overstep-
ping its mandate. Invoking threats to its security, the government's attitude towards
refugees has hardened, with critical implications for access to and enjoyment of
rights.

## Relationships between Humanitarian Agencies and Donors

A second broad factor that inhibits the bolstering of local capacity is the nature of
funding and the attendant relationship between humanitarian actors and donors.
Three processes are relevant here, namely targeted funding practices, intensifying
agency competition for shrinking funds and the contractual implementation structure. All are operationally biased in favour of international actors.

### Targeted Funding

Although more than 60 per cent of African refugees are settled spontaneously among
local communities and depend on scarce local resources, donor policies inhibit attempts at integrating refugee assistance with national and local planning. Integration
would require acknowledging, working with and channelling substantial amounts
of relief aid through government structures. However, as illustrated by all three case
studies, humanitarian action is victim targeted and remains largely set apart from
mainstream development activities. Even in Tanzania, where refuge assistance in the
1960s and 1970s was firmly integrated with national development policy, this policy
fizzled out in the 1990s with the arrivals of large numbers of refugees and, by then,
the existence of a strong international humanitarian regime ready to take on the task
of assistance itself.

Ideas about integrating refugee assistance with development planning are not
new. Mooted in the 1970s and 1980s, refugee integration was a matter of extensive
discussion in the International Conferences on Assistance to Refugees in Africa
(ICARA I in 1981 and ICARA II in 1984). However, while donors expressed appre-
ciation for the idea and pledged support, very few honoured their pledges. Comparatively ICARA I (1981) was more successful in terms of fundraising. It managed to
mobilise $570 million, about 50 per cent of the money requested. However, donors
earmarked most of the money for specific programmes rather than making it avail-

able to host countries. ICARA II failed to generate any significant amounts of funds. While the donors focussed on seeking durable solutions, i.e. repatriation, resettlement and integration, African governments emphasised the burden imposed on them by the refugee presence, the consequences for development and the heavy sacrifices they were being called upon to make (Stein, 1987). This difference in focus was never resolved then, nor has it come near to being resolved later as the experience of Tanzania after the 1994 influx indicates.

As this approach failed to attract support, resources available for camp-targeted assistance through international actors increased manyfold. The failure of the ICARA process was a missed opportunity for adopting the affected area approach and bolstering the capacity of both states and local institutions at a time when the scale of the crisis was manageable. As experience was to show, long-term displacement has multiple effects on the host environment and calls for a broad-based intervention strategy. Unfortunately, even as this awareness grows, agencies such as UNHCR face difficulties in attracting adequate funds for such programmes.

The camp remains strategically the more favoured framework of intervention. Compared to spontaneous settlements, camps ensure visibility, which is critical for fund raising purposes, are administratively convenient and remain useful organising units. As the camp model prevails as the structure for organising assistance to refugees, mounting evidence indicates that encampment impacts negatively on the enjoyment of refugee rights. Artificially created, camps are by nature exclusive and insensitive to local institutions and capacities that typically are over-stretched and weakened, particularly during the initial phase of the emergency (Chambers, 1993). Camps contribute neither to the empowerment of the refugees nor the local agencies seeking to assist and protect them. Owing to the levels of impoverishment in most hosting areas, targeted assistance has been a source of great tension and acrimony between the locals and refugee or IDP populations. Visibility of populations within camps has also exposed them to increasing xenophobia.

Animosity towards refugees takes place against a disturbing imbalance created by programs in areas of intervention. For example, in Adjumani district of Uganda refugees number some 67,000 against 137,000 locals, a ratio of 1:2 (Kathina Juma, 2000). Humanitarians have constructed 22 well-staffed and equipped health facilities for refugees, compared to 7 ill-equipped, poorly staffed health centres that lack basic medicine and equipment for the local community. While in principle these health centres are open to the local community, in practice the latter are expected to pay for treatment. A notice on one of the notice boards indicating this distinction reads: "Free medical services is for refugees only. Locals are required to pay in line with the cost sharing policy". Owing to poverty levels most locals are unable to afford these services, although they continue to live among refugees who access them freely. Kakuma refugee camp in northern Kenya, which has an area of 12 square kilometres, has 22 schools (20 pre- and primary schools and 2 secondary schools). This compares with 3 primary schools for the entire Kakuma division, which has an area of more than 100 square kilometres. As the locals collect and use untreated water from the seasonal river, Tarach, into which the camp hospital and health centres dispose their waste, refugees have more than 6 boreholes generating approximately 71.3 cubic metres (71,000 litres) of water daily, with over 10 water collection points, ensuring between 18–21 litres of water per person per day. As Jeff Crisp aptly demonstrates, such disparities exacerbate resentment of refugees and contribute to insecurity in and around Kakuma camp (1999).

In an attempt to redress this imbalance, UNHCR has funded construction of water systems in Kakuma division and allows a certain proportion of the locals to access social services such as hospitals and schools within the camp. In Tanzania, this redress has taken the form of refocusing on an affected area approach, which addresses common needs rather than targeting refugees to the exclusion of their hosts. However, these measures are exceptions rather than the rule; they represent attempts to ameliorate situations of great disparity rather than forming constitutive elements of humanitarian action. A radically different approach—such as that envisaged in the ICARA meetings—puts the African state at the centre of the process, rather than at its margins to where the international humanitarian regime has progressively pushed it. The alternative approach entails giving more responsibility and more resources to the state for responding to humanitarian emergencies. In effect, it means scaling down or bypassing the international humanitarian regime. While the approach would necessarily have to be adjusted to the nature of the state and the emergency in question, a shift in this direction seems necessary for building local capacity whether this is in the public or private sectors.

## Shrinking Funding, Agency Competition vis-à-vis Institutional Survival

Although funding trends indicate a general increase in resources available for use in relief operations, the multiplication of emergencies as well as the exponential growth of actors has precipitated intense competition resulting in a dramatic reduction of resources available to some agencies. The managing of the resource kitty in terms of who has access to resources has a direct impact on local capacity issues. Throughout the 1990s, resources available to East Africa dwindled as attention turned to more dramatic emergencies in Rwanda and elsewhere. For instance, UNHCR's general programme budget in Kenya dropped from $56 million in 1993 to approximately $20 million in 1999. From being a major donor at the beginning of the emergency, UNHCR was receiving less than the total relief funds administered by any three international NGOs by 2000.

In general, the culture of the international humanitarian regime is one where pressure to be present or perish, to do or die, leads the agencies to aggressively and constantly defend their turf. Among tactics employed for survival is defending resource flows by blocking access of other agencies to resource kitties. Larger actors cultivate intermediary roles between donors and local agencies and engage in high-level media campaigns to drum up support for their programs. Unsurprisingly, the 1990s became a decade of media, publicity and public relations officers as agencies began to operate under what Alex de Waal (1997) calls a humanitarian Gresham's law, according to which programs that are good for generating funds drive out those that may be more effective or sensitive but that cannot obtain publicity. This resulted in intensive use of social networks and "cartels" that generated an "imperfect" market, as the larger, well-connected actors locked the smaller weaker ones out of the performance arena. New to the specifications and requirements of most donor agencies, local actors found their capacity to access resources limited and fell out of the resource loop.

Donor practices of channelling resources through some favoured NGOs worsened the situation. More than two thirds of resources disbursed by DFID-UK for the rehabilitation of internally displaced persons in Kenya in 1997 was spent by two UK based NGOs, namely Action Aid and International Child Trust (ICT). This pattern was also evident in Tanzania and Uganda in the 1990s, where resources donated by the UK were spent exclusively by or through Oxfam—UK and Ireland. An increasing number of multilateral donors were also adopting this trend and demanding that local actors create partnerships with international counterparts in order to access their funds. Invariably these 'partnerships' are 'headed' by the international (Northern-based) partners. These partnerships have one common characteristic: while justification for seeking funding is local needs and agencies, Northern 'partners' are exclusively the lead agencies in accounting and directing utilisation of funds.

This structure creates a layer of powerful INGOs that act as resource gatekeepers. Being conduits for funds gives international agencies enormous power to define humanitarian aid structures. In East Africa, this system of resource patronage extended to operational levels where all local NGOs, except those affiliated to international structures such as the churches, were relegated to being sub-contractors of the larger well-connected international agencies. In a significant way the determination of aid strategies, allocation of resources and planning of specific projects were thereby controlled by external agencies, without reference to overall national planning or local aid structures (Harrell-Bond, Hussein and Matlou, 1992).

## Contractual Implementation Structure

As with other forms of aid, humanitarian work is increasingly being characterised by stringent 'contractual' demands for financial accountability and realisation of tangible outputs. Donor pressure for agencies to demonstrate financial accountability is steadily taking precedence over issues of altruism and "doing good" missions. Pressure to show quick results means issues intrinsic to capacity building, including the creation and retention of human resources, are given low priority as actors privilege activities with measurable output indicators. To ensure the desired performance while at the same time cutting costs in training, an activity which donors are reluctant to fund, international actors engaged in poaching from the relatively small pool of trained and experienced local staff from various sectors. For instance, at the height of the Somali refugee emergency in 1993, UNHCR employed the Director of the Refugee Secretariat in Kenya to head its Sub-Office in Ngara, Tanzania. While this bolstered UNHCR's capacity, it was a major setback for the Refugee Secretariat, which remained dormant for nearly a year. Kenyan nationals who worked in Dadaab refugee camp complex at various times during this emergency provided a large reservoir of experience for international agencies that operated in the Goma camps for Rwandese refugees after 1994. This had an immediate negative impact on programs in Kenya because agencies were forced to recruit people with little or no experience in refugee-related work. Reflecting on the effect of the rapid staff turnover, the Head of UNHCR Sub-Office in Kakuma told this author in 1999 that "UNHCR is constantly engaged in 'baby sitting' new NGO staff that have no clue what to do, because NGO hiring goes on throughout the year".

Differences in pay packets and conditions of work between international and local NGOs contribute to high staff turn-over, especially among the latter, and poaching of local staff by international agencies. Without exception all INGOs pay higher salaries than their local counterparts. There is also a further incentive in moving to another country, which turns a local into an "international," employee. In most cases, this translates into more than three times the local staff salary, even if job responsibility is similar. Reflecting on this disparity, a Ugandan humanitarian staff member described to this author her reaction after her first salary in Goma as an international employee: "When my first salary came, I thought there had been a big mistake.

Although I had been doing the same job as local staff in Uganda, I earned much, much, much less." The ongoing poaching leads to depletion of local capacity and reduction in the capacity of host communities and institutions to deal with the consequences of refugee emergencies.

UNHCR's contracting policy towards implementing partners was particularly key in inhibiting the creation or retention of local capacity. As a rule, UNHCR demands that NGOs agencies seeking partnership demonstrate experiences in emergency response, credit worthiness and ability to cater for their overhead costs (see UNHCR 1984). On a prima facie basis, these conditions exclude most local NGOs for lack of experience beyond their countries. Nearly all NGOs have limited capacity in accessing resources from international sources. Further, the interpretation of these requirements in East Africa was left largely to the discretion of the Resident Representatives, resulting in a systematic bias during the selection of "partners" that favoured international actors. Consequently, during the entire emergency period (1990–1997), less than 10 per cent of local actors were given the status of lead agencies throughout the region.

While UNHCR cited experience as one of the core requirements for partnership, only one international NGO, the Lutheran World Federation (LWF), had amassed experience working in emergencies in Tanzania before the 1990s. Care International, the lead agency in the Dadaab refugee camps since 1991, operated in Kenya as a development agency. Oxfam, which had some experience with famine relief in Turkana, was contracted for a year to help establish water supply systems. In Uganda, the Deutsche Entwicklungs Dienst (German Development Service—DED) ascended to the lead agency status in Rhino camp in northern Uganda without any prior experience with emergency relief. As will be argued later, these agencies may have accumulated experiences in other parts of the world, however, such experience did not necessarily transfer to the East African context.

In contrast, attempts by local NGOs to become partners of UNHCR were rejected for "lack of capacity" and the actors "urged" to create capacities as a prerequisite for partnership. This produced a vicious circle that generated frustration for local NGO staff and partly explains the prevailing desire to become international staff. Capturing the frustration resulting from the UNHCR interpretation of capacity, the Chief Executive of one local NGO observed:

> If an agency asks for a budget of Kshs. 1 million ($15,000) funding, agencies (INGOs) say that reflects lack of capacity. When you ask for a budget of more than Kshs. 5 million ($45,000) you are told you lack capacity to handle such resources. Whichever way you go, you lose (Communication to the author, 1994).

Whether an actor was perceived to have experience (capacity) determined its positioning in the humanitarian power structure. Presumed to be most experienced, lead agencies were bestowed with immense power and authority. They were the gatekeepers to camp(s) and operational areas under their control, had power to approve the participation of other agencies or visits by individuals to these areas and had authority to supervise and oversee the activities of other agencies on behalf of UNHCR. In the chain of command, they were de facto deputies to UNHCR and held the second most powerful position within the humanitarian structure. Even when UNHCR in the mid-1990s began to reassert its supervisory and monitoring position and expanded its presence to all refugee hosting areas in East Africa, it continued to depend heavily on the reports of lead agencies in making operational decisions.

Unsurprisingly, lead agencies were not eager to relegate or share their power, but sought instead to maintain and expand the power that came with their privileged position. When in 1996 LWF, then the lead agency in Kakuma, was stripped of its status following a series of scandals and growing unease within UNHCR as well as among other actors about its increasing power, the organisation experienced a drastic reduction in power. In less than a year, 30 per cent of its jobs were lost as two of its largest programs, health provision and community rehabilitation services, were contracted out to another INGO, the International Rescue Committee (IRC).

In response, LWF engaged in a damage control campaign. A new Country Representative was appointed and the head of field programmes replaced. Accompanying these changes there was intense networking and lobbying of the UNHCR Branch Office (Nairobi) and Headquarters (Geneva). Soon LWF was back in the fold. By June 1998, its social services division was expanding rapidly, sometimes duplicating activities of other agencies. Arguing that the LWF rehabilitation had nothing to do with its ability, experience or expertise (capacity), one UNHCR officer observed:

> Really LWF should have gone... but there was immense lobbying at Geneva and Nairobi levels. The current Country Director is very close to the UNHCR Resident Representative and good at lobbying. So LWF is still here but we all know its presence has nothing to do with performance... it is politics...that is what keeps agencies in the field.

Ability to network and cultivate patrons among powerful actors was key in determining the positioning of an agency within the humanitarian arena. Lacking in influential patrons, local NGOs became the subordinated clients and had to be content with the status of sub-contractors for international NGOs.

UNHCR funding trends, in particular the development of the rationalisation policy, accelerated the marginalisation of local organizations in the late 1990s. Justified as a means of facilitating a smooth transition from relief to rehabilitation, the rationalisation policy required a multi-sectoral agency to implement all programs in an operational area. Local NGOs became the immediate victims of the policy as they implemented small (appendage) programs, usually sub-contracted by INGOs. By 1998, rationalisation had been implemented in most refugees hosting areas across East Africa, and in all except Nakivale in South West Uganda, UNHCR partners were international NGOs.

While this policy favoured INGOs, its implementation sparked off power struggles among larger actors in the humanitarian arena. In Kakuma refugee camp an attempt at rationalisation resulted in a dilemma for UNHCR when both LWF and IRC expressed interest in being multi-sectoral operators, necessitating making a choice between them that was difficult. One local aid official aptly summarised the situation:

> If any of these agencies were local, the decision for rationalisation would have been very easy and already accomplished. But that is not the case. LWF has built impressive lobbying networks. But IRC is American and enjoys leverage at the national and international levels. It is real politics at work and UNHCR is in a real dilemma. There is no way of implementing rationalisation in Kakuma without losing a friend! (Communication to author, 1998).

On the ground, agency rivalry translated into animosity between the staff of these organisations. Team leaders issued guidelines prohibiting co-operation between their staff and those of other organisations, even when they were involved in similar activities. This denied programs coherence and the benefits of complementarity.

The rationalisation policy raises the question of the threshold for exit. In the late 1990s, the numbers of operational international NGOs had been reduced considerably throughout East Africa, yet those present were more entrenched and operated larger programs. While rationalisation may have some operational advantages such as maximising performance of the more able agencies, it affects local capacity issues negatively by encouraging the entrenchment of international NGOs. This causes further marginalisation and destruction of local capacity.

Rather than nurturing local capacities in ways that could facilitate a smooth take-over by local actors when INGOs withdrew, evidence from Kenya suggests that INGO expansion and entrenchment weakened local capacities. This was particularly the case in situations of IDPs where international actors killed local initiatives and capacities. On the whole, areas that had minimal presence of international agencies rehabilitated faster and better than where full-scale intervention occurred. One such case is the Mt. Longonot area in Kenya where victims of displacement were assisted through local community structures. Within a few months most returned to their homes. In Thessalia, (Kisumu) Kenya, three agencies facilitated the relocation of the victims (without being physically there) and encouraged local agricultural experts to register a local NGO that would provide extension services to them. Soon, the impact of this agency was evident in the dramatic increase in yield and quality of production from plots that were much smaller than the vacated farms (Kathina Juma and Masika, 1997). Responding to high demand, this agency expanded its services to three neighbouring districts.

These two experiences contrast starkly with examples of areas that witnessed large-scale intervention by outsiders. For instance, in an effort to respond to displacement in Enoosupukia, humanitarian agencies created Maela camp in 1993. Highly visible, Maela became a pitch for 'games' between UNDP and the government of Kenya, at the expense of the victims (HRW, 1997). In Burnt Forest, large-scale intervention not only killed local initiatives but caused further impoverishment of the victims of displacement. Typical to areas that witnessed massive intervention was lack of co-ordination as a local priest in Burnt Forest observes:

> UNDP, MSF-Belgium, MSF-France, NCCK, Catholic Church, Red Cross, human rights organisations, mention them, all of them were here...all of us. Then every agency was doing anything it wanted. There was no co-ordination, no listening to each other... nothing. It was not unusual to find a family with 6 tins of oil from 6 different agencies when they did not have a blanket. By the end of it the displacee was far worse than when he/she fled here for help. Now I have been left with a parish that is worse off and a 'refugee' camp in the parish compound, with no one to help. I think the intervening agencies helped themselves more than the victims. The whole issue of helping has been politicised and this has only multiplied problems here ... child prostitution, refusal to return and hence occupation of farm lands, dependency etc. I really wish all these agencies had not come to Burnt Forest...Vulnerability is higher today than it was when the emergency began.

The moral of this experience is clear. As Eade and Williams argue, interventions ran the risk of leaving a trail of weakened victims and local institutions (1995:861).

## Partnership between Local and International Actors

The marginalisation of state structures, and relations between humanitarian agencies and donors are mediated by a humanitarian techno-speak that justifies the patronage of international actors over local actors and capacities. The logic driving partnerships is the fact that international agencies are resource rich, have experiences, are technically appropriate and able to mobilise and manage resources. In contrast, local actors are perceived as weak, lacking in the requisite capacities and as partisan in crises. Ideologically, international experts are assumed to have sufficient credentials to get on with the work, whatever the local nuances. Somewhat ironically, few expatriate staff had previous management experience of the kind required for relief operations in the 1990s.

On the whole, the experience from East Africa shows that local staff, whether employed by international or local agencies, ran field operations and remained crucial to programme continuity. While local staff rarely rose to top decision-making positions, and remained at programme positions, on average they held higher levels of training, experience in related fields and more than half had at least one postgraduate qualification. Their international counterparts, who held policy and decision-making positions, were a mixed bag. While some were highly trained, at any one time, a majority were recent graduates or student interns, with hardly any emergency or related experience and comparatively much younger than their local counterparts. Aware of this reality, international 'experts' depended largely on local (junior) staff to run programs, but this dependency was neither acknowledged officially nor rewarded.

One case is particularly instructive. A Kenyan who had worked as a programme officer with UNDP's internally displaced persons programme, was employed by UNHCR as an Assistant Protection Officer at the Sub-Office level. After two years of undertaking protection work he was replaced with a young law graduate. Trained in Belgium, the new protection officer had limited, if any, familiarity with the relevant common law, let alone the network of traditional practices at play in any refugee camp. This replacement was justified with the argument that the Kenyan did not have a law degree and therefore could not undertake protection work effectively. Six months after the arrival of the Belgian-trained protection officer, the Kenyan was still doing most protection duties in addition to his responsibilities as an assistance programme officer. Yet his salary was less than a quarter of that of his colleague. In this case, capacity was evidently being built in reverse, without being acknowledged. Such was the typical pattern in the humanitarian scene of the 1990s. Inexperience was also evident among officers given leadership positions. Exasperated by this pattern, one UNHCR field officer in Dadaab refugee camp exclaimed:

> Aid workers, especially UNHCR people, come in with no experience in managing and leading a community, yet that is what their job is. They must immediately become a leader and most are not prepared to do that. They don't have the experience, skills, or knowledge to do what the job requires.

In all these cases, most expatriates lacked knowledge of the local environment, including rules, social regulation mechanisms or social customs. Their ignorance was a cause of great frustration for those they worked with. Although infrequent, tensions arose from such situations and sometimes led to clashes between international and local staff. In one case, the conduct of some European medical officers, unfamiliar with tropical diseases, ended in a physical confrontation between them and the Kenya medical team in the Dadaab camp, causing great embarrassment for UNHCR. This anomaly was pervasive in a system that remained insensitive and generated great inequalities. As noted by one IRC leader in Kakuma (1993–94):

> There are thousands of good Kenyan health care employed who today are traumatised by insensitive expat nurses who come in thinking they know it all and that the locals are incompetent and don't want to work hard. For an NGO to put that kind of inexperienced person in charge is absolutely mad, but it happens all the time (Walkup 1994).

The lack of a clear merit-based system translated into institutional competition where actors jostled for performance space and needed to cultivate patrons and clients to ensure survival. Nowhere was the effect of this on local capacity as well exemplified as by the Partnership in Action (PARinAc) process.

As noted at the outset of this chapter, the international community took an initiative in the early 1990s to improve "partnership" in relief assistance and development cooperation. UNHCR followed up in 1993 with a PARinAc initiative that aimed at increasing and sustaining local capacity, especially in emergency prone situations, and creating in-country resource data bases as reservoirs from where emergency "rapid" response teams could be drawn. Local actors, making up these databases, would be the entry points for international actors; together they would create a framework for partnerships that would enhance effective and efficient humanitarian operations.

The methodology proposed in pursuing the PARinAc objectives was building trust between international and local actors, especially NGOs. Critics of this methodology argue that the structure of the humanitarian regime is in fact predicated not on trust, but on an authority structure that is maintained and legitimised by the very absence of trust between givers and recipients. Accordingly, it is implausible to inject trust by wishing it into a structure that is fraught with competition, suspicion and mistrust (Harrell-Bond, Voutira and Leopold, 1992). To operate in politically charged political environments, actors are in reality compelled to play political games, be manipulative, negotiate their presence and create networks that strengthen their positions vis-à-vis other agencies. When such activities take place among states they are labelled realpolitik. In the humanitarian sphere, they are defended as unintended consequences. The experience with PARinAc in Kenya exemplifies the manner in which power issues, reinforced by patronizing attitudes and insensitivity of international agencies, can weaken local initiatives and diminish local capacity.

### Before and after Oslo: Building or Destroying Capacity?

Prior to the initiation of the UNHCR PARinAc process, Kenya was host to large numbers of refugees whose presence attracted numerous humanitarian actors. (Kathina Juma, 1995:89–113). Unprecedented in scale, this emergency generated multiple challenges for policy makers as well as practitioners. In response to performance-related issues a group of individuals and agencies from human rights organisations and academic institutions created a forum to provide space for implementing agencies to debrief each other, share information on programs and present their work to interested parties that were not necessarily operational. Known as the Ad-hoc Refugee Advocacy Group (ARAG), this group was housed within the Kenyan Chapter of the International Commission of Jurists (ICJ). Starting from a small group of volunteers, ARAG expanded to include all humanitarian agencies, as well as the Government of Kenya, which was granted observer status. Within a short time, the forum began to inject accountability into the humanitarian arena.

Out of the credibility it earned itself, ARAG gained a stature as a legitimate and independent arbitrator within this arena. It began to receive complaints, listen, investigate and adjudicate disagreements between actors, and to intercede and make petitions on behalf of refugees and NGOs (particularly the local ones) to the government and UNHCR. In undertaking these tasks ARAG established formal and informal networks with various sectors of the society including the media and the AG chambers and its influence grew noticeably. It was ARAG that pushed for the withdrawal of the first three refugee draft bills (1990, 1992, 1993) as each favoured state security rather than refugee protection. By the beginning of 1993, ARAG was injecting a measure of transparency into the humanitarian arena in Kenya. In reality, therefore, a central element of the PARinAc process was alive in Kenya long before its conceptualisation and initiation by UNHCR. However, the fact of this organisation being local, a cause for great pride among those who conceived and ran it independent of the humanitarian industry, caused much unease among powerful actors, as would become apparent.

In March 1994, ICJ was invited to the African regional PARinAc consultative meeting in Addis Ababa. At the meeting, Kenyan delegates reported on the progress of "their" PARinAc process in Kenya. In spite of its critical role, neither the ICJ nor the ARAG were invited to the final PARAinAc meeting held in Oslo in June 1994. Nonetheless, considering the matter of establishing a PARinAc focal point as a fait accompli, Kenyan delegates to Oslo endorsed ARAG cum ICJ as the country focal point. This was not to be. The UNHCR Branch Office in Nairobi together with some international NGOs blocked the endorsement of ARAG as Kenya's PARinAc focal point on two counts. First, UNHCR argued that a PARinAc focal point had to be field-based and, second, UNHCR insisted that the nomination of ARAG was undemocratic and demanded demonstration of democracy—with elections of a focal point. Encouraged by UNHCR, one international (Islamic) organisation organised an election in which it was itself 'elected' as the national and regional PARinAc focal point. This agency then started calling "PARinAc" meetings on the same days as ARAG, causing immense confusion within the humanitarian arena. Interestingly, UNHCR sent representatives to both meetings, creating confusion both ways.

In April 1995, the Geneva based International Council of Voluntary Agencies (ICVA), the NGO global PARinAc focal point, organised a follow-up meeting in Nairobi. However, neither ICJ nor ARAG were invited to this meeting. Protests against the omission were raised at the beginning of the meeting and information dispatched to ICJ, following which the programme officer heading the human rights and refugee programme, who doubled up as liaison and secretary to ARAG, was sent to the meeting. When she arrived at the venue, she was refused entry to the meeting hall, an act that heightened tensions throughout the meeting and effectively put the last nail in the coffin of the PARinAc process in Kenya. The UNHCR sponsored focal point never called a meeting after this incident, feeding suspicions that UNHCR's key objective was to kill the local initiative. Since then no such forum has come into existence and UNHCR as well as other large agencies deal with local NGOs individually. The death of ARAG not only heightened cynicism of Kenyans towards the commitment of international agencies to follow through on the objective of building local relief capacity, but also carried a painful lesson. It indicated clearly that when local interests conflict or threaten those of international actors, the latter can effectively neutralise local capacity.

The pattern of destruction of local capacity was replicated with grave consequences in situations of internal displacement where local actors initially played a critical role. The example most cited is the destruction of the Western Province Co-ordination Committee (WPCC). Created in 1993 by NGOs operating in Western Kenya in response to the displacement that swept the region in 1991–92, WPCC was mandated to co-ordinate relief, rehabilitation and resettlement of the victims. WPCC began to register success in making agencies accountable, ensuring that the government delivered on security issues and instituting a division of labour that reduced duplication and wastage of resources. These successes contributed to a remarkable degree of resettlement and rehabilitation of displaced populations in this part of the country.

The entry of UNDP as the national co-ordinator for the internally displaced persons programme halted the success of WPCC, starting in 1994. After promising to

fund and provide logistical assistance to the Committee, as well as to support rehabilitation and development programmes, UNDP assumed the driver's seat and began
to overshadow WPCC. In an attempt to establish a functional relationship with
UNDP, the WPCC co-ordinator isolated the Committee from its initial members,
namely, the local actors. Meanwhile, donor pledges to the reconstruction process fell
through and funding for WPCC became indeterminate. Unable to fulfil its promises
or to secure the WPCC, UNDP cut the funding of the Committee abruptly and asked
the co-ordinator to close the office within a fortnight in March 1995. With this closure, WPCC had effectively collapsed.

## What Relief Capacity Was Built in the 1990s?

Throughout the 1990s, local capacity building for humanitarian action in East Africa took three ineffectual forms. The first was minimal information sharing, especially when actors felt threatened by the government. While there were numerous calls
for agency co-ordination, the larger and better-funded INGOs remained reluctant,
arguing that they derived limited or no benefit from co-ordination. Instead, they preferred to cultivate patrons and clients independently across the humanitarian and
political systems. This practice inhibited the promotion of policy in the humanitarian arena and led each actor to protect its objectives and using its resources to enhance its presence. At the end of the 1990s, aware of this anomaly and still claiming
commitment to capacity building, UNHCR recommended a wide range of informal
and formal training, conducted by its officers and its consultants. A major component of this training involved issues related to financial probity and reporting mechanisms. The basic aim was to ensure that agencies met donor-reporting requirements
in the face of dwindling resources and increasingly complicated accounting procedures. In Tanzania for instance, the Norwegian Red Cross reporting demands were
such that the local Red Cross Society was often either behind in the reporting sched-
ule or engaged in reporting, as an on-going activity. Another UNHCR capacity
building activity took the form of internship programs, whose chief beneficiaries
were students from outside of East Africa. The most popular of these was the Ogata
camp programme, which recruited students from the developed world and sponsored them to stay in camps for periods of 1–3 months.

UNHCR also conceived capacity building in the form of funding some select activities of a few local actors, including the official Refugee Secretariats in the three
East African countries. While the level of support varied, most of it was confined to
paying for consumables such as fuel, transport, and topping up salaries (called incentives) for officers in local structures or seconded to international humanitarian
actors. Based on an unclear system of determination, the incentive structure failed
to ensure sustainability and created divisions and tensions between those who benefited from it and the rest who perceived it as outright discriminatory (Kathina
Juma, 2000:Chapter 5). While benefiting select individuals, the incentive system did
not focus on institutional building.

Finally, capacity building involved limited training that was conceived and guided by the workshop model. Workshops were one-off events, facilitated mainly by international "experts" and rarely built on each other in any coherent way that would
facilitate accumulation of critical knowledge. For instance, workshops in trauma
healing in Northern Uganda were based on a Harvard-generated model that hardly
tapped local knowledge, expertise or resources. The local people responded by mak-

ing continued use of their traditional mechanisms, as illustrated in Chapter 7 on Uganda.

Glaringly absent in this catalogue of capacity building is the notion of learning from local skills and expertise. The starting point for any empowerment programme is the realisation that no matter how well intentioned, the structure of administering assistance has important implications for the host state and the local environment. It may reinforce the dominant top-down approach, exacerbate processes of institutional marginalisation and destruction, permit outside agencies to gain great control over policies and practice, and may fail to enhance the capacity of government institutions, local institutions or community-based organisations. If not well structured, empowerment programs may have the effect of destroying rather than creating or bolstering capacity.

Further, there is a need to appreciate that empowering local structures involves major political decisions. To situate capacity building within the expanding anti-political arena of humanitarianism is to cloak a real political issue in the language of 'humanitarianism' and 'development' techno-speak. It is mystification in its elementary form. The language seeks to present the aid apparatus as an 'anti-politics machine' and interprets empowerment as a technical rather than a fundamentally political process (Fergusson, 1990). In this framework, creating capacity easily becomes another name for avoiding the critical issues of democratisation and opening up real participation of the South to determine the manner in which it should be assisted, if at all. It means failure to focus on issues of power and establishing whether there is a commitment to situate it where it ought to be, i.e. with local actors, if empowerment is the ultimate objective of these programs.

Locating capacity building in empowerment terms allows the asking of pertinent questions. What should be the threshold of intervention? What level of empowerment should be created by the time agencies phase out? What time is required for this process? As observed elsewhere, when an intervention begins without determination of why, when or how it will be phased out (as most are), interveners are unable to relinquish control and instead expand and entrench their presence. Their operations create needs that require further intervention. In such situations, it is clearly doubtful that the presence of outside capacity is empowering to either the people or their institutions (Eade and Williams, 1995).

Patronage created by humanitarian systems can only be countered by injecting participation that will make aid actors accountable to the beneficiaries of their programs. Actors whose capacity is being created hardly know who is funding their capacity building or how many resources are available. The mystery that covers humanitarianism systems should be unveiled by strengthening the accountability of those who seek to provide relief and build capacity. Transparency would also counter the obscurity and power that characterises the resource transfer process. Transfer of goods from donors to recipients creates a long chain of hands and networks of power, all seeking to exercise power, patronage and control. If there is no accountability and genuine participation of stakeholders, such power can be and has been abused. The powerful actors will become reluctant to surrender it. In contributing to this debate de Waal (1997) argues that democratisation of aid is a necessary imperative because conceptually it would remove assistance from aid-speak, which consists of trying to talk about power without mentioning it by name. According to de Waal, it is only in acknowledging that aid is essentially a political process with political consequences (up to now mostly anti-democratic) that change can come.

Change will only result from efforts to change power relations within aid establishments, and this is likely to be met by resistance.

Further, democratisation would call for recognition of all stakeholders. The prevailing notion among some humanitarian agencies that African governments are bad, inept, failing, obstructive and should therefore be excluded from interventions is not conducive to capacity building. It is a position that marginalises and threatens an actor that is critical in the creation of an enabling environment for empowerment. It also leads agencies to turn their back on an institution with capacities that can, if well utilised, facilitate empowerment of various sectors across society (Atampugre, 1994).

Finally, democratisation calls for the overhauling of token projects such as piecemeal Africanisation programs. It calls for full devolution of power, which is least observed in the humanitarian arena for the very reason that it counters the logic of assistance: patronage. In all these processes, the role of information needs emphasising. As it stands, information is generated by Northerners, stored and used by Northern agencies. The need to establish systems of generating knowledge at the local level, sharing and utilising it is critical to any empowerment process, if only for the fact that information is power.

# References

## Chapter 1. Introduction

Duffield, Mark, 1994, "Complex Emergencies and the Crisis of Developmentalism", *IDS Bulletin* 25, 4.

Duffield, M., 2001. *Global Governance and the New Wars*. London: Zed Books.

Gellner, Ernst, 1988, *Plough, Sword and Book. The Structure of Human History*. Chicago: University of Chicago Press.

Kathina Juma, Monica, 2001, *The Politics of Humanitarian Assistance: States, NGOs and Displacement in Kenya and Uganda (1989–1999)*. D. Phil. Thesis, University of Oxford.

Maynard, Kimberly, 1999, *Healing Communities in Conflict*. Columbia University Press.

Smillie, Ian, (ed.) 2001, *Patronage or Partnership. Local Capacity Building in Humanitarian Crises*. Bloomfield, CT: Kumarian Press.

Sollenberg, Margareta and Peter Wallensteen, 1999, "Armed Conflict, 1989–99", *Journal of Peace Research*, 37, 5.

de Waal, Alex, 1997, *Famine Crimes. Politics and the Disaster Relief Industry in Africa*. Bloomington: Indiana University Press.

www.ifrc.org/where/appeals/index.asp.


## Chapter 2. From relief to social services. An international humanitarian regime takes form.

ASIL, 2000, "Guiding Principles on Internal Displacement", *Studies in Transnational Legal Policy*, No. 32. Washington D.C.: The American Society of International Law.

Baitenmann, Helga, 1990, "NGOs and the Afghan War: The Politicisation of Humanitarian Aid", *Third World Quarterly*, 12, 1.

Barber, Ben, 1997, "Feeding Refugees or War?" *Foreign Affairs*, 76, 4.

Berdal, Mats and David I. Malone, 2000, *Greed and Grievance. Economic Agendas in Civil Wars*. Boulder, Colo.: Lynne Rienner.

Brauman, Rony, 1996, *Le dilemme humanitaire. Entretient avec Philippe Petit*. Paris: Éditions Textuel.

Burr, J. Millard and Robert O. Collins, 1995, *Requiem for the Sudan: War, Drought, and Disaster Relief on the Nile*. Boulder, Col.: Westview Press.

Cohen, Roberta and Francis Deng, 1998, *Masses in Flight*. Washington, D.C.: Brookings.

Cutts, Mark, 1999, *The Humanitarian Operation in Bosnia 1992–95: Dilemmas of Negotiating Humanitarian Access*. Geneva: UNHCR.

Daedring, Jürgen, 1996, "Humanitarian Coordination", in Jim Whitman and David Peacock, (eds), *After Rwanda: The Coordination of United Nations Humanitarian Assistance*. London: Macmillan.

Danida, 1996, *Joint Evaluation of International Emergency Assistance to Rwanda*. Copenhagen: Ministry of Foreign Affairs.

Danida, 1999, *Evaluation of Danish Humanitarian Assistance. UN and International Organizations*. Vol. 8. Copenhagen: Ministry of Foreign Affairs. www.um.dk./danida/evalueringsrapporter/1999-9/index.asp.

Danida, 1999a, *Evaluation of Danish Humanitarian Assistance. Evaluation of Danish Humanitarian Assistance to Sudan, 1992–98*. Vol. 7. Copenhagen: Ministry of Foreign Affairs. www.um.dk./danida/evalueringsrapporter/1999-9/index.asp..

Duffield, Mark, 2001, *Global Governance and the New Wars*. London: Zed Books.

Eliasson, Jan, 1992, "Humanitarian Assistance and Development". Unpublished address to the Governing Council of the UNDP, May 12,1992.

Ellwood, Sheelagh M., 1991, *The Spanish Civil War*. Oxford: Blackwell.

Forman, Shepherd and P. Steward, (eds), 2000, *Good Intentions. Pledges of Aid for Post-Conflict Recovery*. Boulder/London: Lynne Rienner.

Forsythe, David, 1977, *Humanitarian Politics: The International Committee of the Red Cross*. Baltimore: Johns Hopkins University Press.

Haas, Ernst, B., 1990, *When Knowledge Is Power*. Berkeley: University of California Press.

Haas, Peter M., Robert O. Keohane and Marc A. Levy. (eds),1993, *Institutions for the Earth. Sources of Effective International Environmental Protection*. Cambridge, Mass.: MIT Press.

Higgins, Rosalyn, 1993, "The New United Nations and Former Yugoslavia", *International Affairs*, 69, 3.

Hobsbawm, Eric, 1996, *The Age of Extremes. A History of the World, 1914–1991*. New York: Vintage Books.

ICRC, 1985, *Annual Report*. Geneva: International Committee of the Red Cross.

Kaul, Inge et al., (eds),1999, *Global Public Goods: International Cooperation in the 21st Century*. New York: Oxford University Press.

Keen, David, 1994, "The Functions of Famine in Southwestern Sudan: Implications for Relief," in Joanna Macrae and Anthony Zwi, *War and Hunger*. London: Zed Books.

Kratochwil, Friedrich, 1993, "Contract and Regimes: Do Issue Specificity and Variations of Formality Matter?", in Volker Rittberger, (ed.) *Regime Theory and International Relations*. Oxford: Clarendon Press.

Loescher, Gil, 1993, *Beyond Charity*. Oxford: Oxford University Press.

Loescher, G., 2001, *The UNHCR and World Politics: A Perilous Path*. Oxford: Oxford Univ Press.

Macrae, Joanne and M. Bradbury, 1998, *Aid in the Twilight Zone. A Critical Analysis of Humanitarian-Development Aid Linkages in Situations of Chronic Instability*. London: Overseas Development Institute.

Maren Michael, 1997, *The Road to Hell. The Ravaging Effects of Foreign Aid and International Charity*. New York: The Free Press.

Mason, Linda and Roger Brown, 1983, *Rice, Rivalry and Politics: Managing Cambodian Relief*. Notre Dame, Indiana: University of Notre Dame Press.

ODI, 2001, *Humanitarian Coordination: Lessons from Recent Field Experience*. London: Overseas Development Institute.

Prendergast, John, 1997, *Crisis Response. Humanitarian Band-Aids in Sudan and Somalia*. London: Pluto Press.

Ramsbotham, Oliver and Tom Woodhouse, 1996, *Humanitarian Intervention in Contemporary Conflict: A Reconceptualization*. Cambridge: Polity Press.

Rieff, David, 1996, *Slaughterhouse. Bosnia and the Failure of the West*. New York: Simon and Schuster.

Rittberger, Volker, (ed.), 1993, *Regime Theory and International Relations*. Oxford: Clarendon Press.

Roberts, Adam, 1996, *Humanitarian Action in War*, Adelphi Paper no. 305. London: International Institute of Strategic Studies.

Rufin, Jean-Christophe, 1996, "Les économies de guerre dans les conflicts internes", in Francois Jean and Jean-Christophe Rufin, (eds), *Économie des guerres civiles*. Paris: Hachette.

Shawcross, William, 1984, *The Quality of Mercy: Cambodia, Holocaust, and Modern Conscience*. New York: Simon and Schuster.

Smillie, Ian, (ed.), 2001, *Patronage or Partnership. Local Capacity Building in Humanitarian Crises*. Bloomfield, CT: Kumarian Press.

Sollenberg, Margareta and Peter Wallensteen, 1997, "Armed Conflict, 1989–99", *Journal of Peace Research*, 37, 5.

Stremlau, John, 1977, *The International Politics of the Nigerian Civil War, 1967–1970*. Princeton: Princeton University Press.

Suhrke, Astri, 1995, "Responding to Global Refugee Problems: The Role of UNHCR," in Lydio Tomasi, (ed.), *In Defense of the Alien*. Vol.XVII. New York: Center for Migration Studies.

Suhrke, Astri et al., 2000, *The Kosovo Refugee Crisis. An independent evaluation of UNHCR's emergency preparedness and response*. www.unhcr.ch/epau/eval.

Terry, Fiona, 2000, *Condemned to Repeat? The Paradoxes of Humanitarian Action*. Ph.D. thesis. Australian National University, Canberra.

Thomas, Hugh, (ed.), 1986, *The Spanish Civil War*. New York: Simon and Schuster.

Tvedt, Terje, 1998, *Angels of Mercy*. Trenton, N.J.: Africa World Press.

United Nations, 1998, *Report of the Secretary-General on protection for humanitarian assistance to refugees and others in conflict situations*. S/1998/883.

United Nations, 1999, *Secretary-General's Annual Report to the General Assembly*. SG/SM/ 7136,GA/9596.

UNHCR, 1993, *The State of the World's Refugees*. UNHCR. Geneva/Oxford: Penguin.

de Waal, Alex, 1997, *Famine Crimes. Politics and the Disaster Relief Industry in Africa*. Bloomington: Indiana University Press.

Weiss, Thomas G. and Cindy Collins, 1996, *Humanitarian Challenges and Intervention*. Boulder, Col.: Westview Press.

Weiss, Thomas G. and Leon Gordenker, 1996, *NGOs, the UN & Global Governance*. Boulder, Col.: Lynne, Rienner.

Woodward, Susan, 1995, *The Balkan Tragedy*. Washington, D.C.: Brookings Institution.

WFP, 1999, *Partnership with NGOs*. Rome. World Food Programme. WFP/EB.1/99/3-A.

World Bank, 1998, *The World Bank's Experience with Post-Conflict Reconstruction*. Washington, D.C.: The World Bank.

Zolberg, Aristide, A. Suhrke and S. Aguayo, 1989, *Escape from Violence*. New York: Oxford University Press.

www.pcpafg.org.

## Chapter 3. International Humanitarian law in the African context

Abi-Saab, Georges, 1988, "Non-International Armed Conflicts", in *International Dimensions of Humanitarian Law*. Paris, Geneva, Dordrecht: Unesco, Henry Dunant Institute and Martinus Nijhoff.

Abi-Saab, G., 1979, "Wars of National Liberation in the Geneva Conventions and Protocols", *Recueil*, The Hague Academy of International Law, 165, 353.

Alliot, Michel, 1965, "Les résistances traditionnelles au droit moderne", in Jean Poirier (ed.), *Etudes de droit africain et de droit malgache*. Toulouse: Cujas.

Alliot, M., 1997, *Democratic Republic of the Congo: Deadly Alliances in Congolese Forests*. London: Amnesty International.

Ankumah, Evelyn A., 1996, *The African Commission on Human and Peoples' Rights: Practice and Procedure*. The Hague, London and Boston: Kluwer Law International.

Ayissi, Anatole, (ed.), 2001, *Cooperating for Peace in West Africa. An Agenda for the 21st Century*. Geneva: UNIDIR.

Bedjaoui, Mohammed, 1979, "Asylum in Africa". Unpublished paper submitted to the Pan-African Conference on Refugees, Arusha, May 1979. Geneva (UNHCR).

Bello, Emmanuel G., 1984, "Shared Legal Concepts between African Customary Norms and International Conventions on Humanitarian Law", *The Military Law and Law of War Review*, 23, 286.

Bello, E.G., 1984, "A Proposal for the Dissemination of International Humanitarian Law in Africa. Pursuant to the 1977 Protocols Additional to the Geneva Conventions of 1949", ibid., 311.

Bello, E.G., 1980, *African Customary Humanitarian Law*. Geneva: Oyez and ICRC.

Boisson de Chazournes, Laurence, 1996, "Les résolutions des Nations Unies, et en particulier celles du Conseil de sécurité, en tant que source du droit humanitaire", in Luigi Condorelli et al., (eds), *United Nations and the Implementation of International Humanitarian Law*. Paris: Pedone.

Boumedra, Tahar, 1981, "International Regulation of the Use of Mercenaries in Armed Conflicts", *The Military Law and Law of War Review*, 20, 35.

Condorelli, Luigi and Laurence Boisson de Chazournes, 1984, "Quelques remarques à propos de l'obligation des Etats de 'respecter et faire respecter' le droit international humanitaire en 'toutes circonstances'", in Christophe Swinarski (ed.), *Studies and Essays on International Humanitarian Law and Red Cross Principles in Honour of Jean Pictet*. Geneva and The Hague: ICRC and Martinus Nijhoff.

David, Eric, 1977, "Les mercenaires en droit international (Développements récents)", *Belgian Review of International Law*, 13, 201.

Diallo, Yolande, 1976, "Humanitarian Law and Traditional African Law", *International Review of the Red Cross*, 16, 57.

Diallo, Y., 1976, "African Traditions and Humanitarian Law", ibid., 387.

Djiena-Wembou, Michel C., 1993, "Validité et portée de la résolution 794 (1992) du Conseil de sécurité", *African Journal of International and Comparative Law*, 5, 340.

Fall, Ibrahima, 1972, "Contribution à l'étude du droit des peuples à disposer d'eux-mêmes en Afrique". Paris. Unpublished doctoral thesis.

Human Rights Watch/Africa, 1997, *Transition, War and Human Rights*. New York: Human Rights Watch.

Human Rights Watch/Africa, 1997, *Attacked by All Sides. Civilians and the War in Eastern Zaïre*. New York: Human Rights Watch.

Human Rights Watch and FIDH, 1997, *Democratic Republic of the Congo. What Kabila is Hiding: Civilian Killings and Impunity in Congo*. New York and Paris: Human Rights Watch and FIDH.

ICRC, 1997, *National Implementation of International Humanitarian Law*, Annual Report 1996. Geneva: ICRC.

ICRC, 1997, *Hannibal, Idris 1er, l'Emir Abdelkader. Leur contribution au droit international humanitaire*. Tunis: ICRC.

ICRC, 1997, *Implementing International Humanitarian Law: From Law to Action*. Geneva: ICRC.

ICRC, 1995, "Synthèse des observations reçues par les autorités suisses au sujet de la liste des mesures envisageables pour promouvoir le respect du droit international humanitaire". Unpublished document, Geneva.

ICRC, 1992, *Pan-African Conference of Red Cross and Red Crescent Societies, Mbabane, Swaziland, 28 September–2 October 1992*, p. 590. Geneva: ICRC.

ICRC, 1991, *Implementation of International Humanitarian Law: National Measures*. Geneva: ICRC.

ICRC, 1989, "Pan-African Conference of National Red Cross and Red Crescent Societies", Dakar, 21–23 November 1988. Geneva: ICRC.

ICRC, 1988, "National Measures to Implement International Humanitarian Law: A New Move by the ICRC. Annex 1: Resolution V of the Twenty-fifth International Conference of the Red Cross, Geneva, 1986". ICRC, 1988: 127.

ICRC and Henry Dunant Institute, 1986, "Final Report of the Fifth African Seminar on International Humanitarian Law, Yaoundé, 26 November-4 December 1986". Geneva and Yaoundé. Unpublished report.

ICRC and Henry Dunant Institute, 1979, "Report on the Second African Seminar on International Humanitarian Law, Yaoundé, 27 November–5 December 1979". Geneva and Yaoundé. Unpublished report.

ICRC and Henry Dunant Institute, 1977, "Rapport du premier séminaire africain sur le droit international humanitaire, Yaoundé, 18 novembre-3 décembre 1977". Geneva and Yaoundé. Unpublished report.

Kalongo, Mbikayi, 1972, "Individualisation et collectivisation du rapport juridique de responsabilité civile en droit zaïrois", *Annales de la Faculté de droit de l'Université de Kinshasa*, 1, 39.

Kleine-Ahlbrant, Stéphanie, 1996, *The Protection Gap in the International Protection of Internally Displaced Persons: The Case of Rwanda*. Geneva: Graduate Institute of International Studies.

Lavoyer, Jean P., (ed.), 1996, *Internally Displaced Persons*. Geneva: ICRC.

Martin, Guy, 1995, "International Solidarity and Cooperation in Assistance to African Refugees: Burden-Sharing or Burden-Shifting?", *International Journal of Refugee Law*, 6, 250.

M'Baye, Kéba, 1992, *Les droits de l'homme en Afrique*. Paris and Geneva: Pedone and International Commission of Jurists.

M'Baye, Kéba and Birame Ndiaye, 1982, "The Organization of African Unity (OAU)", in Karel Vasak (ed.), *The International Dimensions of Human Rights*. Paris: Unesco.

Meriboute, Zidane, 1995, "Le CICR et le respect de la personne humaine: illustration de cas en Afrique", *African Yearbook of International Law*, 3, 121.

Minta, Ige, 1996, "The Rwanda Conflict: With the Failure of Peacekeeping, Is Peacemaking Still Possible?", *African Yearbook of International Law*, 4, 19.

Mubiala, Mutoy, 2001, "La Convention de l'Organisation de l'Unité Africaine de 1969 sur les aspects spécifiques des problèmes de réfugiés en Afrique et ses liens avec la Convention de Genève de 1951 sur le statut des réfugiés", in Vincent Chetail (ed.), *La Convention de Genève de 1951 cinquante ans après: bilan et perspectives*. Brussels: Bruylant.

Mubiala, M., 1996, "Les Nations Unies et la crise des réfugiés rwandais", *Belgian Review of International Law*, 33, 493.

Mubiala, M., 1995, "L'opération des Nations Unies pour les droits de l'homme au Rwanda", *African Yearbook of International Law*, 3, 277.

Mubiala, M., 1990, "L'individu devant la justice au Zaïre. De l'arbre à palabres aux cours et tribunaux", *Penant*, 102, 184.

Mubiala, M, 1989, "African States and the Promotion of Humanitarian Principles", *International Review of the Red Cross*, 29, 93.

Ndam Njoya, Adamou, 1988, "The African Conception", in *International Dimensions of Humanitarian Law*. Geneva, Paris and Dordrecht: Henry Dunant Institute, Unesco and Martinus Nijhoff.

Ntampaka, Charles, 1995, "Le retour à la tradition dans le règlement des différends: le gacaca", *Dialogue*, 28, 95.

OAU and UNHCR, 1995, *The Addis Ababa Document on Refugees and Forced Population Displacements in Africa*. Geneva: UNHCR.

Okoth-Obbo, George, 1988, "Traditional' African Humanitarian Law and the Other Issues Concerning the Humanitarian Law", *Lesotho Law Journal*, 4, 199.

Omotoso, Kole, 1997, *Woza Africa: Music Goes to War*. Johannesburg: Jonathan Ball Publishers.

Ouguergouz, Fatsah, 1993, *La Charte africaine des droits de l'homme et des peuples. Une approche juridique entre tradition et modernité*. Paris: Presses Universitaires de France.

Owona, Joseph, 1982, "Droit international humanitaire", in *Encyclopédie juridique de l'Afrique*. Abidjan, Dakar et Lomé: Les Nouvelles Editions Africaines.

Palwankar, Umesh, 1994, "Measures Available to States for Fulfilling their Obligation to Ensure Respect for International Humanitarian Law", *International Review of the Red Cross*, 36, 9.

Poulton, Robin E. and Ibrahim ag Youssouf, 1998, *A Peace of Timbuktu. Democratic Governance, Development and African Peacemaking*. Geneva and New York: UNIDIR.

Prunier, Gérard, 1995, *The Rwanda Crisis 1959–1994. History of a Genocide*. London: Hurst and Company.

Sandoz, Yves, Christophe Swinarski and Bruno Zimmermann, 1996, *Commentary on the Additional Protocols of 8 June 1977*. Geneva and The Hague: ICRC and Martinus Nijhoff.

Sohier, Antoine, 1955, *Traité élémentaire du droit coutumier du Congo Belge*. Bruxelles: Larcier.

Sommaruga, Cornelio, 1997, "Humanitarian Action and Peacekeeping Operations", *International Review of the Red Cross*, 37, 178.

Torrelli, Maurice, 1995, "Les zones de sécurité", *Revue générale de droit international public*, 99, 810.

Touré, Amadou T., 1997, "La négociation médiatisée, une technique démocratique de résolution des conflits", in *Génocides et violences dans l'Afrique des Grands Lacs*. Montpellier: Coopération internationale pour la démocratie.

Wodie, Francis V., 1986, "Africa and Humanitarian Law", *International Review of the Red Cross*, 26, 249.

Yusuf, Abdulqawi A., 1994, "Reflections on the Fragility of State Institutions in Africa", *African Yearbook of International Law*, 2, 3.

## Chapter 4. Regional co-operation for humanitarian action:
## The potential of the East African community

Allot, Magaga, 1999, "The Role of Defence and Security in the East African Cooperation". Presentation to the Workshop on Humanitarian Assistance and Conflict: A Nordic African Dialogue, Nairobi Kenya 15–18 August, 1999.

Beyani, Chaloka, 1997, "Refugee Protection and Burden Sharing in the Context of International Cooperation between States". Briefing Paper written for the GAP Consultations on the International Protection of Refugees, Division of International Protection, UNHCR, Geneva, 3–5 December 1997.

Bronnee, Stern, 1993, "The History of the Comprehensive Plan of Action", *International Journal of Refugee Law*, 5, 534.

EAC, 1996, "Final Report of the 6th Commission Meeting", 6 December 1996.

EAC, 1997, "EAC Meeting of Immigration and Refugee Chiefs", Arusha, Tanzania, 29–30. September 1997, (EAC/SR/97/26).

European Commission, Proposal to the Council for a Joint Action based on Article K.3 2(b) of the Treaty on European Union concerning Temporary Protection of Displaced Persons.

Fonteyne, Jean-Pierre, 1987, "Burden Sharing: An Analysis of the Nature and Function of International Solidarity in Cases of Mass Influx." 10 *Australian Yearbook of International Law*.

Goodwin-Gill, Guy, (ed.), 1996, *The Refugee in International Law 2*. Oxford: Oxford University Press.

Gorman, Robert, 1987, *Coping with Africa's Refugee Burden: A Time for Solutions*. Dordrecht/ London: Nijhoff and UNITAR.

IGC, 1995, *Study on the Concept of Burden-Sharing*. Geneva: Secretariat of the Inter-Governmental Consultations on Asylum, Refugee and Migration Policies in Europe, North America and Australia.

Kibreab, Gaim, 1991, *The State of the Art Review of Refugee Studies in Africa,* Uppsala Papers in Economic History, Research Report No 26, Department of Economic History, Uppsala.

OAU, 1993, "Declaration of the Assembly of Heads of States and Governments on the Establishment, within the OAU of a Mechanism for Conflict Prevention, Management and Resolution". Cairo, Egypt, June 1993.

Stein, B.J., 1987, "ICARA II: Burden-Sharing and Durable Solutions", in Rogge, J.R., *Refugees, A Third World Dilemma*,Totowa, N. J.: Rowman and Littlefield.

**Chapter 5. The Marginalisation of local relief capacity in Tanzania.**

Ayok, Chol, 1983, *Refugee Law and Practice in Africa with Emphasis on the Tanzanian Experience,* LL.M Thesis, University of Dar es Salaam.

Borton, John et al., 1996, *Humanitarian Aid and Its Effects*, Study 3 of Joint Evaluation of Emergency Assistance to Rwanda. Danida.

von Bernuth, Rudolp, 1996, "The Voluntary Agency Response and the Challenge of Coordination" in *Journal of Refugee Studies* 9, 3.

Connelly, Maureen, 1995, "The International Response to the Refugee Emergency in Tanzania, October 199–July 1994". Paper presented at an international workshop on the refugee crisis in the Great Lakes Region, organised by the Centre for Study of Forced Migration, University of Dar es Salaam, August, 1995, paras 3.3 and 3.4.

Daley, Patricia, 1989, *Refugees and Underdevelopment in Africa: The Case of Burundi Refugees in Tanzania*, D.Phil Thesis, Oxford University.

Gasarasi, C., 1987, "The Tripartite Approach to the Resettlement and Integration of Rural Refugees in Tanzania" in Rogge, J.R., *Refugees, A Third World Dilemma*. Roman and Littlefield.

Gasarasi, C., 1984, *The Tripartite Approach to the Resettlement ans Integration of Rural Refugees in Tanzania*. Research Report No. 71. Uppsala: The Scandinavian Institute for African Studies.

Gasarasi, C., 1976, "The Life of a Refugee Settlement: The Case of Muyenzi in Ngara District Tanzania", Research Project Written for the UNHCR.

Government of Tanzania, 1995, The Tanzania Refugee Policy, Implementation Record and the Tanzania Position on the Rwanda and Burundi Refugee Related Problems.

Harrell-Bond, Barbara and Bonaventure Rutinwa, 1996, "The Situation of Rwandese Refugees in Tanzania Planning Implications for Non-Governmental Organisations", Report for the Norwegian People's Aid, November 1996.

Hyden, Göran, 1995, "Bringing Voluntarism Back In: East Africa in Comparative Perspective", in Semboja, J., and Therkildsen, O., *Service Provision under Stress in East Africa*. London: James Currey.

Ishumi, G.M. Abel, 1995, "Provision of Secondary Education in Tanzania: Historical Background and Current Trends", in Semboja, J., and Therkildsen, O., *Service Provision under Stress in East Africa*. James Currey, London.

Matthews, Z.K., 1967, "The Role of Voluntary Organisations in Refugee Situations in Africa", in Hamrell, S. (ed.). *Refugee Problems in Africa*. Uppsala: The Scandinavian Institute of African Studies.

Mwakasege, Christopher, 1995, *Impact of Refugees on Host Communities. The Case of Kasulu, Ngara and Karagwe Districts in Tanzania*. A Report of a Study Commissioned by Oxfam, Tanzania, January 1995.

Neldner, Brian, 1981, "Settlement of Rural Refugees in Africa", in Eriksson, Melander and Nobel, (eds), *An Analysing Account of the Conference on the African Refugee Problem, Arusha, May 1979*. Uppsala: Scandinavian Institute of African Studies.

Norwegian People's Aid, 1996, *NPA and Support to the NGO Sector in Tanzania. A Consultancy Report*. Oslo:NPA.

NSCNPN, 1999, "The Fifth Draft of Tanzania National Policy on Non-Governmental Organisations". June 1999.

Nyerere, J. Kambarage, 1981, "Inaugural Speech at the Conference on the African Refugee Problem, Arusha, May 1979", in Eriksson, L-G, Melander, G. and Nobel, P., (eds), *An Analyising Account of the Conference on the African Refugee Problem, Arusha, May 1979.* Uppsala: Scandinavian Institute of African Studies.

Nyerere, J., 1983, "Opening Address by the President of the United Republic of Tanzania, Mwalimu Julius Kambarage Nyerere" in Nobel, P., (ed.), *Meeting of the OAU-Secretariat and Voluntary Agencies on African Refugees, Arusha, March 1983.* Uppsala: The Scandinavian Institute of African Studies.

Rutinwa, Bonaventure, 1996, "The Tanzanian Government's Response to the Rwandan Emergency", in *Journal of Refugee Study,* 9, 3.

Sivalon, Joseph, 1995, "The Catholic Church and the State in the Provision of Social Services", in Semboja, J. and Therkildsen, O., *Service Provision under Stress in East Africa.* James Currey, London.

Sterkenburg, J., Kirby, J. and O'Keefe, P., 1991, "Refugees and Rural Development: A Comparative Analysis of Project Aid in Sudan and Tanzania", in Adelman, H., and Sorenson, J., *African Refugees, Development Aid and Repatriation.* Boulder: West View Press.

UN, 1996, *The United Nations and Rwanda, 1993–1996.* New York: UN Department of Public Information.

UNHCR, 1982, *Mishamo Mid-Term Review.*

United States Institute of Peace, 1996, *Humanitarian Assistance and Conflict in Africa.* Washington D.C.

Wohlgemuth, Lennart et al., 1998, "Introduction" in Wohlgemuth, et al., *Institution Building and Leadership in Africa.* Uppsala: Nordiska Afrikainstitutet.

Yeld, Rachel, 1996, Rwanda: *Unprecedented Problems Call for Unprecedented Solutions.* RSP Occasional Paper. Oxford: Refugee Studies Programme, Univ of Oxford.

## Chapter 6. Strengthening local relief capacity in Kenya: Challenges and prospects

African Rights, 1993, *The Nightmare Continues. Abuses against Somali Refugees in Kenya,* London: African Rights.

Bravo, E. Q., 1999, *The Problems of Refugees in Africa: Boundaries and Borders.* London: Ashgate.

Carlebach, J., 1962, *The Jews of Nairobi, 1903–1962.* Nairobi: The Nairobi Hebrew Congregation.

Carver, R., 1994, "Kenya: Aftermath of the Elections", in *Refugee Survey Quarterly.* 13, 1. Spring.

Cohen, R., 1996, "Protecting the Internally Displaced", in *World Refugee Survey, 1996.* US Committee for Refugees, Washington, D.C.: Immigration and Refugee Service of America.

Crisp, J., 1999, "A State of Insecurity: The Political Economy of Violence in Refugee-Populated Areas of Kenya" Unpublished Paper, UNHCR, Geneva, October.

Deng, F., 1993, *Protecting the Displaced: A Challenge for the International Community.* Washington, D.C.: Brookings Institute.

Edwards, M., 1994, "International NGOs and Southern Governments in the New World Order", in Clayton , A. (ed.), *Governance, Democracy & Conditionality: What Role for NGOs.* Oxford: INTRAC.

Fowler, A., 1995, "NGOs and Globalization of Social Welfare: Perspectives from East Africa", in Semboja, J. and Therkildsen, O. (eds), *Services Provision under Stress: States and Voluntary Organizations in Kenya, Tanzania and Uganda.* London: James Currey.

Fowler, Alan., 1993, "Non-Governmental Organizations as Agents of Democratization: An African Perspective", in *Journal of International Development* 5,3.

Fowler, A., 1991, "The Role of NGOs in Changing the State-Society Relations: Perspectives from Eastern and Southern Africa" in *Development Policy Review* 9,1.

Gallagher, D. and Martin, S. F., 1992, *The Many Faces of the Somali Crisis: Humanitarian Issues in Somalia, Kenya and Ethiopia.* Canada: Refugee Policy Group, Center for Policy Analysis and Research on Refugee Issues.

Harris, Joseph E., 1987, *Repatriates and Refugees in a Colonial Society: Case of Kenya.* Washington, D.C.: Howard University Press.

Headley, W. R., 1988, "A Hand Look and a Fresh Start: Local Response to the Refugee in Kenya and Implications for African Refugee Services". Silver Jubilee Conference of the African Studies Association (UK) London: 14–16, September.

Human Rights Watch (HRW), 1997a, *Failing the Displaced: The UNDP Displaced Persons Program*. New York: Human Rights Watch.

Human Rights Watch, 1997b, *Uncertain Refuge: International Failure to Protect Refugees*. New York: Human Rights Watch.

Human Rights Watch, 1993a, *Divide and Rule: State-Sponsored Ethnic Violence in Kenya*. New York: Human Rights Watch.

Human Rights Watch, 1993b, *Seeking Refuge, Finding Terror: The Widespread Rape of Somali Women Refugees in North Eastern Kenya*. New York: Human Rights Watch.

Hyndman, J., 2000, *Managing Displacement: Refugees and the Politics of Humanitarianism*. Minneapolis: University of Minnesota Press.

Hyndman, J. and Nylund V., 1998, "UNHCR and the Status of Prima Facie Refugees in Kenya" in *International Journal of Refugee Law*, 10, 1–2.

International Commission of Jurists, 1998, *Protecting Refugee Rights in Kenya*. Nairobi: ICJ (Kenya Section).

INTRAC, 1998, *Direct Funding from a Southern Perspective: Strengthening Civil Society?* Oxford; International Non-Governmental Training and Research Center (INTRAC).

ICRC, 1995, *Situation Report No 6*, July–August 1995. http://gopher.ifrc.org:70/0/sitreps/all/039506.txt

ICRC, 1996, "Internally Displaced Persons Symposium", Geneva, 23–25 October, 1995. Geneva: ICRC.

Jesuit Refugee Service, 1997, "Kenya: Urban Refugee Population Explosion." http://www.jesuit.org/refugee/nrb701.html.

Jesuit Refugee Service, 1997, "JRS Kenya Projects" http://www.jesuit.org/refugee/jrskeny.html.

Kagwanja, Peter., 1999, "Humanitarianism in an Imperial Shark-Tank: British Response to Ethiopian and Eritrean Refugees in Kenya, 1935–1941." Submitted to International Journal of African Historical Studies.

Kagwanja, P, 1998a, "Investing in Asylum: Ethiopian Forced Migrants and the Matatu Industry in Nairobi", in *IFRA: Les Cahiers* March/April, 10.

Kagwanja, P., 1998b, Killing the Vote: State-Sponsored Violence and Flawed Elections in Kenya. Report Published by the Kenya Human Rights Commission, Nairobi.

Kathina Juma, Monica, 1999a, "The compromised Brokers: NGOs and protection of Human Rights in Situations of Population Displacement in East Africa." Paper presented at the symposium on *Human Rights and Development in Africa: Establishing the Rule of Law*, held at the University of Illinois at Urbana-Champaign, July 8–10.

Kathina Juma, M. 1999b, "Building Capacity during Relief Interventions: Illustrations from Kenya and Uganda." Unpublished paper presented at Chr. Michelsen Institute, Bergen, Norway.

Kenya Human Rights Commission, 1999, *Haven of Fear: The Plight of Women Refugees in Kenya*. Nairobi.

Kenya Human Rights Commission, 1998, *Where Terror Rules: Torture by Kenya Police in Northeastern Kenya*. Nairobi.

Kibreab, Gaim, 1996, "Eritrean and Ethiopian Urban Refugees in Khartoum: What the Eye Refuses to See", in *African Studies Review*, 39,3.

Kirkby, J., Kliest, T., Frerks, G., Flikkema, W. and O'Keefe, P., 1997, "UNHCR's Cross Border Cooperation in Somalia: The Value of Quick Impact Projects for Refugee Settlement", in *Journal of Refugee Studies*. 10,2.

Lawyers Committee for Human Rights, 1995, *African Exodus: Refugee Crisis, Human Rights and the 1969 OAU Convention*. New York.

Lwanga-Lunyiigo, S., 1998, "Uganda's Long Connection with the Problem of Refugees: From the Polish Refugees of World War Two to the Present" in Gingyera-Pinycwa, A.G.G. (ed.), *Uganda and the Problem of Refugees*. Kampala: Makerere University Press.

Mbogori, E., 1994, "NGO Programming: A Kenyan NGO Perspective", in Clayton, A. (ed.) *Governance, Democracy & Conditionality: What Role for NGOs?*. Oxford: INTRAC.

M'Inoti, Kathurima, 1992, "Beyond the 'Emergency' in North Eastern Province: An Analysis of the Use and Abuse of Emergency Powers", in *Nairobi Law Monthly* 41(February/ March).

Ndegwa, S. N., 1996, *The Two Faces of the Civil Society: NGOs and Politics in Africa*. West Hartford: Kumarian Press.

Nelson, Robert E., 1983, "Report on Small Enterprise Development for Refugees in Kenya". Sponsored by UNHCR and Management Development Branch of International Labor Office, Geneva, September.

NCCK, 1985–1995, *Annual Reports of the Refugee Service Unit*. Nairobi.

Organization of African Unity, 1969, *Convention Governing the Specific Aspects of Refugee Problems in Africa*. 10 September.

Osodo, P. and Matsvai, S., 1998, *Partners or Contractors? The Relationship netween Official Agencies and NGOs: Kenya and Zimbabwe*. Oxford: INTRAC.

Pirouet, L., 1979, "Urban Refugees in Nairobi: Small Numbers, Large Problems". Paper Presented at the African Studies Conference (UK), London, September.

Sahley, C., 1995, *Strengthening the Capacity of NGOs: Cases of Small Enterprise Development Agencies in Africa*. Oxford: INTRAC.

Shaw, R. and Gatheru, W., 1998, "Emergency Response—Too Little, Too Late", in *Our Problems, Our Solutions: An Economic and Public Policy Agenda for Kenya*. Nairobi: Institute of Economic Affairs.

Suhrke, Astri, 1998, "Burden Sharing During Refugee Emergencies: The Logical of Collective versus National Action", in *Journal of Refugee Studies*, 11,4.

Tandon, Yash, 1984, "Ugandan Refugees in Kenya: A Community of Enforced Self-Reliance", in *Disaster* 8, 4.

Verdirame, G., 1999, "Human Rights and Refugees: The Case of Kenya", in *Journal of Refugee Studies*, 12, 1.

Wilkin, David, 1980, "Refugees and British Administrative Policy in Northern Kenya, 1936–1938", in *African Affairs*, 79, 317.

Zarjevski, M., 1988, *A Future Preserved: International Assistance to Refugees*. Geneva: UNHCR.

Chapter 7. Revitalising relief capacity as part of the general reconstruction programme in Uganda

ACORD/UWONET, 1997, *The Challenge of Peace in Northern Uganda: A search for solutions*. Report of the Peace Conference 26–27 February, 1997. Kampala.

Action-Aid Uganda, 1998, *Kitgum Emergency Initiative in Education Review Report*. Kampala.

Action-Aid Uganda, 2000, *Country Strategy Paper II*. Kampala.

Amaza, Ondoga Oris, 1998, *Museveni's Long March: From Guerrilla to Statesman*. Kampala: Fountain Publishers.

Amnesty International, 1999, *Uganda Breaking the Circle: Protecting Human Rights in the Northern War Zone*. AFR 59/0199.

Appe, J., 1994, *The Dynamics of Factional Politics and Its Effects in the Political Development of Uganda and Kenya since Independence*. Ph.D. thesis, University of Edinburgh.

Banugire, F.R., 1989, "Uneven and unbalanced development: Development strategies and conflict", in Kumar Rupesinghe (ed.), *Conflict Resolution in Uganda*. London: James Currey.

Behrend, Heike, 1991, "Is Alice Lakwena a witch? The Holy Spirit Movement and its fight against evil in the north", in Holger Bernt Hansen and Michael Twaddle (eds)*Changing Uganda*. London: James Currey.

European Platform for Conflict Prevention and Transformation, 1999, *Searching for Peace in Africa. An Overview of Conflict Prevention and Management Activities*. Utrecht, The Netherlands.

Finnström, Sverker, 1999, *Living with Bad Surroundings: War and Uncertainty in Northern Uganda*. Working Paper in Cultural Anthropology, No.9, Department of Cultural Anthropology and Ethnology. Uppsala: Uppsala University.

Global IDP Survey and Norwegian Refugee Council, 1999, *A workshop on the Guiding Principles on Internal Displacement*. Final Report, 3–29 March. Kampala.

Government of Uganda/UNICEF, 1998, *Northern Uganda Psycho-Social Needs Assessment Report*. Kampala.

Gundel, Joakim, 1999, *Humanitarian Assistance: Breaking the Waves of Complex Political Emergencies, A Literature Survey*. CDR Working Papers. 99.5. Copenhagen: Centre for Development Research.

Harrell-Bond, Barbara, 1986, *Imposing Aid*. Oxford: Oxford University Press.

Human Rights Watch Africa, 1997, *The Scars of Death: Children Abducted by the LRA in Uganda.* New York.

Human Rights Watch Africa, 1994, *Abuses by all parties in the war in Southeren Sudan.* New York.

Kabera, J., 1987, "The Refugee Problem in Uganda," in John Rogge, (ed.), *Refugees: A Third World Dilemma.* New Jersey: Rowman and Littlefield.

Kathina Juma, Monica and Aida Mengistu, 2002, *The Infrastructure of Peace Building in Africa. Assessing the Capacity of African Institutions to Respond to Crisis and Conflict.* New York: International Peace Academy.

Kitgum District Disaster Relief Committee, 1998, *Situation Report.* Kitgum.

Kitgum Distrct, 1998, *Report of the Peace Initiative Interim Committee, April–July.* Kitgum.

Lawanga-Luyiigo, S., 1993, "Polish Refugees in Uganda 1942–1952". Paper presented at a Workshop on Uganda and Refugee Problems, Makerere University, 20 December.

Matovu, J.M. and Stewart F., 2000, "The Social and Economic Costs of Conflict. Uganda—A Case Study", in Stewart, F. and Fitzgerald, V. (eds), *War and Underdevelopment: Case Studies of Countries in Conflict,* vol. 2. London: Oxford University Press.

Mudoola, Dan, 1991, "Institution-building: The case of the NRM and the military 1986–69", in Holger Bernt Hansen and Michael Twaddle (eds), *Changing Uganda.* London: James Currey.

Museveni, K.Y., 1997, *Sowing the Mustard Seed. The Struggle for Freedom and Democracy in Uganda.* London: Macmillan.

Nabuguzi, Emmanuel, 1995, "Popular Initiatives in Service Provision in Uganda", in Joseph Semboja and Ole Therkildsen (eds), *Service Provision under Stress in East Africa: The State, NGOs and People's Organisations in Kenya, Tanzania, and Uganda.* Copenhagen: Centre for Development Research in association with Fountain Publishers.

Okwe, C. A. and Amisi, B., 1997, "Analysis on the Human and Economic Cost of War in Northern Uganda, NGO Advocacy and Lobby for Peace in Northern Uganda". Unpublished report. Kampala: MUK and Emergency Response Information Centre, ActionAid.

Oloya, John, J., Judy Adoko and Jamie Balfour-Paul, 1997, *An Oxfam Needs Assessment of Kitgum and Gulu Districts.* Kampala: OXFAM.

Omara-Otunnu, A., 1987, "The Struggle for Democracy in Uganda", in *Journal of Modern African Studies* 30 (2)

Pinychwa, G., 1998. "Sharing with Refugees in our Midst: The Experience of Uganda", in *Makerere Political Science Review* Vol.1.

Pirouet, M. Louise, 1991, "Human Rights Issues in Museveni's Uganda", in Holger Bernt Hansen and Michael Twaddle (eds), *Changing Uganda.* London: James Currey.

Republic of Uganda/UNICEF, 1998, *Northern Uganda Psyco-Social Needs Assessment Report. Kampala,* November 1998.

Tandon Y., 1987, "Ugandan Refugees in Kenya. A Community of Enforced Self-Reliance", in *Disasters,* 81.

Tidemand, Per, 1995, "Popular versus State Provision of Local Justice", in Joseph Semboja and Ole Therkildsen (eds), *Service Provision under Stress in East Africa: The State, NGOs and People's Organisations in Kenya, Tanzania, and Uganda.* Copenhagen: Centre for Development Research in association with Fountain Publishers.

Torrente, Nicolas de and Frederick Mwesigye, 1999, *The Evolving Roles of the State, Donors and NGOs in Providing Health Services in a Liberal Environment: Some Insights from Uganda.* Occasional Paper, 2. Kampala: Centre for Basic Research (CBR).

UNHCR, 1999, *Country Programme 1998/1999 (Uganda).* Kampala.

UNHCR, 2000, *The State of the World's Refugees. Fifty Years of Humanitarian Action.* London: Oxford University Press.

United States Committee for Refugees, 1985, *Human Rights in Uganda.* Washington DC.

World Vision International, 1996, *Baseline Survey Report,* Kitgum Integrated Programme. Kitgum.

## Chapter 8. Humanitarianism and spoils politics in Somalia

Abdillahi, Mohamed Sheikh, 1998, "The Emergence of Local NGOs in the Recovery and Development Process of Somaliland (Northwest Somalia)", in *Voices from Africa,* 8.

Adam, Hussein M., 1992, "Somalia: Militarism, Warlordism and Democracy?", in *Review of African Political Economy,* 54.

African Rights, 1992, *Operation Restore Hope: A Preliminary Assessment*. London.

African Rights, 1997, *Food and Power in Sudan: A Critique of Humanitarianism*. London.

Allen, Chris, 1995, "Understanding African Politics", in *Review of African Political Economy*, 65.

Anderson, Mary B., 1995, "Humanitarian NGOs in Conflict Intervention", in Chester Crocker, Fen Osler Hampson and Pamela All (eds), *Managing Global Chaos—Sources of and Responses to International Conflict*. Washington D.C.: United States Institute of Peace.

Anderson, M. B., 1996, *Do No Harm: Supporting Local Capacities for Peace through Aid*. Cambridge, MA: The Collaborative for Development Action, Inc.

Anderson, M. B., 1999, *Do No Harm: How Aid Can Support Peace or War*. London: Lynne Rienner.

Augelli, Enrico and Craig N. Murphy, 1995, "Lessons of Somalia for Future Multilateral Humanitarian Assistance Operations", in *Global Governance*, 1.

Berman, Bruce, 1998, "Ethnicity, Patronage and the African State: The Politics of Uncivil Nationalism". *African Affairs*, 97.

Bradbury, Mark and Coultan, Vincent, 1998, *Somalia Inter-Agency Flood Response Operation Phase I, Nov–Dec. 1997*. Nairobi.

Bryden, Matt, 1995, "The Wages of Failure". *Current History*, April.

Bryden, Matt and Martina Steiner, 1998, *Somalia between peace and war, Somali women on the eve of the 21st century*, UNIFEM.

Chabal, P. and J. F. Daloz, 1998, "Africa Works Disorder as Political Instrument", in *African Issues*.

Chazan, Naomi et al., 1999, *Politics and Society in Contemporary Africa*, 3. edition. Boulder, Col.: Lynne Rienner.

Clarke, Walter and Jeffrey Herbst (eds), 1997, *Learning from Somalia—The Lessons of Armed Humanitarian Intervention*. Oxford: Westview.

Cliffe, Lionel and Robin Luckham, 1999, "Complex Political Emergencies and the State: Failure and the Fate of the State", in *Third World Quarterly Special Issue on Complex Political Emergencies*, 20,1.

Cremer, Georg, 1998, "Humanitarian Aid for Warlords? The Dilemma of Relief Organizations in Violent Conflict Situations", in *Forum, D+C*, 5.

Cremer, G., 1998, "On the Problem of Misuse in Emergency Aid", Caritas Germany, International Department, and University of Freiburg, in *Journal of Humanitarian Assistance* posted on 15 June 1998 as http://www-jha.sps.cam.ac.uk/a/a772.htm.

DHA (United Nations Department for Humanitarian Affairs) and OCHA (Office for the Coordination of Humanitarian Afffairs, 1998, www.reliefweb.int/artfs/finarchive.htm #Link94/95/96.

Doornbos, Martin and John Markakis, 1994, "Society and State in Crisis: What Went Wrong in Somalia", in *Review of African Political Economy*, 59.

Duffield, Mark, 1999, "The Crisis of International Aid", in Pirotte, Husson and Grunewald (eds) *Responding to Emergencies and Fostering Development—The Dilemmas of Humanitarian Aid*. London: Zed Books.

Fennell, James, 1998, "Hope Suspended: Morality, Politics and War in Central Africa", in *Disasters*, 22,2.

Gundel, Joakim, 1995, *An Analysis of Local Reflections on the Introduction of Multiparty Politics in Tanzania*. Institute of Political Science MA dissertation, University of Copenhagen.

Gundel, J., 1999a, *Humanitarian Assistance: Breaking the Waves of Complex Political Emergencies: A Literature Survey*. CDR Working Papers 99.5, Copenhagen: Centre for Development Research.

Gundel, J., 1999b, "Input paper to a seminar on humanitarian principles in Nairobi". Mimeo, November.

Gundel, J., 2000, "Byggestensmodellen i Somalia", in *Den Ny Verden*, 33(4): 99–121.

Heinrich, Wolfgang, 1997, *Building the Peace*. Uppsala: Life and Peace Institute.

Helander, Bernhard, 1995, "Somalia: Aid Fuels the Conflict", *News from the Nordic Africa Institute*, 3.

Keen, David, 1998, *The Economic Functions of Violence in Civil Wars*, Adelphi Paper 320. Oxford: International Institute of Strategic Studies.

Lewis, I.M., 1961, *A Pastoral Democracy*. Oxford: Oxford University Press.

Marchal, Roland, 1996, *Final Report on the Post-Civil War Somali Business Class*. EU/Somalia Unit.

Maren, Michael, 1997, *The Road to Hell—The Ravaging Effects of Foreign Aid and International Charity*. The Free Press.

Menkhaus, Ken and Roland Marchal (eds), 1998, *Human Development Report Somalia*. Nairobi: UNDP Somalia.

Menkhaus, Ken and Prendergast, John., 1995,"Governance and Economic Survival in Post-Intervention Somalia", in *Trocaire Development Review*: 47–61.

Natsios, Andrew S., 1997, "Humanitarian Relief Intervention in Somalia: The Economics of Chaos", in Clarke, Walter and Jeffrey Herbst (eds), *Learning from Somalia—The Lessons of Armed Humanitarian Intervention*. Oxford: Westview.

Netherlands Development Cooperation, 1994, *Humanitarian Aid to Somalia. Evaluation Report*.

Pirotte, Husson and Grunewald, 1999, *Responding to Emergencies and Fostering Development— The Dilemmas of Humanitarian Aid*. London: Zed Books.

Prendergast, John, 1997, *Crisis Response—Humanitarian Band-Aids in Sudan and Somalia*. London/Chicago: Pluto Press.

Prendergast, John, and Colin Scott, 1996, *Aid with Integrity—Avoiding the Potential of Humanitarian Aid to Sustain Conflict: A Strategy For USAID/BHR/OFDA in Complex Emergencies*. Occasional Paper. Washington D.C.: USAID

Raghe, Abdirahman Osman, "Somali NGOs", in Hussein M. Adam and Richard Ford (eds), *Mending Rips in the Sky*.Trenton, N.J.: Red Sea Press.

Refugee Policy Group, 1994, *Hope Restored? Humanitarian Aid in Somalia 1990–1994*.

Reno, William, 1998, *Warlord Politics and African States*. Boulder, Col.: Lynne Rienner.

SACB, 1999, *Somalia Aid Coordination Body*. SACB Secretariat, Nairobi, August.

Sahnoun, Mohamed, 1994, *Somalia—The Missed Opportunities*. 2nd.print. Washington D.C.: US Institute of Peace Press,.

Samatar, Said and David Laitin, 1987, *Somalia: Nation in Search of a State*. Boulder, Col.: Westview Press.

SCPD, 1999, *Rebuilding from the Ruins: A Self-Portrait of Somaliland, SCPD/War-Torn Societies Project*. Hargeysa: Somaliland Centre for Peace and Development.

Simons, Anna, 1998, "The Structures of Dissolution", in Villalon and Huxtable (eds) *The African State at a Critical Juncture*. Boulder, Col.: Lynne Rienner.

Tin, Hjalte, 1999, *Aid Under Fire in Somalia. A report from the research project on major constraints for the peace inducing impact of humanitarian aid in complex emergencies. Danish humanitarian aid to Somalia, Afghanistan, and Bosnia in 1992 and 1997*. Copenhagen: Danish Institute of International Affairs.

Uvin, Peter, 1998, *Aiding Violence—The Development Enterprise in Rwanda*. West Hartford: Kumarian Press.

de Waal, Alex, 1997, *Famine Crimes—Politics and the Disaster Relief Industry in Africa*. Oford: African Rights/James Currey.

Yannis, Alexandros, 1999, "Humanitarian Politics in Collapsed States: A critical appraisal of the role of international NGOs in the Somali Crisis". Mimeo. Geneva, July 1999.

## Chapter 9. The political economy of building local capacity in Africa

Atampugre, N. 1994, "In the Cobweb of Money, Politics and Development", in *Africa World Review*. London: Arib May–Sept.

Betts, T.F., 1993, "Evolution and Promotion of the Integrated Rural Development Approach to Refugee Policy in Africa", in *Africa Today* 31 (1): 7–24.

Borton, J. 1993, "Recent Trends in the International Relief System", in *Disasters* 17(3).

Bratton, M., 1987, "The Politics of Government-NGO Relations in Africa", in *World Development* Vol.17 (4).

Chambers, R., 1993, "Hidden Losers? The Impact of Rural Refugees and Refugee Programs on Poorer Hosts" in Robert F. Gorman (ed), *Refugee Aid and Development. Theory and Practice*. Westpoint: Greenwood Press.

Chambers, R., 1979 "Rural Refugees in Africa: What the Eye Does Not See", in *Disasters* 3 (4).

Crisp, J., 1999, *A State of Insecurity: The Political Economy of Violence in Refugee-Populated Areas of Kenya*. Geneva: UNHCR.

Cuenod, J., 1989, "Refugees: Development or Relief", in Loescher G., & Monahan L., *Refugees and International Relations*. Oxford: Oxford University Press.

Cuny, F.C., 1981, "The UNHCR and Relief Operations: A Changing Role", in *International Migration Review* 15(1).

Eade, D.., and S. Williams, 1995, *The Oxfam Handbook of Development and Relief,  Vol. 1*. Oxford: Oxfam.

Eriksson, John, et al., 1996. *Humanitarian Aid and Effects (Study III): The International Response to Conflict and Genocide. Lessons from the Rwanda Experience*. Joint Evaluation of Emergency Assistance to Rwanda. Copenhagen: Danida.

Fergusson, J., 1990, *The Anti-Politics Machine: Development, Depoliticization and Bureaucratic Power in Lesotho*. Minneapolis: University of Minnesota Press.

Fowler, Alan and Rick James, 1994, *The Role of Southern NGOs in Development Cooperation*. INTRAC Occasional Papers No.2. Oxford: INTRAC.

Gariyo, Zie, 1992, *The Press and the Democratic Struggles in Uganda, 1900–1962*. Working Paper No. 24. Kampala: Center for Basic Research.

Gingyera-Pinycwa, A.G.G. (ed.), 1998, *Uganda and the Problem of Refugees*. Kampala: Makerere University Press.

Gorman, Robert F., 1993, "Linking Refugee Aid to Development in Africa", in Robert F. Gorman (ed.), *Refugee Aid and Development Theory and Practice*. Westport: Greenwood Press.

Gulgielmo, V., 1998, "Human Rights and Refugees: The Case of Kenya", in *Journal of Refugee Studies* 12(1).

Hansen, A, B. Holger and M. Twandle (eds), 1995, *Religion and Politics in East Africa. The Period Since Independence*. London: James Currey.

Harrell-Bond, Barbara, 1985, "Humanitarianism in a Straight Jacket", in *African Affairs*, 334.

Harrell-Bond, Barbara, E. Voutira and M. Leopold , 1992, "Counting Refugees: Gifts, Givers, Patrons and Clients", in *Journal of Refugee Studies* 5(3/4).

Harrell-Bond, Barbara, K. Hussein , and P. Matlou, 1994, "Contemporary Refugees in Africa. A Problem of the State". Unpublished manuscript, Refugee Studies Programme, Oxford University.

Harrell-Bond, Barbara and E. Voutira, 1995, "In Search of the Locus of Trust: The Sound World of the Refugee Camp". Unpublished RSP manuscript. Oxford.

Harrell-Bond, Barbara, 1996, "The Ikafe Refugee Settlement Project in Iringa County". Unpublished report to Oxfam.

Hyden Göran, 1980, *Beyond Ujamaa in Tanzania. Underdevelopment and Uncaptured Peasantry*. London: Heinemann.

Hyndman, J. and V. Nylund, 1998, "UNHCR and the Status of Prima Facie Refugees in Kenya", in *International Journal of Refugee Law*, 10 (1–2).

Human Rights Watch, 1997, *Failing the Internally Displaced: THE UNDP Displaced Persons Program in Kenya*. New York.

Kabera, J., 1987, "The Refugee Problem in Uganda", in John Rogge (ed.), *A Third World Dilemma*. New Jersey: Rowman and Littlefield.

Karadawi, A., 1983, "Constraints on Assistance to Refugees: Some Observations from the Sudan", in *World Development*, 11 (6).

Kathina Juma, Monica, 2000, *The Politics of Humanitarian Assistance. State, NGOs and Displacement in Kenya and Uganda* (1989–1998). D.Phil Thesis, University of Oxford.

Kathina Juma, Monica and A. Masika, 1997,  *Evaluation of DFID's Intervention in the Resettlement of Ethnic Clashes Victims in Kenya*. Nairobi: DFID.

Kathina Juma, Monica, 1995, "NGO Co-ordination in the Somali Emergency Crisis 1990-93", in Jon Bennet (ed.), *Meting Needs. NGO Co-ordination in Practice*. London: Earthscan.

Malloch-Brown, Mark, 1984, "Presentation" at the *International Symposium on Assistance to Refugees: Alternative View Points*. Oxford: Refugee Studies Programme.

Maren, Michael, 1997, *The Road to Hell. The Ravaging Effects of Foreign and International Charity*. New York: Free Press.

Ogata, Sadako, 1994, "Address to the PARinAc Global Meeting in Oslo". June.

Omar, Rakyiat and Alex de Waal, 1994, *Humanitarianism Unbound*. London: African Rights.

Stein, Barry, 1987, "ICARA II: Burden Sharing and Durable Solutions", in John R. Rogge (ed.), *Refugees. A Third World Dilemma*. New Jersey: Rowman and Littlefield.

UNHCR, 1993, "Joint NGOs/INGOs/UN meeting". 24–28 January.

UNHCR, 1984, *Guidelines on cooperation between non-governmental organisations and UNHCR in the planning and implementation of UNHCR-funded projects.* Geneva: UNHCR.

UNHCR, 1996, *Partnership: A Programme Management Handbook for UNHCR's Partners.* Geneva: UNHCR.

de Voe, D., 1981, "Framing Refuges as Clients", in *International Migration Review* 15 (1–2).

de Waal, A., 1997, *Famine Crimes. Politics and the Disaster Relief Industry in Africa.* Oxford: James Currey.

Yaansah, A.E., 1995, *An Analysis of Domestic Legislation to Regulate the Activities of Local and Foreign NGOs in Croatia, Kenya, Rwanda and Uganda.* Oxford: Refugee Studies Programme.

Walkup, Mark, 1994, *Policy Issues in the Management of Humanitarian Assistance.* Oxford: Refugee Studies Programme.

# Contributors .

**Bertha Amisi** is a graduate of the University of Nairobi (B.A., M.A.) and Notre Dame (M.A.), USA. A practitioner in the area of development assistance and peace building, Ms Amisi has extensive experience in developing early warning and response mechanisms for emergencies. She has worked in Kenya, Uganda, Tanzania, Eritrea, Ethiopia, Ghana, Rwanda and Burundi. Currently, Amisi is a doctoral student at the University of Syracuse, USA.

**Joakim Gundel** is a research fellow at the Centre for Development Studies, Copenhagen, and is writing a Ph.D. dissertation on humanitarian relief in Somalia at the University of Copenhagen.

**Peter Mwangi Kagwanja** is a graduate of Kenyatta University (B.Edu., M.A.), Kenya. He is undertaking doctoral work on human rights and forced displacement at the University of Illinois at Urbana-Champaign. A lecturer in the Department of History and a research fellow at the Centre for Refugee Studies, Moi University, Kagwanja has written extensively on various aspects of human rights, electoral violence, labour issues and forced migration. Currently, he is holding a one year fellowship at the Kenya Human Rights Commission, where he is dealing with international advocacy and developing a framework for monitoring and mitigating election-relat-. ed violence in Kenya.

**Monica Kathina Juma** holds a D. Phil. (Oxford University). She has served at Moi University, Kenya, as a senior researcher at the Centre for Refugee Studies and as a senior lecturer at the Department of Political Science, and as a research associate at the International Peace Academy in New York. Dr Juma is currently a senior researcher on peace, security and migrations at SaferAfrica in Pretoria, South Africa.

**Mutoy Mubiala** holds a Ph.D. in International Law from the Graduate Institute of International Studies, Geneva. A human rights officer with the UN the High Commissioner for Human Rights, Geneva, Dr Mubiala has written extensively on the legal aspects of humanitarian and human rights issues in Central Africa.

**Bonaventure Rutinwa** is a graduate of the University of Dar es Salaam (LL.B., Hons.), Queen's University, (Canada) (LL.M.), and University of Oxford, where he obtained a Bachelor of Civil Law (B.CL.), a Postgraduate Certificate in Refugee Studies and Doctorate in International Law. Presently, Dr Rutinwa is a senior lecturer in the Faculty of Law and a researcher at the Centre for the Study of Forced Migration (CSFM), University of Dar es Salaam, Tanzania. He is also an advocate of the High Court of Tanzania.

**Astri Suhrke** holds a Ph.D. in International Relations from the University of Denver (USA). She is a senior research fellow at the Chr. Michelsen Institute in Bergen, Norway, and has written widely on humanitarian issues. Her most recent book is The Path of a Genocide: the Rwanda Crisis from Uganda to Zaire (with Howard Adelman), published by Transaction Publishers and the Nordic Africa Institute, 1999.

# Index

www.ingramcontent.com/pod-product-compliance
Lightning Source LLC
Chambersburg PA
CBHW080611270326
41928CB00016B/3012